PRENTICE HALL

CONCEPTUAL PHYSICS
The High School Physics Program

Reading and Study Workbook

PEARSON

Boston, Massachusetts
Glenview, Illinois
Shoreview, Minnesota
Upper Saddle River, New Jersey

ISBN 978-0-13-364739-6

ISBN 0-13-364739-0

11 16

Contents

Chapter 1 About Science

Summary

THE BIG IDEA : Science is the study of nature's rules.

1.1 The Basic Science—Physics

☑ Physics is about the nature of basic things such as motion, forces, energy, matter, heat, sound, light, and the composition of atoms.

- The study of science today branches into the study of living things and nonliving things—the life sciences and the physical sciences.
- The life sciences branch into areas such as biology, zoology, and botany.
- The physical sciences branch into areas such as geology, astronomy, chemistry, and physics.

1.2 Mathematics—The Language of Science

☑ When scientific findings in nature are expressed mathematically, they are easier to verify or to disprove by experiment.

- Science was transformed in the 1600s when it was learned that nature can be analyzed, modeled, and described mathematically.
- The equations of science provide compact expressions of relationships between concepts.

1.3 Scientific Methods

☑ Scientific methods generally include some, if not all, of the following:

1. Recognize a problem.
2. Make an educated guess—a hypothesis—about the answer.
3. Predict the consequences of the hypothesis.
4. Perform experiments to test predictions.
5. Formulate the simplest general rule that organizes the main ingredients: hypothesis, prediction, and experimental outcome.
    - Galileo Galilei and Francis Bacon are usually credited as the principal founders of the scientific method.
    - **Scientific methods** are extremely effective in gaining, organizing, and applying new knowledge.

1.4 The Scientific Attitude

☑ If a scientist finds evidence that contradicts a hypothesis, law, or principle, then the hypothesis, law, or principle must be changed or abandoned.

- A **fact** is a close agreement by competent observers who make a series of observations of the same phenomenon.
- A scientific **hypothesis** is an educated guess that is not fully accepted until demonstrated by experiment.

- When hypotheses about the relationship among natural quantities are tested over and over again and not contradicted, they may become **laws** or **principles.**
- A scientific **theory** is a synthesis of a large body of information that encompasses well-tested and verified hypotheses about certain aspects of the natural world.

1.5 Scientific Hypotheses

✅ **To determine whether a hypothesis is scientific or not, look to see if there is a test for proving it wrong.**

- A scientific hypothesis must be testable. If there is no test for possible wrongness, then an idea is not a scientific hypothesis.
- In science, it is more important that there be a way of proving a hypothesis *wrong* than there be a way of proving it correct.

1.6 Science, Technology, and Society

✅ **Science is a method of answering theoretical questions; technology is a method of solving practical problems.**

- Science has to do with discovering facts and relationships between observable phenomena in nature and with establishing theories that organize and make sense of these facts and relationships.
- Technology has to do with tools, techniques, and procedures for putting the findings of science to use.

1.7 Science, Art, and Religion

✅ **Science is mostly concerned with discovering and recording natural phenomena, the arts are concerned with the value of human interactions as they pertain to the senses, and religion is concerned with the source, purpose, and meaning of everything.**

- The arts describe emotions and suggest what may be in store for us. Similarly, science tells us what is possible in nature.
- The domain of science is natural order; the domain of religion is nature's purpose.

1.8 In Perspective

✅ **Progress in our age is much quicker than it was thousands of years ago.**

- Thousands of years ago, the building of great structures generally took a very long time. Such structures were probably inspired by a vision that went beyond world concerns.
- Today, efforts are directed toward building spaceships. The time required to build these spaceships is extremely brief compared with the time spent building the structures of the past.

Chapter 1   About Science

Exercises

1.1 The Basic Science—Physics (page 1)

1. The study of science today branches into the study of the
_____ sciences and the _____ sciences.

2. Write *L* or *P* beside each of the following to classify it as a branch of life
science or physical science.

_____ zoology   _____ astronomy

_____ physics   _____ botany

_____ chemistry   _____ geology

_____ biology

3. Complete the following table by identifying each type of science described.

Type of Science	Description
	The study of the nature of things such as motion, forces, energy, matter, heat, sound, light, and the composition of atoms
	The study of how matter is put together, how atoms combine to form molecules, and how the molecules combine to make up matter
	The study of matter that is alive

1.2 Mathematics—The Language of Science (page 1)

4. When the ideas of science are expressed in mathematical terms, they are
_____.

5. Explain why equations are often used in science.

_____

_____

6. Is the following sentence true or false? Scientific findings are harder
to verify or to disprove when they are expressed mathematically.
_____

1.3 Scientific Methods (page 2)

7. Which two scientists are usually credited as the principal founders of the
scientific method? _____ and _____

8. Name five steps that are generally included in scientific methods.

a. _____

b. _____

c. _____

d. _____

e. _____

_____

Chapter 1   About Science

9. Is the following statement true or false? Following the steps of the scientific method exactly is an important part of the success of science.

_____

1.4 The Scientific Attitude (pages 2–3)

Match each term to its definition.

Term	Definition
_____ **10.** law or principle	a. a close agreement by competent observers who make a series of observations of the same phenomenon
_____ **11.** fact	b. a hypothesis that has been tested over and over again and not contradicted
_____ **12.** hypothesis	c. an educated guess that is not fully accepted until demonstrated by experiment

13. What should happen if a scientist finds evidence that contradicts a hypothesis, law, or principle?

_____

_____

14. Which is more reliable, an idea of a scientist who has an excellent reputation or a single verifiable experiment that shows the idea is wrong?

_____

15. In everyday speech, the word *theory* means _____
_____ .

16. In science, the word *theory* means _____
_____
_____

17. Is the following statement true or false? Once an idea becomes a theory, it cannot be changed. _____

1.5 Scientific Hypotheses (page 4)

18. What must be true in order for a hypothesis to be scientific?

_____

19. To determine whether a hypothesis is scientific or not, you should

_____ .

20. Scientists perform a(n) _____ to test a(n) _____ .

21. Is the following hypothesis scientific? Why? "Intelligent life exists on other planets somewhere in the universe." _____

Chapter 1   About Science

1.6 Science, Technology, and Society (page 5)

22. Science is a method of answering _____; technology is a method of solving _____.

23. Write *S* or *T* to indicate whether the following statements describe science or technology.

_____ Involves the design and creation of something for the use and enjoyment of humans

_____ Has to do with discovering facts and relationships between observable phenomena in nature

1.7 Science, Art, and Religion (page 6)

Match each term to its definition.

Term		Definition
_____	**24.** science	a. concerned with the source, purpose, and meaning of everything
_____	**25.** art	b. concerned with the value of human interactions as they pertain to the senses
_____	**26.** religion	c. concerned with discovering and recording natural phenomena

27. The domain of science is _____; the domain of religion is _____.

1.8 In Perspective (page 7)

28. Is the following statement true or false? Progress was much slower thousands of years ago than it is today. _____

29. Thousands of years ago, the building of great structures such as the Pyramids was inspired by _____.

30. Is the inspiration for progress today similar to or different from the inspiration thousands of years ago? _____

Chapter 2   Mechanical Equilibrium

Summary

THE BIG IDEA : An object in mechanical equilibrium is stable, without changes in motion.

2.1 Force

☑ **A force is needed to change an object's state of motion.**

- A **force** is a push or a pull. A force is always required to change an object's state of motion.

- The combination of all forces acting on an object is called the **net force.** The net force on an object changes its motion.

- When you hold a rock at rest in your hand, you are pushing upward on it with as much force as Earth's gravity pulls down on it. The net force on the rock is zero.

- The scientific unit of force is the newton, abbreviated N.

- Tension is a "stretching force."

- Weight is the force of gravity acting downward on an object.

- A **vector** is an arrow that represents the magnitude and direction of a quantity. A **vector quantity** is a quantity that needs both magnitude and direction for a complete description. Force is an example of a vector quantity.

- A **scalar quantity** is a quantity that can be described by magnitude only and has no direction. Time, area, and volume are scalar quantities.

2.2 Mechanical Equilibrium

☑ **You can express the equilibrium rule mathematically as $\sum F = 0$.**

- **Mechanical equilibrium** is a state wherein no physical changes occur; it is a state of steadiness.

- Whenever the net force on an object is zero ($\sum F = 0$), the object is said to be in mechanical equilibrium—this is known as the **equilibrium rule.** The symbol $\sum$ stands for "the sum of" and F stands for "forces."

- For a suspended object at rest, the forces acting upward on the object must be balanced by other forces acting downward to make the vector sum equal zero.

2.3 Support Force

☑ **For an object at rest on a horizontal surface, the support force must equal the object's weight.**

- A **support force** is the upward force that balances the weight of an object on a surface. A support force is often called the *normal force.*

- An upward support force is positive and a downward weight is negative.

- The weight of a book sitting on a table is a negative force that squeezes downward on the atoms of the table. The atoms squeeze upward on the book. The compressed atoms produce the positive support force.

Chapter 2   Mechanical Equilibrium

2.4 Equilibrium for Moving Objects

☑ **Objects at rest are said to be in static equilibrium; objects moving at constant speed in a straight-line path are said to be in dynamic equilibrium.**

- Equilibrium is a state of no change. An object under the influence of only one force cannot be in equilibrium. Only when there is no force at all, or when two or more forces combine to zero, can an object be in equilibrium.

- Both static equilibrium and dynamic equilibrium are examples of mechanical equilibrium.

2.5 Vectors

☑ **The Parallelogram Rule: To find the resultant of two nonparallel vectors, construct a parallelogram wherein the two vectors are adjacent sides. The diagonal of the parallelogram shows the resultant.**

- The sum of two or more vectors is called their **resultant.**

- Combining vectors is simple when they are parallel. If they are in the same direction, they add. If they are in opposite directions, they subtract. To find the resultant of nonparallel vectors, use the parallelogram rule.

- When applying the parallelogram rule to two perpendicular vectors that are equal in magnitude, the parallelogram is a square. The resultant is $\sqrt{2}$, or 1.414, times one of the vectors.

- When an object is suspended at rest from two non-vertical ropes, there are three forces acting on it: a tension in the left rope, a tension in the right rope, and the object's weight. The resultant of rope tensions must have the same magnitude as the object's weight.

Chapter 2   Mechanical Equilibrium

Exercises

2.1 Force (pages 13–14)

1. A force is a _____ or a _____.

2. A force is needed to change the state of _____ of an object.

3. Is the following sentence true or false? If an object is sliding on ice, it will continue sliding until a force slows it down. _____

4. Define net force.

   _____

   _____

Match the applied forces on an object with the letter of the corresponding net force on the object.

Applied Forces	**Net Force**
_____ **5.** 5 N to the right and 5 N to the left	a. 2 N to the left
_____ **6.** 4 N to the right and 6 N to the left	b. 2 N to the right
_____ **7.** 7 N to the right and 5 N to the left	c. 10 N to the right
_____ **8.** 6 N to the right and 4 N to the right	d. 0 N (no change in motion)

9. Describe the forces that act on a rock at rest in your hand.

   _____

   _____

10. Circle the letter that identifies the force acting upward on an object suspended from a spring scale.

    a. gravity   b. equilibrium

    c. tension   d. weight

11. A _____ is an arrow that represents the magnitude and direction of a quantity.

12. Explain the difference between a vector quantity and a scalar quantity.

    _____

    _____

13. Write *V* beside each vector quantity. Write *S* beside each scalar quantity.

    _____ a. time   _____ b. area

    _____ c. force   _____ d. volume

Chapter 2   Mechanical Equilibrium

2.2 Mechanical Equilibrium (page 16)

14. Express the equilibrium rule in words.

_____

_____

_____

15. Express the equilibrium rule mathematically, and explain what the symbol in the rule means.

_____

_____

16. Circle the letter that describes the forces acting on a suspended object at rest.

   a. The forces acting upward on the object are greater than the forces acting downward on the object.

   b. The forces acting upward on the object are less than the forces acting downward on the object.

   c. The forces acting upward and downward on the object are balanced.

   d. No forces are acting on the object.

2.3 Support Force (page 17)

17. Identify the two forces acting on a book at rest on a table. State the direction of each force.

   a. _____

   b. _____

18. The _____ force is the upward force that balances the weight of an object on a surface. Another name for this force is the _____ force.

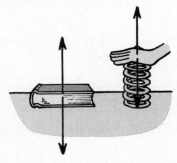

19. Look at the drawing above. Explain how the force of the table pushing up on the book is similar to what happens when the spring is compressed.

_____

_____

_____

Chapter 2   Mechanical Equilibrium

20. Circle the letter that describes an object at rest on a horizontal surface.

    a. The support force is equal to the object's weight.

    b. The support force is greater than the object's weight.

    c. The support force is less than the object's weight.

2.4 Equilibrium for Moving Objects (pages 18–19)

21. If an object is moving at a _____ speed in a
    _____ path, it is in a state of equilibrium.

22. Is the following sentence true or false? If a desk is pushed at a
    constant speed across a horizontal floor, the force of friction
    must be equal in magnitude and opposite in direction to the pushing
    force on the desk. _____

23. Objects at rest are said to be in _____ equilibrium.

24. Objects moving at constant speed in a straight-line path are said to be in
    _____ equilibrium.

2.5 Vectors (pages 19–22)

25. Suppose a gymnast with a weight of 300 N is suspended by a single
    vertical rope. What is the tension in the rope? _____

26. Now suppose the same gymnast hangs from two vertical ropes. What
    are the tensions in the ropes? _____

27. Define resultant. _____

28. State the parallelogram rule.

    _____

    _____

29. The gymnast shown below is suspended from two non-vertical ropes.
    The solid vector represents the gymnast's weight. What does the dashed
    vector represent? _____

    _____

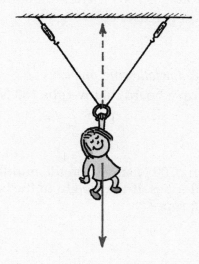

Chapter 2   Mechanical Equilibrium

The Equilibrium Rule

A painter stands on the middle of a board that is suspended at the ends by two vertical ropes. The painter and the board are in mechanical equilibrium. The tension in each rope is 350 N, and the painter's weight is 550 N. What is the weight of the board?

1. Read and Understand

What information are you given?

Tension in rope 1 = T_1 = 350 N

Tension in rope 2 = T_2 = 350 N

Weight of painter = W_1 = 550 N

2. Plan and Solve

What unknown are you trying to calculate?

Weight of the board = W_2 = ?

What mathematical equation can you use to calculate the unknown?

$\Sigma F = 0$

Determine the directions of all forces.

The tension in the ropes is upward. The weights of the painter and the board are downward.

Calculate the sum of the forces, being careful to use the correct signs.

$\Sigma F = 350 \text{ N} + 350 \text{ N} - 550 \text{ N} - W_2 = 0$

$W_2 = 150 \text{ N}$

3. Look Back and Check

Is your answer reasonable?

The sum of the upward forces is 700 N. The sum of the downward forces is 700 N. The answer is reasonable.

Math Practice

On a separate sheet of paper, solve the following problems.

1. Three vertical ropes hold up a board that weighs 180 N. What is the tension in each rope?

2. Suppose a painter weighing 700 N stands on the middle of a board suspended by two vertical ropes. If the weight of the board is 180 N, what is the tension in each rope?

Chapter 3   Newton's First Law of Motion—Inertia

Summary

THE BIG IDEA : Forces cause changes in motion.

3.1 Aristotle on Motion

☑ Aristotle, the foremost Greek scientist, studied motion and divided it into two types: *natural motion* and *violent motion.*

- During Aristotle's time, natural motion on Earth was thought to be either straight up or straight down: It was "natural" for heavy things to fall and for very light things to rise.

- Violent motion was imposed motion and it was the result of forces that pushed or pulled.

- The proper state of objects was thought to be one of rest, unless they were being pushed or pulled or were moving toward their natural resting place.

3.2 Copernicus and the Moving Earth

☑ Copernicus reasoned that the simplest way to interpret astronomical observations was to assume that Earth and the other planets move around the sun.

- Copernicus' idea of motion in space was extremely controversial at the time, because most people believed that Earth was at the center of the universe.

- Copernicus worked on his ideas in secret to escape persecution. At the urging of his close friends, he published his ideas.

3.3 Galileo on Motion

☑ Galileo argued that only when friction is present—as it usually is—is a force needed to keep an object moving.

- One of Galileo's greatest contributions to physics was demolishing the notion that a force is necessary to keep an object moving. A force is any push or pull.

- **Friction** is the force that acts between materials that touch as they move past each other.

- Galileo found that a ball rolling on a smooth horizontal plane has almost constant velocity, and if friction were entirely absent, the ball would move forever. Galileo also stated that the tendency of a moving body to keep moving is natural and that every object resists change to its state of motion.

- The property of a body to resist changes to its state of motion is called **inertia.**

3.4 Newton's Law of Inertia

☑ Newton's first law states that every object continues in a state of rest, or of uniform speed in a straight line, unless acted on by a nonzero net force.

- Isaac Newton's laws of motion replaced the Aristotelian ideas that had dominated thinking for about 2000 years.

- **Newton's first law** is usually called the **law of inertia.**

- Forces are needed to overcome any friction that may be present. Forces are also needed to set objects in motion initially.

- Once an object is moving in a force-free environment, it will move in a straight line indefinitely.

3.5 Mass—A Measure of Inertia

☑ The more mass an object has, the greater its inertia and the more force it takes to change its state of motion.

- **Mass** is the quantity of matter in an object. Mass is a measure of the inertia of an object. Mass is measured in the fundamental unit of **kilograms.**

- **Weight** is the force of gravity on an object. Weight depends on an object's location. The mass of an object is the same whether the object is located on Earth, on the moon, or in outer space.

- Mass and weight are proportional to each other in a given place. Objects with great mass have great weight; objects with little mass have little weight.

- In most parts of the world, the measure of matter is commonly expressed in units of mass. The SI unit of mass is the kilogram and its symbol is kg.

- The SI unit of *force* is the **newton.** The SI symbol *for the* newton is N and is written with a capital letter because it is named after a person.

3.6 The Moving Earth Again

☑ The law of inertia states that objects in motion remain in motion if no unbalanced forces act on them.

- Copernicus announced the idea of a moving Earth in the sixteenth century. This controversial idea stimulated much argument and debate.

- Newton's work showed that objects on Earth move with Earth as Earth moves around the sun. The law of inertia also shows that objects within moving vehicles move with the vehicles.

- Notions of motion today are very different from those of our distant ancestors.

Chapter 3   Newton's First Law of Motion—Inertia

Exercises

3.1 Aristotle on Motion (pages 29–30)

Fill in the blanks with the correct terms.

1. Aristotle divided motion into two types: _____ and _____.

2. Natural motion on Earth was once thought to be either _____ or _____.

3. Aristotle thought that it was natural for heavy things to _____ and for light things to _____.

4. Aristotle also thought that _____ motion was natural for objects beyond Earth and that the planets and stars moved in perfect circles around _____.

5. What force was thought to have caused a horse and cart to experience violent motion? _____

6. Before the 1500s, the proper state of objects was thought to be one of _____, unless they were being pushed or pulled or were moving toward their natural resting place.

7. Is the following statement true or false? Early thinkers thought that violent motion was imposed motion. _____

8. Is the following statement true or false? It was commonly thought by many ancient thinkers that if an object moved "against its nature," then a force of some kind was responsible. _____

3.2 Copernicus and the Moving Earth (page 30)

Determine if each of the following statements is true or false.

_____ 9. Copernicus thought that Earth and other planets move around the sun.

_____ 10. Copernicus thought that Earth was at the center of the universe.

_____ 11. Copernicus did not publish his ideas until he was near death.

_____ 12. Copernicus lived a long and happy life after his works were published.

13. Why did Copernicus do most of his work in secret?

_____

3.3 Galileo on Motion (pages 30–32)

14. What was one of Galileo's great contributions to physics?

_____

15. A force is any _____ or _____.

Chapter 3   Newton's First Law of Motion—Inertia

16. Explain what friction is and how it acts.

_____

_____

_____

17. In the drawings below, describe each type of slope on the top line. On the bottom line, describe the slope's affect on speed.

a. _____   b. _____   c. _____

_____   _____   _____

18. Based on his experiments with rolling balls, Galileo was able to conclude that when friction is present, a _____ is needed to keep an object moving.

19. Describe the property of inertia in your own words.

_____

_____

_____

3.4 Newton's Law of Inertia (pages 33–35)

20. What is another name for Newton's first law of motion?

_____

21. State Newton's first law of motion.

_____

_____

22. Use Newton's first law of motion to explain what happens to dishes on a table when the tablecloth is quickly pulled from beneath them.

_____

_____

_____

23. Objects in a state of rest tend to remain at rest; only a _____ will change that state.

24. Use Newton's first law of motion to explain why an air hockey puck slides on the game table with no apparent loss in speed. Name two things that can cause the puck to change its state of motion.

_____

_____

_____

25. Once an object is moving in a force-free environment, for how long will it move in a straight line? _____

Chapter 3   Newton's First Law of Motion—Inertia

3.5 Mass—A Measure of Inertia (pages 36–38)

26. Circle the letter of each sentence that is true about the mass of an object.

    a. The amount of inertia an object has depends on its mass.

    b. The more mass an object has, the greater its inertia.

    c. Volume and mass are the same quantity.

    d. Mass is usually measured in kilograms.

27. Which item below has more mass? Which has more volume? Which has the greater inertia?

_____

_____

28. Is the following sentence true or false? Mass is a measure of the gravitational force acting on an object. _____

29. _____ is a measure of the amount of material in an object and depends on the number of and kind of atoms that compose it.

30. Is the following sentence true or false? A stone has the same mass on Earth and on the moon, but its weight is less on the moon.
_____

31. _____ is the quantity of matter in an object.

32. _____ is the force of gravity on an object.

Match each phrase with the correct word.

Phrase		Word
_____	**33.** traditional unit of weight in the United States	a. kilogram
_____	**34.** measure of matter in most parts of the world	b. mass
_____	**35.** SI unit of mass	c. pound
_____	**36.** SI unit of force	d. newton

3.6 The Moving Earth Again (pages 38–39)

37. If Earth is rotating at 30 km/s, explain how a bird sitting on a tree can drop down vertically and grab a worm that is crawling on the ground.

_____

_____

_____

Chapter 3   Newton's First Law of Motion—Inertia

38. A girl is sitting on a bus that is traveling at 30 km/h. She is throwing her tennis ball gently into the air and catching it. Circle the letter of each true statement.

a. The tennis ball is moving faster than the girl riding on the bus.

b. The tennis ball is behaving as if the bus were at rest.

c. The inertia of the tennis ball changes when it is thrown.

d. Gravity affects only the vertical motion of the tennis ball.

Match the ideas on motion with the correct scientist.

Idea	Scientist
_____ **39.** did not recognize inertia	a. Aristotle
_____ **40.** developed the law of inertia	b. Newton
_____ **41.** believed that horizontal motion was "unnatural"	c. Galileo
_____ **42.** was one of the first to recognize that no force was needed to keep an object in motion	

Chapter 3   Newton's First Law of Motion—Inertia

Making Unit Conversions

Foods manufactured and packaged outside the United States state the amount in the package in mass units. If a package of cookies manufactured in England contains 0.68 kg, what is the weight in pounds (lb) in the package?

1. Read and Understand

What information are you given?
   Mass of the cookies = 0.68 kg

2. Plan and Solve

What unknown are you trying to calculate?
   Weight of the cookies

What is the relationship between kilograms and pounds?
   1 kilogram = 2.2 pounds

Use this relationship as conversion factors.
   $\dfrac{1 \text{ kg}}{2.2 \text{ lb}}$ or $\dfrac{2.2 \text{ lb}}{1 \text{ kg}}$

Use the value that you know and choose the correct conversion factor.
   $0.68 \text{ kg} \times \dfrac{2.2 \text{ lb}}{1 \text{ kg}} = 1.5 \text{ lb}$

3. Look Back and Check

Is your answer reasonable?
   Yes, the cookies have a mass of less than 1 kg and the calculated number is less than 2.2 pounds. Also, the units canceled correctly, so the correct conversion factor was used.

Math Practice

On a separate sheet of paper, solve the following problems.

   1. A large package of chocolate from Switzerland contains 1.8 kilograms. What is the weight of the chocolate in pounds (lb)?

   2. A canned meat product manufactured in the United States contains 0.75 pound. If the product were sold in Europe, how many kilograms would the label show?

   3. A large instrument used by astronauts weighs 2.50 pounds on Earth. What is the mass of the instrument on the moon? (*Hint*: On the surface of the moon, the object would have only one sixth the weight it has on Earth.)

Chapter 4   Linear Motion

Summary

THE BIG IDEA : You can describe the motion of an object by its position, speed, direction, and acceleration.

4.1 Motion Is Relative

☑ **An object is moving if its position relative to a fixed point is changing.**

- When we describe the motion of one object with respect to another, we say that the object is moving **relative** to the other object.

- Unless stated otherwise, when we discuss the speeds of things in our environment, we mean speed with respect to the surface of Earth.

4.2 Speed

☑ **You can calculate the speed of an object by dividing the distance covered by time.**

- Galileo is credited as being the first to measure *speed* by considering the distance covered and the time it takes.

- **Speed** is how fast an object is moving.

- Any combination of units for distance and time that are useful and convenient are legitimate for describing speed.

- Some units that describe speed are miles per hour (mi/h) and kilometers per hour. The slash symbol (/) is read as "per."

- The speed of an object at any instant is called the **instantaneous speed.**

- The **average speed** of an object is the total distance covered divided by the time.

- Average speed does not indicate variations in the speed that may take place during the trip.

- A simple rearrangement of the definition of average speed gives the total distance covered:

    total distance covered = average speed × travel time

4.3 Velocity

☑ **Speed is a description of how fast an object moves; velocity is how fast and in what direction it moves.**

- **Velocity** is speed in a given direction.

- A quantity such as velocity, which specifies direction as well as magnitude, is called a vector quantity.

- Quantities that require only magnitude for a description are scalar quantities.

- Constant speed means steady speed.

- Constant velocity means both constant speed *and* constant direction, which is in a straight line.

- If *either* an object's speed *or* its direction (or both) is changing, then the object's velocity is changing.

Chapter 4   Linear Motion

4.4 Acceleration

☑ **You can calculate the acceleration of an object by dividing the change in its velocity by time.**

- **Acceleration** is the rate at which the velocity is changing.
- In physics, the term *acceleration* applies to decreases as well as increases in speed.
- Acceleration also applies to changes in *direction*.
- Acceleration is defined as the rate of change in *velocity*, rather than *speed*.
- Acceleration, like velocity, is a vector quantity because it is directional.
- If an object's speed, direction, or both, changes, the object changes velocity and accelerates.
- When the direction is not changing, acceleration may be expressed as the rate at which *speed* changes.
- Since acceleration is the change in velocity or speed per time interval, its units are those of speed per time.

4.5 Free Fall: How Fast

☑ **The acceleration of an object in free fall is about 10 meters per second squared (10 m/s^2).**

- Gravity causes objects to accelerate downward once they begin to fall.
- In real life, air resistance affects the acceleration of a falling object.
- An object moving under the influence of the gravitational force only is said to be in **free fall.** Freely falling objects are affected only by gravity.
- The **elapsed time** is the time that has elapsed, or passed, since the beginning of any motion.
- For free fall, it is customary to use the letter g to represent the acceleration because the acceleration is due to gravity.
- Although g varies slightly in different parts of the world, its average value is nearly 10 m/s^2.
- The instantaneous speed of an object falling from rest is equal to the acceleration multiplied by the amount of time it falls (the elapsed time).
- The instantaneous speed v of an object falling from rest after an elapsed time t can be expressed in equation form as $v = gt$. Note that the letter v symbolizes both speed and velocity.
- At the highest point of a rising object, when the object is changing its direction of motion from upward to downward, its instantaneous speed is zero.
- As an object rises, its speed decreases at the same rate it increases when moving downward—at 10 meters per second each second.
- The instantaneous speed at points of equal elevation in a moving object's path is the same whether the object is moving upward or downward.

Chapter 4   Linear Motion

4.6 Free Fall: How Far

☑ **For each second of free fall, an object falls a greater distance than it did in the previous second.**

- The initial speed of fall is zero and takes a full second to get to 10 m/s.

- Whenever an object's initial speed is zero and the acceleration a is constant, that is, steady and "non-jerky," the equations for the velocity and distance traveled are:

$$v = at \text{ and } d = \tfrac{1}{2}at^2$$

4.7 Graphs of Motion

☑ **On a speed-versus-time graph the slope represents speed per time, or acceleration.**

- On a speed-versus-time graph, if the line forms a straight line, time and speed are directly proportional to each other.

- The *slope* of the line is the vertical change divided by the horizontal change for any part of the line.

- On a distance-versus-time graph for a falling object, the relationship is *quadratic* and the curve is *parabolic*.

4.8 Air Resistance and Falling Objects

☑ **Air resistance noticeably slows the motion of things with large surface areas like falling feathers or pieces of paper. But air resistance less noticeably affects the motion of more compact objects like stones and baseballs.**

- Air resistance can affect the acceleration of objects outside a vacuum.

- In many cases, however, the effect of air resistance is small enough to be neglected.

- With negligible air resistance, falling objects can be considered to be falling freely.

4.9 How Fast, How Far, How Quickly How Fast Changes

☑ **Acceleration is the rate at which velocity itself changes.**

- When we wish to specify how fast something freely falls from rest after a certain elapsed time, we are talking about speed or velocity. The appropriate equation in these cases is $v = gt$.

- When we wish to specify how far an object has fallen, we are talking about distance. The appropriate equation in these cases is $d = \tfrac{1}{2}gt^2$.

Chapter 4   Linear Motion

Exercises

4.1 Motion Is Relative (page 47)

1. Is the following sentence true or false? When we describe the motion of one object with respect to another, we say that the object is moving relative to the other object. _____

2. An object is _____ if its position relative to a fixed point is _____.

3. A driver is going 20 kilometers per hour down the street. What is the driver's speed relative to?

_____

4.2 Speed (pages 48–49)

4. Define speed. _____

5. Complete the following equation: speed = distance/_____.

6. How is the slash symbol read in *km/h*? _____

7. Circle the letters of the sentences that are true of instantaneous speed.

   a. Instantaneous speed is the total distance covered divided by time.

   b. Instantaneous speed is the speed at any instant.

   c. The speedometer on a car shows the instantaneous speed.

   d. If you traveled 30 kilometers in 1 hour, your instantaneous speed would be 30 km/h.

8. How is average speed calculated?

_____

9. If you traveled 80 kilometers in 2 hours, what was your average speed?

_____

10. If your average speed is 30 kilometers per hour and your trip took 1 hour, what was the total distance covered?

_____

4.3 Velocity (page 50)

Determine if each of the following statements is true or false. Write the correct word on the line provided.

_____ 11. Speed is velocity in a given direction.

_____ 12. The speed of a plane can be described as 300 mi/h.

_____ 13. The velocity of a car can be described as 60 km/h to the north.

_____ 14. Speed is a vector quantity.

_____ 15. Velocity is a vector quantity.

Chapter 4   Linear Motion

16. If either the _____ or the _____ is changing (or both are), then the velocity is changing.

4.4 Acceleration (pages 51–52)

17. What is acceleration?

_____

18. How is acceleration calculated?

_____

19. In physics, the term *acceleration* applies to both _____ and _____ in speed.

20. Acceleration is a change in speed, a change in _____, or both.

21. Is the following sentence true or false? Acceleration is a vector quantity.

_____

22. If a car is traveling around a curve on a highway at a constant speed, is the car accelerating? Explain your answer.

_____

23. Circle the letter of the value and units that represent acceleration.

   a. 5 km   b. 15 km/s

   c. 25 s/km   d. 55 km/s^2

4.5 Free Fall: How Fast (pages 53–55)

24. Is the following sentence true or false? In real life, air resistance has no effect on the acceleration of a falling object. _____

25. An object moving under the influence of the gravitational force only is said to be in _____.

26. Define elapsed time.

_____

Match each symbol or value with the correct phrase.

Phrase	Symbol or Value
_____ 27. an approximate value of the acceleration of an object in free fall	a. 10 m/s^2
_____ 28. used to represent acceleration due to gravity	b. *g*
_____ 29. an accurate value of acceleration of an object in free fall	c. *v*
_____ 30. used for both speed and velocity in the equation for instantaneous speed	d. 9.8 m/s^2

Chapter 4   Linear Motion

31. What is the instantaneous speed of an object that is at its highest point when it is thrown straight up in the air? _____

32. When an object is thrown straight up into the air, what is its acceleration when it is moving upward? _____

33. What is the acceleration of the same object in the above question when it is descending? _____

4.6 Free Fall: How Far (page 56)

34. Is the following sentence true or false? For each second of free fall, an object falls a greater distance than it did in the previous second.

_____

35. At the end of time *t*, an object in free fall has fallen a distance equal to

_____

36. What are the equations used to calculate velocity and distance for a freely falling object?

_____

_____

4.7 Graphs of Motion (pages 57–58)

Use the graph below to answer Questions 37–39.

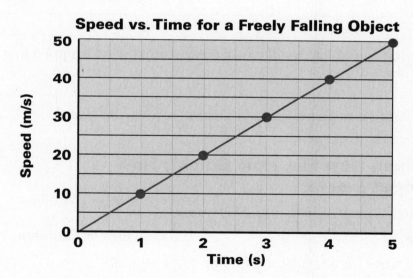

Speed vs. Time for a Freely Falling Object

37. What is the relationship between time and speed on this graph?

_____

38. What does the slope of the line on this graph represent?

_____

39. What is the slope of the graph?

_____

Name _____ Class _____ Date _____

Chapter 4   Linear Motion

Use the graph below to answer Questions 40 and 41.

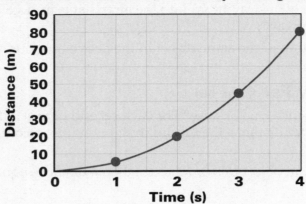

Distance vs. Time for a Freely Falling Object

40. The relationship between distance and time on this graph is
    _____ and the curve is _____.

41. What does the slope of the line at each point represent?
    _____

4.8 Air Resistance and Falling Objects (page 59)

42. Explain why a dropped coin reaches the ground before a feather.

    _____

    _____

43. Explain what would happen if a coin and a feather were dropped in a
    vacuum tube.

    _____

    _____

44. If air resistance is negligible, a falling object can be considered

    _____.

4.9 How Fast, How Far, How Quickly How Fast Changes (page 59)

Match each word or equation with the correct phrase.

Phrase

_____ 45. the word for how fast something
           freely falls from rest after an
           elapsed time

_____ 46. the equation for speed and velocity

_____ 47. the word for how far an object
           has fallen

_____ 48. the equation for distance

_____ 49. the word for the rate at which
           velocity changes

Word or Equation

a. $d = \frac{1}{2}gt^2$

b. $v = gt$

c. acceleration

d. speed

e. distance

Chapter 4   Linear Motion

Speed, Distance, and Acceleration

Calculate the average speed of a jogger who runs 100 meters in 30 seconds.

1. Read and Understand

What information are you given?
  Distance = 100 m
  Time = 30 s

2. Plan and Solve

What are you trying to calculate?

  Average speed

What formula contains the quantities and the unknown?

  $$\text{Average speed} = \frac{\text{total distance covered}}{\text{time interval}}$$

Replace each variable with its known value.

  $$\text{Average speed} = \frac{100 \text{ m}}{30 \text{ s}} = 3.3 \text{ m/s}$$

3. Look Back and Check

Is your answer reasonable?
  Yes, the number calculated is the quotient of distance and time, and the units indicate speed.

Math Practice

On a separate sheet of paper, solve the following problems.

1. Calculate your average speed if you travel 210 kilometers in 7 hours.

2. If your average speed is 40 kilometers per hour and you have traveled for 0.5 hour, what distance have you traveled?

3. Calculate your acceleration if your change in speed is 20 meters per second and the time interval is 5 seconds.

Chapter 5   Projectile Motion

Summary

THE BIG IDEA : Projectile motion can be described by the horizontal and vertical components of motion.

5.1 Vector and Scalar Quantities

☑ **A vector quantity includes both magnitude and direction, but a scalar quantity includes only magnitude.**

- Sketches in physics often include arrows, where each arrow represents the magnitude and the direction of a certain quantity.
- Velocity is a vector quantity, as is acceleration.
- Scalars can be added, subtracted, multiplied, and divided like ordinary numbers.

5.2 Velocity Vectors

☑ **The resultant of two perpendicular vectors is the diagonal of a rectangle constructed with the two vectors as sides.**

- An airplane's velocity is a combination of the velocity of the airplane relative to the air and the velocity of the air relative to the ground (the wind velocity).
- For two velocity vectors that are perpendicular, the result of adding the two vectors, called the *resultant*, is the diagonal of the rectangle described by the two vectors.
- To add equal-magnitude vectors, a square is constructed, and the resultant is the diagonal of the square. For any square, the length of the diagonal is $\sqrt{2}$, or 1.414 times either of its sides.

5.3 Components of Vectors

☑ **The perpendicular components of a vector are independent of each other.**

- Two vectors at right angles that add up to a given vector are known as the **components** of the vector they replace.
- The process of determining the components of a vector is called **resolution.**
- Any vector drawn on a piece of paper can be resolved into vertical and horizontal components that are perpendicular.

5.4 Projectile Motion

☑ **The horizontal component of motion for a projectile is just like the horizontal motion of a ball rolling freely along a level surface without friction. The vertical component of a projectile's velocity is like the motion for a freely falling object.**

- A cannonball shot from a cannon, a stone thrown into the air, a ball rolling off the edge of a table, a spacecraft circling Earth—all of these are examples of projectiles.

Chapter 5   Projectile Motion

- A **projectile** is any object that moves through the air or space, acted on only by gravity (and air resistance, if any).
- When no horizontal force acts on a projectile, the horizontal velocity remains constant.
- The horizontal component of motion for a projectile is completely independent of the vertical component of motion.

5.5 Projectiles Launched Horizontally

☑ **The downward motion of a horizontally launched projectile is the same as that of free fall.**

- When projectiles are launched horizontally, gravity acts only downward, so the only acceleration is downward.
- The vertical distance fallen has nothing to do with the horizontal component of motion.
- The path traced by a projectile accelerating only in the vertical direction while moving at constant horizontal velocity is a *parabola*.

5.6 Projectiles Launched at an Angle

☑ **The vertical distance a projectile falls below an imaginary straight-line path increases continually with time and is equal to $5t^2$ meters.**

- The maximum horizontal range for projectiles is attained at a projection angle of 45°.
- When the effect of air resistance on a projectile's motion is significant, the range is diminished and the path is not a true parabola.
- If air resistance is negligible, a projectile hits the ground with the same speed it had originally when it was projected upward from the ground.

Chapter 5   Projectile Motion

Exercises

5.1 Vector and Scalar Quantities (page 69)

1. Sketches in physics often include arrows, in which each arrow represents the _____ and the _____ of a quantity.

2. What two things are required of a vector quantity?

   a. force and time   b. direction and magnitude

   c. time and temperature   d. direction and mass

3. Is the following sentence true or false? Velocity is a scalar quantity.

   _____

4. Circle the letter of each quantity that is a vector quantity.

   a. velocity   b. time

   c. acceleration   d. momentum

5. A scalar quantity includes only _____.

6. Circle the letter that best describes how two scalar quantities are multiplied.

   a. using scientific notation

   b. like ordinary numbers

   c. by taking the square root of the sum of their squares

   d. multiplying their magnitudes and subtracting their directions

7. In the spaces below, write an example of a vector quantity and a scalar quantity.

   vector: _____

   scalar: _____

8. Circle the letter of each quantity that is a scalar quantity.

   a. 5 liters   b. 10 m/s north

   c. 32 minutes   d. 2 cm south

9. Can a scalar quantity be made into a vector quantity by adding a direction to its magnitude? Explain why or why not and give an example.

   _____

   _____

5.2 Velocity Vectors (pages 70–71)

10. A diagram includes a 3-cm long arrow pointing to the right. The arrow is a vector scaled so that 1 cm = 10 m/s. Circle the letter of the statement that best describes the vector.

    a. 3 cm to the right   b. 30 m/s to the right

    c. to the right   d. 60 km/h to the right

11. An airplane flies in the same direction as the wind. Is the following sentence true or false? The velocity of the airplane is the sum of the airplane's velocity relative to the air and the wind's velocity relative to the ground. _____

Chapter 5   Projectile Motion

12. Is the following sentence true or false? A tailwind increases the velocity of an airplane. _____

13. Is the following sentence true or false? Vectors can only be used to add velocities that are parallel to each other. _____

14. The result of adding two vectors is called the _____.

15. Circle the letter of the resultant of a 3-unit vector and a 4-unit vector that are perpendicular.

   a. 1-unit vector
   b. 3-unit vector
   c. 5-unit vector
   d. 7-unit vector

16. The figure below shows the addition of vectors with equal magnitudes at right angles to each other. Circle the letter that best describes the resultant.

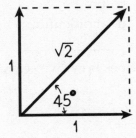

   a. 1 unit upward
   b. 1 unit to the right
   c. $\sqrt{2}$ units at 45°
   d. 2 units upward

17. Is the following sentence true or false? The length of the diagonal of a square is always 1.414 times the length of either side.

   _____

5.3 Components of Vectors (page 72)

18. Any vector can be resolved, or broken, into an equivalent set of two _____ vectors at right angles to each other.

19. Is the following sentence true or false? Component vectors are always at right angles to each other. _____

20. Is the following sentence true or false? The two components of a vector are independent of each other. _____

21. A ball is thrown into the air at an angle. The velocity of the ball can be resolved into _____ and _____ components.

5.4 Projectile Motion (page 73)

22. Circle the letter of each statement about a projectile that is true.

   a. A projectile moves through air or space.
   b. A projectile is always subject to at least two forces.
   c. A projectile is subject to the force of gravity.
   d. A projectile in air is subject to air resistance.

Chapter 5   Projectile Motion

23. Is this sentence true or false? For a projectile, the horizontal component of its motion is like the horizontal motion of a ball freely rolling on a level surface without friction. _____

24. The _____ component of velocity for a projectile always changes with time.

25. Circle the letter that best describes the relationship between the vertical and horizontal components of velocity for a projectile.

    a. equal   b. opposite

    c. independent   d. constant

5.5 Projectiles Launched Horizontally (page 74)

26. Is the following statement true or false? Ignoring air resistance, the horizontal component of velocity of a horizontally launched projectile remains constant. _____.

27. A ball is dropped off the edge of a desk. Another ball rolls off the desk at exactly the same time. Circle the letter that best describes the vertical component of velocity of the balls.

    a. equal   b. opposite

    c. zero   d. constant

28. Circle the letter of each statement about a horizontally launched projectile that is true.

    a. Gravity acts on the projectile.

    b. Ignoring air resistance, horizontal motion is constant.

    c. The projectile accelerates downward.

    d. The vertical motion is the same as a freely falling object.

29. Circle the letter that best describes the path followed by a ball that rolls off the edge of a desk.

    a. straight   b. circular

    c. curved   d. horizontal

30. The path of a projectile with constant horizontal motion and a downward acceleration due to gravity is a(n) _____.

31. A boy drops a rock off a cliff at the same time that his sister throws another rock horizontally from the cliff. Circle the letter of each statement about the two rocks that is true.

    a. Gravity acts on both rocks.

    b. Both rocks hit the ground at the same time.

    c. Both rocks accelerate horizontally and vertically.

    d. Both rocks follow parabolic paths.

Chapter 5   Projectile Motion

5.6 Projectiles Launched at an Angle (pages 75–79)

32. The path of a projectile is also called its _____.

33. Circle the letter that describes the motion of a ball thrown horizontally in the absence of gravity.

    a. diagonally downward   b. vertically downward

    c. parabolic   d. perfectly horizontal

34. The curving path followed by a projectile in air is due to _____.

35. Is the following sentence true or false? The distance a projectile falls below its imaginary straight-line path (in the absence of gravity) is equal to the distance a freely falling object would travel in the same amount of time. _____

36. The equation for the distance a projectile falls below its imaginary straight-line path is _____.

Use the Figure below to answers questions 37–39.

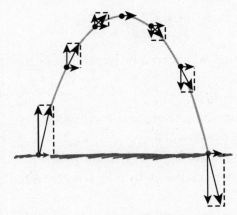

37. Circle the letter that best describes the horizontal component of velocity for the projectile.

    a. zero   b. constant

    c. varying   d. increasing

38. Circle the letter of the vertical component of velocity for the projectile at the peak of its trajectory.

    a. zero   b. positive

    c. negative   d. increasing

39. Is the following sentence true or false? At the beginning of the projectile's trajectory, the magnitude of the vertical component of the velocity is greater than the magnitude of the horizontal component of the velocity. _____

Chapter 5   Projectile Motion

Vector Addition and Resolution

A small rubber-band-powered airplane can fly at a speed of 2.5 m/s in still air. If it flies into a 0.5 m/s headwind, what is its speed relative to the ground? What is its speed in a tailwind with the same magnitude?

1. Read and Understand

What information are you given?
   Speed in still air = 2.5 m/s
   Speed of headwind = 0.5 m/s
   Speed of tailwind = 0.5 m/s

2. Plan and Solve

What unknown are you trying to calculate?
   Speed relative to ground into headwind = ?
   Speed relative to ground with tailwind = ?

What formula contains the given quantities and the unknown?
   Into headwind:
   Speed relative to ground = speed in still air − speed of headwind
   = 2.5 m/s − 0.5 m/s
   = 2.0 m/s

   With tailwind:
   Speed relative to ground = speed in still air + speed of tailwind
   = 2.5 m/s + 0.5 m/s
   = 3.0 m/s

3. Look Back and Check

Is your answer reasonable?
   Yes, a headwind would cause the airplane's speed to decrease, while a tailwind would cause the speed to increase.

Math Practice

On a separate sheet of paper, solve the following problems.

1. A stream flows with a speed of 3.0 m/s relative to the shore. A kayaker paddles downstream with a speed of 1.5 m/s relative to the stream. What is the kayaker's speed relative to the shore?

2. A train travels at a speed of 25.0 m/s relative to the ground. If you walk to the back of the train at a speed of 0.5 m/s relative to the train, what is your speed relative to the ground?

Chapter 5   Projectile Motion

3. Susan can row a boat at 4.0 m/s in still water. While trying to row directly across a river from west to east, Susan is pulled by a current flowing southward at 3.0 m/s. How fast does Susan row relative to the shore?

4. A bird flies at a speed of 9.0 m/s in still air. If the bird flies with a 12 m/s crosswind blowing, how fast does it travel relative to the ground?

Chapter 6   Newton's Second Law of Motion—Force and Acceleration

Summary

THE BIG IDEA : An object accelerates when a net force acts on it.

6.1 Force Causes Acceleration

☑ **Unbalanced forces acting on an object cause the object to accelerate.**

- The combination of forces acting on an object is the net force; acceleration depends on net force.
- Doubling the force on an object doubles its acceleration.
- An object's acceleration is directly proportional to the net force acting on it.

6.2 Mass Resists Acceleration

☑ **For a constant force, an increase in the mass will result in a decrease in the acceleration.**

- The same force applied to twice as much mass results in only half the acceleration.
- For a given force, the acceleration produced is inversely proportional to the mass. Inversely means that the two values change in opposite directions.

6.3 Newton's Second Law

☑ **Newton's second law states that the acceleration produced by a net force on an object is directly proportional to the magnitude of the net force, is in the same direction as the net force, and is inversely proportional to the mass of the object.**

- **Newton's second law** describes the relationship among an object's mass, an object's acceleration, and the net force on an object.
- In equation form, Newton's second law is written as follows:

$$\text{acceleration} = \frac{\text{net force}}{\text{mass}} \quad \text{or} \quad a = \frac{F}{m}$$

- Acceleration is equal to the net force divided by the mass.

6.4 Friction

☑ **The force of friction between the surfaces depends on the kinds of material in contact and how much the surfaces are pressed together.**

- Friction acts on materials that are in contact with each other, and it always acts in a direction to oppose relative motion.
- Liquids and gases are called **fluids** because they flow. Fluid friction occurs when an object moves through a fluid.
- **Air resistance** is the friction acting on something moving through air.
- A diagram showing all of the forces acting on an object is called a **free-body diagram.**

Chapter 6   Newton's Second Law of Motion—Force and Acceleration

6.5 Applying Force—Pressure

☑ **For a constant force, an increase in the area of contact will result in a decrease in the pressure.**

- **Pressure** is the amount of force per unit of area.
- In equation form, pressure is defined as follows:

$$\text{pressure} = \frac{\text{force}}{\text{area of application}} \quad \text{or} \quad P = \frac{F}{A}$$

- Pressure is measured in newtons per square meter, or **pascals** (Pa). One newton per square meter is equal to one pascal.
- The smaller the area supporting a given force, the greater the pressure on that surface.

6.6 Free Fall Explained

☑ **All freely falling objects fall with the same acceleration because the net force on an object is only its weight, and the ratio of weight to mass is the same for all objects.**

- A 10-kg cannonball and a 1-kg stone dropped from an elevated position at the same time will fall together and strike the ground at practically the same time.
- Since mass and weight are proportional, a 10-kg cannonball experiences 10 times as much gravitational force as a 1-kg stone.

6.7 Falling and Air Resistance

☑ **The air resistance force an object experiences depends on the object's speed and area.**

- The force due to air resistance diminishes the net force acting on falling objects.
- **Terminal speed** is the speed at which the acceleration of a falling object is zero because friction balances the weight.
- **Terminal velocity** is terminal speed together with the direction of motion.

Chapter 6   Newton's Second Law of Motion—Force and Acceleration

Exercises

6.1 Force Causes Acceleration (page 87)

1. When a hockey puck is struck with a hockey stick, a(n) _____ acts on the puck and the puck _____.

2. Circle the letter of the type of force that causes acceleration.

    a. balanced   b. negligible

    c. zero   d. unbalanced

3. The combination of forces acting on an object is known as the _____ force.

4. The acceleration of an object is directly proportional to the net force acting on it. This means that, as the net force acting on the object increases, the acceleration of the object _____.

5. Circle the letter of each statement about force and acceleration that is true.

    a. Balanced forces cause constant acceleration.

    b. The forces acting on an object at rest are unbalanced.

    c. A net force acting on an object causes acceleration.

    d. Force is not required for an object to accelerate.

6. Two shopping carts of equal mass are pushed by two different people. One cart accelerates three times as fast as the other cart. Describe the forces acting on each cart.

    _____

    _____

6.2 Mass Resists Acceleration (page 87)

7. For a constant force, how does an increase in an object's mass affect its acceleration?

    _____

8. What does it mean for two quantities to be inversely proportional to one another?

    _____

9. Circle the letter showing how mass and acceleration are related.

    a. acceleration ~ mass   b. acceleration ~ 1/mass

    c. acceleration ~ mass^2 d. acceleration ~ $\frac{1}{2}$ mass

6.3 Newton's Second Law (pages 88–89)

10. Circle the letter of each quantity related by Newton's second law.

    a. mass   b. force

    c. time   d. acceleration

Chapter 6   Newton's Second Law of Motion—Force and Acceleration

11. Circle the letter of each statement related to Newton's second law that is true.

    a. Acceleration is directly proportional to the net force.

    b. The direction of acceleration is the same as the net force.

    c. Acceleration is inversely proportional to mass.

    d. Net force and mass are always equal.

12. When using the equation for Newton's second law, if force is measured in newtons, then the unit for acceleration is _____ and the unit for mass is _____.

13. Is the following sentence true or false? The acceleration of an object is equal to the net force acting on it divided by the object's mass. _____

14. A 100-N force is used to accelerate a large push cart across the floor. Circle the letter of the force required to accelerate the push cart twice as fast.

    a. 50 N   b. 100 N

    c. 150 N   d. 200 N

15. An object accelerates when a net force is applied to it. Circle the letter describing the conditions that would double the object's acceleration.

    a. doubling the mass

    b. halving the force

    c. doubling the mass and halving the force

    d. halving the mass

16. During a lab experiment, a net force is applied to an object and the object accelerates. The mass of the object is then doubled, and the net force applied to it also doubles. Describe the object's acceleration.

    _____

    _____

17. Circle the letter of the equation that describes Newton's second law of motion.

    a. $a = \dfrac{F}{m}$ b. $F = ma^2$

    c. $F = \dfrac{a}{m}$ d. $F = \dfrac{1}{2}(am)^2$

6.4 Friction (page 90–91)

18. Describe what causes friction between two solid surfaces.

    _____

    _____

    _____

19. Is the following sentence true or false? Friction does not depend on the types of materials in contact with each other. _____

20. Is the following sentence true or false? Friction depends on how much the materials in contact are pushed together. _____

Chapter 6   Newton's Second Law of Motion—Force and Acceleration

21. The figure above shows where an out-of-control car might strike a concrete road divider. In terms of friction, explain why the concrete barrier is superior to the steel barrier in the figure.

_____

_____

22. Substances that are liquids or gases are also called _____.

23. Is the following sentence true or false? When friction is present, an object can move with constant velocity even when an outside force is applied. _____

24. A _____ is a diagram in which all of the forces acting on an object are shown.

6.5 Applying Force—Pressure (pages 91–92)

25. Circle the letter of each quantity related to pressure.

   a. time   b. force
   c. weight   d. area

26. Circle the letter that best describes pressure.

   a. the applied force that acts on an object

   b. force per unit of area

   c. the area to which a force is applied

   d. force times surface area

27. Imagine standing on a bathroom scale on two feet and then one foot. Describe the force and pressure exerted in each case.

_____

_____

28. As the area a force acts on increases, the force exerted on each unit of area _____.

29. What is the equation for pressure when the force is perpendicular to the surface area?

_____

30. Circle the letter that describes the unit of pressure known as a pascal.

   a. newtons × area   b. newton · meter
   c. newtons per square meter   d. square meters per second

Chapter 6   Newton's Second Law of Motion—Force and Acceleration

31. Look at the two books resting on a shelf in the illustration shown below. Assume the two books are identical. Circle the letter of each statement about the two books that is true.

    a. Both books have the same mass.

    b. Both books exert the same force on the shelf.

    c. Both books exert the same pressure on the shelf.

    d. Both books have the same weight.

6.6 Free Fall Explained (pages 93–95)

32. An object dropped in air that experiences no air resistance is said to be in

    _____.

33. A 1-kg river rock and a 10-kg small boulder are dropped from the back of a truck at the same time. Identify which rock will strike the ground first.

    _____

34. When an object is in free fall, the only force acting on the object is _____.

35. Circle the letter of each statement about freely falling objects that is true.

    a. They all fall with the same acceleration.

    b. The net force acting on them is their weight.

    c. Their weight-to-mass ratios are always the same.

    d. Their acceleration is g, the acceleration due to gravity.

6.7 Falling and Air Resistance (pages 95–97)

36. Identify the conditions needed for a feather and coin to fall at the same rate.

    _____

37. Circle the letter of each factor that affects the amount of air resistance experienced by an object.

    a. time in contact with the air   b. speed of object through the air

    c. surface area of object   d. weight of object

38. Circle the letter that describes the forces that are in balance when an object reaches its terminal speed.

    a. mass and air resistance   b. air resistance and friction

    c. friction and mass   d. weight and air resistance

39. Define terminal speed and terminal velocity.

    _____

    _____

Chapter 6   Newton's Second Law of Motion—Force and Acceleration

Newton's Second Law

A large mining dump truck has a mass of 40,000 kg. If its engine produces 20,000 N of force, how fast will the truck accelerate?

1. Read and Understand

What information are you given?
  Mass of truck = 40,000 kg
  Force applied = 20,000 N

2. Plan and Solve

What unknown are you trying to calculate?
  Acceleration of truck = ?

What formula contains the given quantities and the unknown?

  Acceleration = $\dfrac{\text{force}}{\text{mass}}$ or $a = \dfrac{F}{m}$

Replace each variable with its known value and solve.

  $a = \dfrac{20,000 \text{ N}}{40,000 \text{ kg}} = \dfrac{20,000 \text{ kg} \cdot \text{m/s}^2}{40,000 \text{ kg}} = 0.5 \text{ m/s}^2$

3. Look Back and Check

Is your answer reasonable?
  Yes, the number calculated is the quotient of force and mass and the units are those of acceleration.

Math Practice

On a separate sheet of paper, solve the following problems.

1. The truck described above dumps its load and its mass is reduced to 10,000 kg. What is the acceleration of the truck? Assume its engine still produces the same amount of force.

2. How much force must the engine of the dump truck described above develop to achieve an acceleration of 3.5 m/s^2?

3. A toy car has a mass of 1500 g. If a 3-N force is applied to the car, what will its acceleration be?

Chapter 7   Newton's Third Law of Motion—Action and Reaction

Summary

THE BIG IDEA : For every force, there is an equal and opposite force.

7.1 Forces and Interactions

☑ A force is always part of a mutual action that involves another force.

- A mutual action is an **interaction** between one thing and another.
- An example of interaction occurs when a hammer exerts a force on a nail, and the nail exerts a force on the hammer.

7.2 Newton's Third Law

☑ Newton's third law states that whenever one object exerts a force on a second object, the second object exerts an equal and opposite force on the first object.

- **Newton's third law** describes the relationship between two forces in an interaction. Newton's third law is often stated: "To every action there is always an equal opposing reaction."
- In an interaction, one force is called the **action force.** The other force is called the **reaction force.** The action and reaction forces are equal in strength and opposite in direction.
- When you walk on a floor, you push against the floor, and the floor simultaneously pushes against you.

7.3 Identifying Action and Reaction

☑ To identify a pair of action-reaction forces, first identify the interacting objects A and B, and if the action is A on B, the reaction is B on A.

- When a boulder falls to Earth, the *action* is Earth exerting a force on the boulder, and the *reaction* is the boulder simultaneously exerting a force on Earth.
- A rocket accelerates because the rocket pushes exhaust gas and the exhaust gas pushes on the rocket.

7.4 Action and Reaction on Different Masses

☑ A given force exerted on a small mass produces a greater acceleration than the same force exerted on a large mass.

- Recall that Newton's second law states that acceleration is proportional to the net force and inversely proportional to the mass.
- When a boulder falls toward Earth, Earth also moves toward the boulder. Because Earth has a huge mass, its acceleration toward the boulder is infinitesimally small. A rocket accelerates because it continually recoils from the exhaust gases ejected from its engine.

Chapter 7   Newton's Third Law of Motion—Action and Reaction

7.5 Defining Systems

☑ **Action and reaction forces do not cancel each other when either of the forces is external to the system being considered.**

- Consider an imaginary system consisting of an orange sitting on a cart. An external force, provided by an apple pulling the cart, causes the system to accelerate in accord with Newton's second law.

- The fact that the orange simultaneously exerts a force on the apple, which is external to the system, may affect the apple (another system), but not the orange. You can't cancel a force on the orange with a force on the apple.

- Now consider a larger system, enclosing both the orange and the apple. The force pair is internal to the orange-apple system. Therefore these forces do not cancel each other.

- A force external to the system, in this case friction, is needed for acceleration. When the apple pushes against the floor, the floor simultaneously pushes on the apple—an external force on the system—and the system accelerates.

7.6 The Horse–Cart Problem

☑ **If the horse in the horse–cart system pushes the ground with a greater force than it pulls on the cart, there is a net force on the horse, and the horse-cart system accelerates.**

- Imagine a horse that believes its pull on a cart carrying a farmer will be canceled by the opposite and equal pull by the cart on the horse, thus making acceleration impossible.

- From the farmer's point of view, the net force on the cart, divided by the mass of the cart, will produce an acceleration.

- In the system of the horse, the opposite reaction force by the cart on the horse restrains the horse. The horse moves forward by interacting with the ground. When the horse pushes backward on the ground, the ground simultaneously pushes forward on the horse.

- In the horse–cart system as a whole, the pull of the horse on the cart and the reaction of the cart on the horse are forces that act and react within the system. They cancel and can be neglected. It is the outside reaction by the ground that pushes the system.

7.7 Action Equals Reaction

☑ **For every interaction between things, there is always a pair of oppositely directed forces that are equal in strength.**

- Suppose that, for some reason, you punch a wall. You cannot hit the wall any harder than the wall can hit you back.

- Hold a sheet of paper in midair and tell your friends that the heavyweight champion of the world could not strike the paper with a force of 200 N (45 pounds). The paper is not capable of exerting a reaction force of 200 N, and you cannot have an action force without a reaction force.

Chapter 7   Newton's Third Law of Motion—Action and Reaction

Exercises

7.1 Forces and Interactions (page 107)

1. A force is always part of a(n) _____ that involves another force.

2. Define **interaction.** _____

3. Describe the interaction forces between a nail and a hammer that hits it.

   _____

   _____

7.2 Newton's Third Law (page 108)

4. State Newton's third law.

   _____

   _____

5. Is the following sentence true or false? It doesn't matter which force we call *action* and which we call *reaction.* _____

6. Action and reaction forces are equal in _____ and opposite in _____.

7. Is the following sentence true or false? In every interaction, the forces always occur in pairs. _____

8. Complete the table by writing the reaction for each action.

Action	Reaction
When you walk, you push against the floor.	
The tires of a car push against the road.	
When swimming, you push the water backward.	
A dog wags its tail.	
You push on a wall.	
When a batter swings, the bat exerts a force on the ball.	

9. Use the idea of action and reaction forces to explain why a person trying to walk on ice may not have any forward motion.

   _____

   _____

   _____

Chapter 7   Newton's Third Law of Motion—Action and Reaction

7.3 Identifying Action and Reaction (pages 108–109)

10. What are the two steps you can take to identify a pair of action-reaction forces?

a. _____

b. _____

11. Identify the action–reaction forces of a boulder falling off a cliff by answering the following questions.

a. What are the two interacting objects? _____

b. What is the action of A on B? _____

c. What is the action of B on A? _____

12. Complete the table by identifying the reaction forces. In each case, specify the direction of the reaction force.

Action	Reaction
As a car moves along a road, the tires of the car push backward against the road.	
As a spaceship moves through space, it pushes gas out behind.	
A ball rolls across a table and exerts a force against a second ball.	

7.4 Action and Reaction on Different Masses (pages 110–111)

13. Is the following sentence true or false? If you drop a pencil, the pencil pulls Earth upward with a much smaller force than that with which Earth pulls the pencil downward. _____

14. State Newton's second law.

_____

_____

15. When a boulder falls off a cliff toward the ground, Earth accelerates toward the boulder. Circle the letter that explains why we don't sense this acceleration.

a. The boulder's pull on Earth is much smaller than Earth's pull on the boulder.

b. Earth's huge mass causes its acceleration to be infinitesimally small.

c. Earth's acceleration is in the same direction as the boulder's acceleration.

d. The boulder's acceleration is much smaller than the Earth's acceleration.

Chapter 7   Newton's Third Law of Motion—Action and Reaction

16. When a cannonball is fired from a cannon, the force the cannon exerts on the cannonball is exactly _____ and _____ to the force the cannonball exerts on the cannon.

17. Name the three factors that you must consider in order to understand why a cannonball moves much faster than the cannon when the cannonball is shot from the cannon.

_____

18. The picture above shows a cannonball being shot from a cannon. Explain why the change in velocity of the cannonball is much greater than the change in velocity of the cannon.

_____

_____

_____

19. How is the acceleration of a rocket similar to the acceleration of a cannonball that is fired from a cannon?

_____

_____

_____

_____

20. Is the following sentence true or false? A rocket is propelled by the impact of exhaust gases against the atmosphere. _____

21. The upward force that causes helicopters, birds, and airplanes to fly is called _____.

22. A helicopter has a lifting force because its blades are shaped to force air particles _____, and the air forces the blades _____.

Match each condition on the left to the result on the right.

Condition	Result
_____ **23.** Lift equals the helicopter's weight.	a. The helicopter moves downward.
_____ **24.** Lift is greater than the helicopter's weight.	b. The helicopter moves upward.
_____ **25.** Lift is less than the helicopter's weight.	c. The helicopter hovers in midair.

Chapter 7   Newton's Third Law of Motion—Action and Reaction

26. Describe the action and reaction forces that cause a bird to fly.

_____

_____

27. Describe two action–reaction pairs that cause an airplane to move upward and forward.

   a. _____

   b. _____

7.5 Defining Systems (pages 112–113)

28. In order to understand why action and reaction forces don't cancel to zero, you must consider the _____ involved.

For questions 29 and 30, refer to the figure below.

29. The figure shows a force exerted by an apple. The dashed line identifies the system that accelerates because of this force. Explain why the force that the orange exerts on the apple doesn't cancel the force that the apple exerts on the orange.

_____

_____

30. Suppose the system includes both the orange and the apple. Explain why the force of the orange on the apple cancels the force of the apple on the orange.

_____

_____

31. Is the following sentence true or false? The trillions and trillions of interatomic forces that hold a baseball together do play a role in accelerating the ball. _____

32. Is the following sentence true or false? If the action–reaction forces are internal to a system, then the forces cancel and the system does not accelerate. _____

33. When a football player kicks a ball, the player's foot exerts a force on the ball, and the ball exerts a force on the player's foot. Why does the ball accelerate, even though the forces are equal and opposite?

_____

Chapter 7   Newton's Third Law of Motion—Action and Reaction

7.6 The Horse–Cart Problem (pages 114–115)

34. Describe the horse–cart problem.

_____

_____

_____

35. Name the three points of view from which you can consider the horse–cart problem.

a. _____

b. _____

c. _____

36. The farmer is only concerned with the force that is exerted on the _____.

37. According to the farmer, the _____ on the cart, divided by the _____ of the cart, will produce a(n) _____.

38. The horse believes that the reaction force by the _____ on the horse restrains the horse.

39. From the horse's point of view, the horse moves forward by interacting with _____.

40. If the horse in the horse–cart system pushes the ground with a greater force than it pulls on the cart, then _____, and the horse–cart system accelerates.

41. Consider the horse–cart system as a whole.

a. Which action–reaction pair contributes nothing to the acceleration of the system?

_____

b. Which interaction is responsible for moving the system?

_____

7.7 Action Equals Reaction (page 116)

42. Is the following sentence true or false? You cannot hit a wall any harder than the wall can hit you back. _____

43. Explain why it is impossible to strike a sheet of paper that is held in midair with a force of 200 N.

_____

_____

44. For every interaction between things, there is always a pair of oppositely directed forces that are _____.

Chapter 7   Newton's Third Law of Motion—Action and Reaction

Reaction Force

A 28-kg skater slides across ice at a speed of 2.0 m/s, pushes against a sled, and slows to 1.0 m/s in 0.50 s. What is the force of the skater on the sled?

1. Read and Understand

What information are you given?

the skater's mass = m = 28 kg

initial speed = v_i = 2.0 m/s

final speed = v_f = 1.0 m/s

time = t = 0.5 s

2. Plan and Solve

What unknown are you trying to calculate?

The force of the skater on the sled = F_2

What do you already know?

The force that slows the skater, F_1, is equal and opposite to the force of the skater on the sled, F_2.

What mathematical equations can you use to calculate the unknown?

Newton's second law of motion: F = ma

Since a = $(v_f - v_i)/t$, F = ma = $m(v_f - v_i)/t$

Newton's third law of motion: F_1 = $-F_2$

Apply Newton's second law of motion.

F_1 = (28 kg)(1.0 m/s − 2.0 m/s)/0.5 s = −56 N

Apply Newton's third law of motion.

F_1 = $-F_2$ = −(−56 N) = 56 N

3. Look Back and Check

Is your answer reasonable?

The force that the skater exerts on the sled is in the same direction as the skater's motion (positive), as it should be.

Math Practice

On a separate sheet of paper, solve the following problems.

1. A 38-kg boy is rollerskating at a speed of 1.8 m/s when he bumps against a box. The box slows the boy's speed to 1.2 m/s in 0.40 s. What is the force of the boy against the box?

2. An 18-kg ball rolls across a smooth floor and strikes a wall with a force of 9.0 N. What is the recoil acceleration of the ball?

Chapter 8   Momentum

Summary

THE BIG IDEA : Momentum is conserved for all collisions as long as external forces don't interfere.

8.1 Momentum

☑ **A moving object can have a large momentum if it has a large mass, a high speed, or both.**

- **Momentum** is the mass of the object multiplied by its velocity.
- A moving truck has more momentum than a car moving at the same speed because the truck has more mass.
- A fast car can have more momentum than a slow truck.
- A truck at rest has no momentum at all.

8.2 Impulse Changes Momentum

☑ **The change in momentum depends on the force that acts and the length of time it acts.**

- The quantity *force × time interval* is called **impulse**. In short-hand notation, impulse = $F\Delta t$.
- The greater the impulse exerted on something, the greater will be the change in momentum. The exact relationship is impulse = change in momentum or $Ft = \Delta(mv)$.
- To increase the momentum of an object, apply the greatest force possible for as long as possible. A golfer teeing off and a baseball player trying for a home run do both of these things when they swing as hard as possible and follow through with their swings.
- In the case of decreasing momentum, a longer contact time reduces the force and decreases the resulting deceleration. A padded dashboard in a car is safer than a rigid, metal one because the padded dashboard increases the time of contact.

8.3 Bouncing

☑ **The impulse required to bring an object to a stop and then to "throw it back again" is greater than the impulse required merely to bring the object to a stop.**

- It takes a greater impulse to catch a flower pot and throw it back up than merely to catch it.
- A karate expert strikes the bricks in such a way that her hand is made to bounce back, yielding as much as twice the impulse to the bricks.

Chapter 8   Momentum

8.4 Conservation of Momentum

✅ **The law of conservation of momentum states that, in the absence of an external force, the momentum of a system remains unchanged.**

- The **law of conservation of momentum** describes the momentum of a system.

- If a system undergoes changes wherein all forces are internal—for example, in atomic nuclei undergoing radioactive decay, cars colliding, or stars exploding—the net momentum of the system before and after the event is the same.

- The momentum before firing a cannon is zero. After firing, the momentum is still zero because the momentum of the cannon is equal and opposite to the momentum of the cannonball.

8.5 Collisions

✅ **Whenever objects collide in the absence of external forces, the net momentum of both objects before the collision equals the net momentum of both objects after the collision.**

- When objects collide without being permanently deformed and without generating heat, the collision is said to be an **elastic collision.**

- Colliding *objects* bounce perfectly in perfect elastic collisions.

- A collision in which the colliding objects become distorted and generate heat during the collision is an **inelastic collision.**

- Whenever colliding objects become tangled or couple together, a totally inelastic collision occurs.

- Perfectly elastic collisions are not common in the everyday world. At the microscopic level, however, perfectly elastic collisions are commonplace. For example, electrically charged particles bounce off one another without generating heat.

8.6 Momentum Vectors

✅ **The vector sum of momenta is the same before and after a collision.**

- Momentum is conserved even when the interacting objects don't move along the same straight line.

- The momentum of a car wreck is equal to the vector sum of the momenta of each of the cars before the collision.

- When a firecracker bursts, the vector sum of the momenta of its fragments adds up to the firecracker's momentum just before bursting.

Chapter 8   Momentum

Exercises

8.1 Momentum (page 125)

1. Define momentum. _____

2. What is the equation for momentum? _____

3. A moving object can have a large momentum if it has a(n) _____, a(n) _____, or both.

8.2 Impulse Changes Momentum (pages 125–129)

4. Is the following sentence true or false? If the momentum of an object changes, either the mass or the velocity or both change. _____

5. If a force is increased on an object, what happens to the velocity and the momentum? _____

6. The change in momentum depends on the _____ that acts and the length of _____ it acts.

7. What is the short-hand notation for impulse? _____

8. What is the formula that relates impulse and change in momentum? _____

9. Explain why a baseball player follows through with his or her swing. _____ _____

10. Is the following sentence true or false? By hitting a soft object, such as a haystack, instead of a hard object, such as a concrete wall, you extend the contact time in which the momentum is brought to zero. _____

11. Circle the letter of each sentence that is true about impulse and momentum.

    a. When jumping from an elevated position down to the ground, you should keep your legs stiff to decrease the momentum.

    b. A wrestler thrown to the floor should extend his time hitting the mat by relaxing his muscles and spreading the impulse to his foot, knee, hip, ribs, and shoulder.

    c. When a boxer gets punched, she should move her head away from the punch to increase the contact time and reduce the force.

    d. A dropped dish is more likely to survive a fall on carpet rather than concrete, because the softness of the carpet leads to increased contact time.

Chapter 8   Momentum

8.3 Bouncing (pages 129–130)

12. Is the following sentence true or false? The impulse required to bring an object to a stop and then to "throw it back again" is less than the impulse merely to bring the object to a stop. _____

13. Explain how a person practicing karate can break bricks with his or her bare hand.

_____

_____

Impulse

14. Use the diagram of the Pelton Wheel above to explain how the blades work.

_____

_____

8.4 Conservation of Momentum (pages 130–131)

Match each phrase with another phrase that makes the statement true.

_____ **15.** If you wish to change the momentum of an object,

_____ **16.** The force or impulse must be exerted on the object

_____ **17.** If no outside force is present,

_____ **18.** The force on the cannonball inside the cannon barrel is equal

a. no change in momentum is possible.

b. exert an impulse on it.

c. and opposite to the force causing the cannon to recoil.

d. by something outside the object.

19. Explain why the total momentum of a cannon–cannonball system is zero after firing.

_____

_____

Chapter 8   Momentum

20. Is momentum a vector or a scalar quantity? _____

21. Is the following sentence true or false? The law of conservation of momentum states that, in the absence of an external force, the momentum of a system remains unchanged. _____

22. Is the following sentence true or false? If a system undergoes changes wherein all the forces are internal, such as an atomic nuclei undergoing nuclear decay, the net momentum of the system before and after the event is the same. _____

8.5 Collisions (pages 132–134)

23. Is the following sentence true or false? Whenever objects collide in the absence of external forces, the net momentum of both objects before the collision does not equal the net momentum of both objects after the collision. _____

24. When objects collide without being permanently deformed and without generating heat, the collision is said to be a(n) _____.

25. Describe how the velocities of each of the billiard balls changes in the elastic collisions below.

Before Collision   Collision   After Collision

a.

b.

c.

a. _____

_____

b. _____

_____

c. _____

_____

Chapter 8   Momentum

26. A collision in which the colliding objects become distorted and generate heat during the collision is a(n) _____.

27. What is the equation for the conservation of momentum?

_____

28. Since there is no air resistance in space, what is the only opposing force that affects two docking space stations? _____

29. What is an example of a perfectly elastic collision at the microscopic level?

_____

8.6 Momentum Vectors (pages 135–136)

30. Is this sentence true or false? Momentum is conserved only when interacting objects move along the same straight path.

_____

31. Circle the letter of each sentence that is true.

   a. The vector sum of the momenta is the same before and after a collision.

   b. The momentum of the car wreck is not equal to the vector sum of the momenta of car A and car B before the collision.

   c. When a firecracker bursts, the vector sum of the momenta of its fragments add up to the firecracker's momentum just before bursting.

   d. Momentum is not conserved for high-speed elementary particles in bubble chambers.

32. What two conservation laws are the most powerful tools in the study of mechanics?

_____

Chapter 8   Momentum

Momentum

A 0.5-kg toy truck moving at a velocity of 0.5 m/s collides head-on with a 0.75-kg toy truck that is at rest. The trucks become entangled and lock together. What is the velocity of the two toy trucks after the collision?

1. Read and Understand

What information are you given?

$m_{toy\ 1} = 0.5$ kg

$v_{toy\ 1} = 0.5$ m/s

$m_{toy\ 2} = 0.75$ kg

$v_{toy\ 2} = 0$ m/s

2. Plan and Solve

What unknown are you trying to calculate?

$v_{after} = ?$

What formula contains the given quantities and the unknown?

$(net\ mv)_{before} = (net\ mv)_{after}$

Replace each variable with its known value.

$(0.5$ kg$)(0.5$ m/s$) + (0.75$ kg$)(0$ m/s$) = (0.5$ kg $+ 0.75$ kg$)(v_{after})$

0.25 kg $\cdot$ m/s $= (1.25$ kg$)(v_{after})$

$v_{after} = 0.2$ m/s

3. Look back and check

Is your answer reasonable?

Yes, the number calculated is the quotient of distance and speed, and the units indicate a velocity.

Math Practice

On a separate sheet of paper, solve the following problems.

1. A 0.25-kg ball rolling at 1.0 m/s rolls and overtakes a 0.3-kg ball rolling in the same direction at 0.5 m/s. The balls stick together on impact. What is the velocity of the two balls after the collision?

2. A 5.0-kg puppy running at 2.0 m/s picks up a 1.0-kg stick that is sitting on the ground. What is the momentum of the puppy and the stick after the puppy picks up the stick?

Chapter 9   Energy

Summary

THE BIG IDEA : Energy can change from one form to another without a net loss or gain.

9.1 Work

☑ **Work is done when a force acts on an object and the object moves in the direction of the force.**

- **Work** is the product of the force on an object and the distance through which the object is moved.

- In the simplest case, when the force is constant, the motion takes place in a straight line in the direction of the force: work = force × distance. In equation form, $W = Fd$.

- Work generally falls into two categories: work done against another force and work done to change the speed of an object. In both categories, work involves a transfer of energy between something and its surroundings.

- The unit of work is the newton-meter (N·m), also called the **joule.** One joule (J) of work is done when a force of 1 N is exerted over a distance of 1 m.

9.2 Power

☑ **Power equals the amount of work done divided by the time interval during which the work is done.**

- **Power** is the rate at which work is done:

$$power = \frac{work\ done}{time\ interval}$$

- A high-power engine does work rapidly. If an engine has twice the power of another engine, this means that it can do twice the work in the same amount of time or the same amount of work in half the time.

- The unit of power is the joule per second, which is also known as the **watt.** One watt (W) of power is expended when one joule of work is done in one second.

- In the United States, we customarily rate engines in units of horsepower and electricity in kilowatts, but either may be used. One horsepower (hp) is the same as 0.75 kW.

9.3 Mechanical Energy

☑ **The two forms of mechanical energy are kinetic energy and potential energy.**

- The property of an object or system that enables it to do work is **energy.**

- Like work, energy is measured in joules.

- **Mechanical energy** is the energy due to the position of something or the movement of something.

Chapter 9   Energy

9.4 Potential Energy

✔ **Three examples of potential energy are elastic potential energy, chemical energy, and gravitational potential energy.**

- Energy that is stored and held in readiness is called **potential energy** (PE) because in the stored state it has the potential for doing work.

- A stretched or compressed spring, a bow that is drawn back, and a stretched rubber band have *elastic potential energy*.

- The chemical energy in fuels is potential energy at the submicroscopic level. This energy is available when a chemical change in the fuels takes place.

- The potential energy due to the elevated position of an object is *gravitational potential energy*.

- The amount of gravitational potential energy possessed by an elevated object is equal to the work done against gravity in lifting it. Gravitational potential energy = weight × height. In equation form, PE = *mgh*. The height in this equation is the distance above some chosen reference level.

9.5 Kinetic Energy

✔ **The kinetic energy of a moving object is equal to the work required to bring it to its speed from rest, or the work the object can do while being brought to rest.**

- The energy of motion is **kinetic energy** (KE).

- The kinetic energy of an object is equal to half the object's mass multiplied by the square of its speed. In equation form, this is

$$KE = \frac{1}{2}mv^2.$$

- The net force on an object multiplied by the distance along which the force acts equals the object's kinetic energy. In equation form, this is

$$Fd = \frac{1}{2}mv^2.$$

9.6 Work-Energy Theorem

✔ **The work-energy theorem states that whenever work is done, energy changes.**

- The **work-energy theorem** describes the relationship between work and energy.

- Work equals change in kinetic energy. In equation form, Work = ΔKE, where the delta symbol, Δ, means "change in." The work in this equation is the *net* work.

- If you push a box across a floor at a constant speed, you are pushing just hard enough to overcome friction. In this example, the net force and net work are zero, and KE = 0.

- Kinetic energy often appears hidden in different forms of energy. Random molecular motion is sensed as *heat. Sound* consists of molecules vibrating in rhythmic patterns. *Light* energy originates in the motion of electrons in atoms. Electrons in motion make *electric currents.*

Chapter 9   Energy

9.7 Conservation of Energy

✅ **The law of conservation of energy states that energy cannot be created or destroyed. It can be transformed from one form into another, but the total amount of energy never changes.**

- The study of the various forms of energy and the transformations from one form into another is the **law of conservation of energy.**

- Everywhere along the path of a pendulum bob, the sum of potential energy and kinetic energy is the same. At the highest points, the energy is only potential energy. At the lowest point, the energy is only kinetic energy.

- The sun shines because some of its nuclear energy is transformed into radiant energy. In nuclear reactors, nuclear energy is transformed into heat.

- Some electric-generating plants transform the energy of falling water into electrical energy. Electrical energy then travels through wires to homes.

9.8 Machines

✅ **A machine transfers energy from one place to another or transforms it from one form to another.**

- A **machine** is a device used to multiply forces or to change the direction of forces. A machine cannot put out more energy than is put into it.

- A **lever** is a simple machine made of a bar that turns about a fixed point.

- If heat from friction is negligible, the work put into a machine equals the work put out by the machine: work input = work output.
  $$(force \times distance)_{input} = (force \times distance)_{output}$$

- The pivot point of a lever is the **fulcrum.**

- The ratio of output force to input force for a machine is called the **mechanical advantage.**

- A type 1 lever has the fulcrum between the input force and the load. If the fulcrum is closer to the load, a small input force exerted through a large distance produces a larger output force over a shorter distance. The directions of input and output are opposite.

- For a type 2 lever, the load is between the fulcrum and the input force. Force is increased at the expense of distance. Input and output forces have the same direction.

- In a type 3 lever, the fulcrum is at one end and the load is at the other. The input force is applied between them. The input and output forces have the same direction.

- A **pulley** is a kind of lever that can be used to change the direction of a force.

- A single pulley with a fixed axis behaves like a type 1 lever. A single pulley with an axis that moves behaves like a type 2 lever.

- A system of pulleys multiplies the force and it may change the direction of the force. The mechanical advantage for a simple pulley system is the same as the number of strands of rope that actually support the load.

Chapter 9   Energy

9.9 Efficiency

✔ **In any machine, some energy is transformed into atomic or molecular kinetic energy—making the machine warmer.**

- The **efficiency** of a machine is the ratio of useful energy output to total energy input, or the percentage of the work input that is converted to work output. No real machine can be 100% efficient. The wasted energy is dissipated as heat.

- An inclined plane is a machine. Its *theoretical* mechanical advantage, assuming negligible friction, is the length of the incline divided by the height of the inclined plane.

- Efficiency can also be expressed as the ratio of actual mechanical advantage to the theoretical mechanical advantage.

- To convert efficiency to percent, express it as a decimal and multiply by 100%.

9.10 Energy for Life

✔ **There is more energy stored in the molecules in food than there is in the reaction products after the food is metabolized. This energy difference sustains life.**

- Most living organisms on this planet feed on various hydrocarbon compounds that release energy when they react with oxygen. In metabolism of food in the body, carbon combines with oxygen to form carbon dioxide.

- Only green plants and certain one-celled organisms can make carbon dioxide combine with water to produce hydrocarbon compounds such as sugar. This process is called *photosynthesis* and requires an energy input, which normally comes from sunlight.

9.11 Sources of Energy

✔ **The sun is the source of practically all our energy on Earth.**

- Sunlight is directly transformed into electricity by photovoltaic cells or in the flexible solar shingles on the roofs of buildings. We use the energy in sunlight to generate electricity indirectly as well.

- Wind, caused by unequal warming of Earth's surface, is another form of solar power. Wind can be used to turn generator turbines within specially equipped windmills.

- Hydrogen is the least polluting of all fuels. Because it takes energy to make hydrogen (to extract it from water and carbon compounds), it is not a *source* of energy. In a **fuel cell,** hydrogen and oxygen gas are compressed at electrodes to produce water and electric current.

- The most concentrated form of usable energy is stored in nuclear fuels.

- Earth's interior is kept hot by producing a form of nuclear power, radioactivity.

- Geothermal energy is held in underground reservoirs of hot water.

Chapter 9   Energy

Exercises

9.1 Work (pages 145–146)

1. Circle the letter next to the correct mathematical equation for work.

   a. work = force ÷ distance   b. work = distance ÷ force

   c. work = force × distance   d. work = force × distance^2

2. You can use the equation in Question 1 to calculate work when the force is _____ and the motion takes place in

   _____.

3. You do work if you lift a book one meter above the ground. How does the amount of work change in each of the following cases?

   a. You lift the book twice as high. _____

   b. You lift two identical books one meter above the ground. _____

4. Complete the table by naming the two general categories of work and giving an example of each.

Category of Work	Example

5. The unit of work is the _____.

6. Suppose that you apply a 50-N horizontal force to a 25-kg box, pushing the box 6 meters across the floor. How much work do you do on the box?

   _____

9.2 Power (pages 146–147)

7. Power is the rate at which _____ is done.

8. Power equals _____ divided by _____.

9. The unit of power is the _____.

10. One megawatt (MW) equals _____ watts.

11. In the United States, we customarily rate engines in units of _____, which is equivalent to _____ kilowatt.

9.3 Mechanical Energy (page 147)

12. Define energy.

   _____

   _____

13. What is the SI unit of energy? _____

Chapter 9   Energy

14. Mechanical energy is the energy due to the _____ or
_____ of something.

15. What are the two forms of mechanical energy?

a. _____

b. _____

9.4 Potential Energy (pages 148–149)

16. On each line, write *elastic*, *chemical*, or *gravitational* to identify the type of potential energy described.

_____ a. fossil fuels

_____ b. a compressed spring

_____ c. water in a reservoir

_____ d. a stretched rubber band

_____ e. food

_____ f. a bow drawn back

_____ g. electric batteries

17. The amount of gravitational potential energy possessed by an elevated object is equal to the work done against _____ in lifting it.

18. What are two ways to calculate gravitational potential energy?

a. _____ × height

b. _____ × _____ × height

19. Explain what the height is when you calculate an object's gravitational potential energy.

_____

_____

20. How do hydroelectric power stations make use of gravitational potential energy?

_____

_____

_____

9.5 Kinetic Energy (page 150)

21. Kinetic energy is energy of _____.

22. Circle the letter for the equation you can use to find the kinetic energy of an object.

a. $KE = 2mv$

b. $KE = \frac{1}{2}mv$

c. $KE = 2mv^2$

d. $KE = \frac{1}{2}mv^2$

23. Kinetic energy equals the _____ on an object multiplied by the distance the object moves.

24. Is the following sentence true or false? If the speed of an object doubles, the kinetic energy of the object also doubles. _____

Chapter 9   Energy

9.6 Work-Energy Theorem (pages 151–152)

25. Express the work-energy theorem.

_____

26. Explain this equation: Work = ΔKE.

_____

27. Is the following sentence true or false? If you push against a heavy refrigerator, and it doesn't slide, then you are not doing work on the refrigerator.

_____

28. Suppose you push against a box so that it moves across a horizontal surface. Explain how to determine the change in kinetic energy in each of the following cases.

a. The surface has no friction. _____

_____

b. The surface has some friction. _____

_____

c. The box moves at a constant speed across a surface that has some friction.

_____

29. Is the following sentence true or false? The maximum friction that the brakes of a car can supply is nearly the same whether the car moves slowly or quickly.

_____

Match each form of hidden kinetic energy with its description.

Form of Kinetic Energy	Description
_____ **30.** heat	a. consists of molecules vibrating in rhythmic patterns
_____ **31.** sound	b. produced by electrons in motion
_____ **32.** electricity	c. results from random molecular motion

9.7 Conservation of Energy (pages 153–154)

33. The energy an arrow delivers to a target is slightly less than the energy it had when it was flying toward the target. What happened to the lost energy?

_____

_____

34. Express the law of conservation of energy.

_____

_____

_____

35. The wound spring of a toy car has 10 J of potential energy. Only 8 J of this energy changes to kinetic energy as the car moves. What happens to the remaining 2 J of energy?

_____

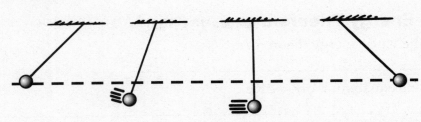

36. The figure above shows the energy of a swinging pendulum bob at different points along its path.

   a. If you ignore friction, how does the energy of the bob at the highest points of its path compare to the energy at the lowest point of its path?

   _____

   _____

   b. How does friction affect the pendulum?

   _____

37. The sun shines because some of its nuclear energy is transformed into _____ energy.

38. In nuclear reactors, nuclear energy is transformed into _____.

39. Suppose a person in distress leaps from a burning building onto a firefighter's trampoline near the ground.

   a. Describe the change in potential energy, kinetic energy, and total energy as the person falls.

   _____

   b. Suppose the person has 10,000 J of potential energy just before jumping. What are the person's potential energy and kinetic energy upon reaching the trampoline?

   _____

9.8 Machines (pages 155–157)

40. A machine is a device used to _____ or _____.

41. Circle each letter that describes something a machine can do.

   a. puts out more energy than is put into it

   b. transfers energy from one place to another

   c. transforms energy from one form to another

   d. destroys or creates energy

42. Describe a lever.

   _____

43. Complete the following mathematical equation for a lever.

   $$\frac{(\underline{\hspace{2cm}} \times \underline{\hspace{2cm}})_{input}}{(\underline{\hspace{2cm}} \times \underline{\hspace{2cm}})_{output}} =$$

44. The pivot point of a lever is called a _____.

Chapter 9   Energy

45. What are two ways to calculate the mechanical advantage of a machine?

a. _____

b. _____

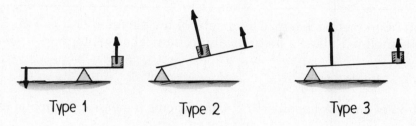

Type 1   Type 2   Type 3

46. The figures above show three types of levers. Give an example of each type.

a. Type 1: _____

b. Type 2: _____

c. Type 3: _____

47. Describe a pulley.

_____

48. Complete the table about pulleys.

Type of Pulley	Changes direction of the input force?	Multiplies the input force?	Mechanical Advantage
Single pulley with fixed axis			
Single pulley with movable axis			
System of pulleys			

9.9 Efficiency (pages 158–160)

49. Is the following sentence true or false? No real machine can be 100% efficient.

_____

50. When a simple lever rocks about its fulcrum, or a pulley turns about its axis, a small fraction of input energy is converted into _____ energy.

51. What are two ratios used to relate the efficiency of a machine to energy and work?

a. _____

b. _____

52. Suppose you put in 100 J of work on a lever and get out 93 J of work.

a. What is the efficiency of the lever? _____

b. How much of the work input is lost as heat? _____

Chapter 9   Energy

53. Is the following sentence true or false? The lower the efficiency of a machine, the greater the amount of energy wasted as heat. _____

54. Which requires less force: sliding a load up an incline or lifting the load vertically?

_____

55. The length of an incline is 8 m. The height of the elevated end is 2 m. Circle the letter of the inclined plane's theoretical mechanical advantage.

    a. 2   b. 4

    c. 8   d. 16

56. If the friction of an object against an inclined plane increases, the actual mechanical advantage _____ and the efficiency _____.

57. What ratio can you use to relate the efficiency of a machine to its mechanical advantage?

_____

58. The efficiency of a machine is always less than _____.

59. How can you convert efficiency to percent?

_____

_____

60. Is the following sentence true or false? An automobile engine is a complex machine that transforms mechanical energy into chemical energy.

_____

9.10 Energy for Life (page 160)

61. Most living organisms on this planet feed on various _____ compounds that release energy when they react with _____.

62. Is the following sentence true or false? The amount of energy stored in gasoline is greater than the amount of energy in the products of its combustion.

_____

63. Is the following sentence true or false? There is less energy stored in the molecules of food than there is in the reaction products after the food is metabolized.

_____

64. How does the metabolism of food in the body compare to the burning of fossil fuels in mechanical engines? How are the processes different?

_____

_____

_____

65. What makes life possible on Earth?

_____

_____

_____

Chapter 9   Energy

9.11 Sources of Energy (pages 161–162)

66. _____ is the source of practically all our energy on Earth.

67. Sunlight is directly transformed into electricity by

_____.

68. Sequence the steps by which sunlight can be used indirectly to generate electricity.

    a. _____

    b. _____

    c. _____

    d. _____

69. Wind can be considered a type of solar power because wind is caused by

_____.

70. Circle the letter of each correct statement about wind energy.

    a. Wind is a steady form of energy.

    b. Wind power can provide all of our energy needs.

    c. Wind can make a substantial contribution to the energy we use.

    d. Wind energy is practical when the energy is stored for future use.

71. Is the following sentence true or false? Hydrogen is a source of energy.

    _____

72. In a _____, hydrogen and oxygen gas are compressed at electrodes to produce water and electric current.

73. Earth's interior is kept hot by _____.

74. _____ energy is held in underground reservoirs of hot water.

Chapter 9   Energy

Gravitational Potential Energy

Calculate the increase in potential energy when a crane lifts a 2,000-kg car a vertical distance of 10 m. The acceleration due to gravity (g) is 10 m/s^2.

1. Read and Understand

What information are you given?

Mass of the car, m = 2,000 kg

Height of the car, h = 10 m

2. Plan and Solve

What unknown are you trying to calculate?

Gravitational potential energy = PE

What mathematical equation can you use to calculate the unknown?

Gravitational potential energy, PE = mgh

Substitute the information you know into the equation.

PE = mgh

  = (2,000 kg)(10 m/s^2)(10 m)

Multiply to find the unknown.

PE = 200,000 J = 200 kJ

3. Look Back and Check

Is your answer reasonable?

The magnitude of the potential energy is 100 times the mass of the car. This is reasonable because the car is lifted 10 m.

Math Practice

On a separate sheet of paper, solve the following problems.

1. A football player throws a ball with a mass of 0.34 kg. What is the gravitational potential energy of the ball when it is 5.0 m above the ground?

2. A 2.0-kg book is on a shelf that is 1.6 m high. What is the gravitational potential energy of the book relative to the ground?

3. A 36-kg girl walks to the top of stairs that are 2.0-m high. How much gravitational potential energy does the girl gain?

4. A can of soup has a mass of 0.35 kg. The can is moved from a shelf that is 1.2 m off the ground to a shelf that is 0.40 m off the ground. How does the gravitational potential energy of the can change?

Chapter 10   Circular Motion

Summary

THE BIG IDEA : Centripetal force keeps an object in circular motion.

10.1 Rotation and Revolution

☑ **Two types of circular motion are rotation and revolution.**

- An **axis** is the straight line around which rotation takes place.

- When an object turns about an *internal* axis—that is, an axis located within the body of the object—the motion is called **rotation,** or spin. A Ferris wheel rotates about an axis.

- When an object turns about an *external* axis, the motion is called **revolution.** Riders *revolve* about the axis of a Ferris wheel.

- Earth undergoes both types of circular motion. It revolves around the sun once every 365 1/4 days, and it rotates around an axis passing through its geographical poles once every 24 hours.

10.2 Rotational Speed

☑ **Tangential speed depends on rotational speed and the distance from the axis of rotation.**

- **Linear speed** is the distance traveled per unit of time. The linear speed is greater on the outer edge of a rotating object, such as a merry-go-round, than it is closer to the axis.

- **Tangential speed** is the speed of something moving along a circular path. For circular motion, the terms *linear speed* and *tangential speed* are interchangeable.

- **Rotational speed,** which is sometimes called angular speed, is the number of rotations per unit of time. All parts of a merry-go-round have the same rotational speed.

- Tangential speed and rotational speed are related.

  Tangential speed ~ radial distance × rotational speed

  $$v \sim r\omega$$

- As you move away from the axis of a rotating platform, your tangential speed increases while your rotational speed stays the same.

- Wheels of a train stay on the track because their rims are slightly tapered. So when a train rounds a curve, wheels on the outer track ride on the wider part of the tapered rims (and cover a greater distance in the same time) while opposite wheels ride on their narrow parts (covering a smaller distance in the same time).

Chapter 10   Circular Motion

10.3 Centripetal Force

☑ **The centripetal force on an object depends on the object's tangential speed, its mass, and the radius of its circular path.**

- Any object moving in a circle undergoes an acceleration that is directed to the center of the circle. This is centripetal acceleration. *Centripetal* means "toward the center."

- The force directed toward a fixed center that causes an object to follow a circular path is called **centripetal force.**

- Centripetal forces can be exerted in a variety of ways. Anything that moves in a circular path is acted on by a centripetal force.

- Centripetal force can be calculated using the following equation:

$$\text{Centripetal force} = \frac{\text{mass} \times \text{speed}^2}{\text{radius of curvature}} \quad \text{or}$$

$$F_c = \frac{mv^2}{r}$$

- Centripetal force F_c is measured in newtons when mass m is expressed in kilograms, speed v in meters/second, and radius of curvature r in meters.

- The centripetal force acting on a circularly moving object is the net force that acts exactly along the radial direction—toward the center of the circular path.

10.4 Centripetal and Centrifugal Forces

☑ **The "centrifugal-force effect" is attributed not to any real force but to inertia—the tendency of the moving body to follow a straight-line path.**

- The apparent outward force on a rotating or revolving body is called **centrifugal force.** *Centrifugal* means "center-fleeing," or "away from the center."

- If you are in a car that rounds a sharp corner to the left, you tend to pitch outward against the right door. This happens not because of some outward or centrifugal force, but because there is no centripetal force holding you in circular motion.

- Likewise, the only force exerted on a whirling can at the end of a string is a centripetal force. No outward force acts on the can.

10.5 Centrifugal Force in a Rotating Reference Frame

☑ **Centrifugal force is an effect of rotation. It is not part of an interaction and therefore it cannot be a true force.**

- Because centrifugal force is merely an effect of rotation, it is not a true force like gravitational, electromagnetic, and nuclear forces.

- Physicists refer to centrifugal force as a "fictitious force."

- To observers in a rotating system, however, centrifugal force is very real.

Chapter 10   Circular Motion

Exercises

10.1 Rotation and Revolution (page 171)

Match each term to its definition.

Term	Definition
_____ 1. rotation	a. straight line around which rotation takes place
_____ 2. axis	b. motion about an axis located within the body of the object
_____ 3. revolution	c. motion about an axis located outside the body of the object

4. Circle the letter that best describes Earth's motion around the sun.

   a. spin

   b. rotation

   c. revolution

   d. linear

5. When you ride a bicycle, the bicycle wheels _____ around their axles.

6. Circle each letter that is an example of rotation.

   a. a Ferris wheel in motion

   b. Earth moving around the sun

   c. an ice skater doing a pirouette

   d. riders on a Ferris wheel in motion

10.2 Rotational Speed (pages 171–174)

Match each term to its definition.

Term	Definition
_____ 7. linear speed	a. speed of something moving along a circular path
_____ 8. rotational speed	b. number of rotations per unit of time
_____ 9. tangential speed	c. distance traveled per unit of time

10. Circle the letter that describes the direction of motion associated with tangential speed.

   a. toward the center of rotation   b. tangent to the circular path

   c. outward from the center   d. downward toward Earth

11. Is the following sentence true or false? The terms *linear speed* and *rotational speed* can be used interchangeably. _____

12. Is the following sentence true or false? All parts of a spinning merry-go-round have the same angular speed. _____

Chapter 10   Circular Motion

13. The abbreviation RPM stands for _____.

14. The diagram below shows the velocity vector for a can spun on a string at the moment that the string breaks.

Circle the letter that best describes the quantity represented by the vector.

a. rotational speed

b. radial speed

c. tangential speed

d. axial speed

15. Is the following sentence true or false? Tangential speed is directly proportional to rotational speed. _____

16. Circle the letter of each action that results in an increase in a circularly moving object's tangential speed.

a. moving farther from the axis of rotation

b. decreasing the RPM

c. increasing the rotational speed

d. moving closer to the axis of rotation

17. Circle the letter of the equation or description that describes the relationship between tangential speed, radial distance, and rotational speed.

a. $V \sim IR$

b. tangential speed ~ radial distance × rotational speed

c. $\omega \sim vr$

d. tangential speed ~ radial distance × (rotational speed)^2

18. Is the following sentence true or false? Your tangential speed while standing at the axis of rotation of a spinning platform is zero.

_____

19. As your radial distance from the center of a rotating platform increases, your _____ speed also increases.

20. Circle the letter that best describes how a train stays on the tracks when going around a curve.

a. Wheels rotate at the same rate but cover different distances as they roll.

b. Raised edges on the outside of each wheel keep them from coming off of the tracks.

c. Wheels rotate at different rates so each wheel travels a different distance.

d. The train tracks are banked so both wheels cover the same distance.

Chapter 10   Circular Motion

10.3 Centripetal Force (pages 175–177)

21. Is the following sentence true or false? Any object moving in a circle is constantly accelerating. _____

22. *Centripetal* means _____.

23. The force directed toward a fixed center that causes an object to follow a circular path is _____.

24. If centripetal force ceased to act on an object moving in a circular path, the object would _____.

25. Explain where the centripetal force that holds a car in a curved path while rounding a corner comes from.

_____

26. Is the following sentence true or false? In a washing machine's spin cycle, water is forced away from the clothes. _____

27. Circle each letter that identifies a factor that affects the amount of centripetal force acting on an object.

　a. tangential speed　　　b. radius of curvature

　c. mass　　　　　　　　d. force of gravity

28. A race car is driven around a banked track as shown in the drawing below. Circle the letter of the answer that identifies the centripetal force vector.

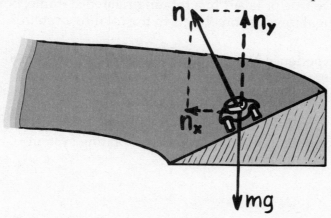

　a. *n*　　　b. n_y
　c. n_x　　　d. *mg*

10.4 Centripetal and Centrifugal Forces (pages 178–179)

29. The apparent outward force on a rotating or revolving body is _____ force.

30. Circle the letter that best describes the meaning of the word *centrifugal*.

　a. toward the center

　b. center-seeking

　c. circle-like

　d. away from the center

Chapter 10   Circular Motion

31. Describe why you are pressed against the door of a car as it rounds a sharp corner.

_____

_____

32. Is the following sentence true or false? When a can tied to a string is swung in a circle, an outwardly directed force acts on the can.

_____

33. What causes the centrifugal-force effect?

_____

_____

10.5 Centrifugal Force in a Rotating Reference Frame (pages 179–180)

34. Imagine riding on a fast-moving train. Describe your speed from the reference frame of the train and from a reference frame of the ground outside the train.

_____

_____

_____

35. Is the following sentence true or false? In a rotating reference frame, both centripetal and centrifugal force act on objects in the rotating system.

_____

36. The centrifugal force experienced in a rotating reference frame is not a _____ force.

37. Circle the letter of each true force.

    a. nuclear force   b. gravitational force

    c. electromagnetic force   d. centrifugal force in a rotating system

Chapter 10   Circular Motion

Centripetal Force

A child ties a string tightly around an orange and swings it in a circle over her head. The radius of the circle is 1.0 m and the mass of the orange is 0.25 kg. If the orange has a speed of 4.0 m/s, what is the tension on the string?

1. Read and Understand

What information are you given?

   Mass of orange = 0.25 kg

   Radius of circle = 1.0 m

   Speed of orange = 4.0 m/s

2. Plan and Solve

What unknown are you trying to calculate?

   Tension in string = ?

What formula contains the given quantity and the unknown?

   Centripetal force, $F_c = \dfrac{mv^2}{r}$

Replace each variable with its known value and solve.

$$F = \frac{(0.25 \text{ kg})(4.0 \text{ m/s})^2}{1.0 \text{ m}} = \frac{4.0 \text{ kg} \cdot \text{m}^2/\text{s}^2}{1.0 \text{ m}} = 4.0 \text{ kg} \cdot \text{m/s}^2 \text{ or } 4.0 \text{ N}$$

3. Look Back and Check

Is your answer reasonable?

   Yes, the tension value is fairly small, as expected, and the calculated answer has the correct units.

Math Practice

On a separate sheet of paper, solve the following problems.

1. How does the tension change in the solved sample question above if the radius of the circle doubles?

2. How does the tension change in the solved sample question above if the mass of the orange doubles?

3. How does the tension change in the solved sample question above if the speed of the orange doubles?

Chapter 11   Rotational Equilibrium

Summary

THE BIG IDEA : An object will remain upright if its center of mass is above the area of support.

11.1 Torque

✓ **To make an object turn or rotate, apply a torque.**

- **Torque** is produced by a turning force and tends to produce rotational acceleration.

- Force and torque are different; forces tend to make things accelerate whereas torques produce rotation.

- A torque is produced when a force is applied with "leverage." You use leverage when you use a screwdriver to open the lid of a paint can.

- The **lever arm** is the distance from the turning axis to the point of contact.

- Torque can be calculated using the following equation:

$$\text{torque} = \text{force}_\perp \times \text{lever arm}$$

11.2 Balanced Torques

✓ **When balanced torques act on an object, there is no change in rotation.**

- Children of unequal weight can balance on a seesaw by sitting at different distances from the pivot point.

- Scale balances with sliding weights are based on balanced torques.

11.3 Center of Mass

✓ **The center of mass of an object is the point located at the object's average position of mass.**

- The point where all of the mass of an object can be considered concentrated is called the **center of mass.**

- For a symmetrical object, the center of mass is at the geometric center of the object. For irregularly shaped objects, the location of the center of mass varies.

- Spin can be applied to an object by applying a force that does not pass through the object's center of mass. Kicking a football in the middle, for example, will make it travel without rotating. Kicking the football above or below its center will make it rotate.

11.4 Center of Gravity

✓ **For everyday objects, the center of gravity is the same as the center of mass.**

- The **center of gravity,** or CG, is the average position of all of the particles of *weight* that make up an object. For most objects on and near Earth, the terms *center of mass* and *center of gravity* are interchangeable.

Chapter 11   Rotational Equilibrium

- If you throw a wrench so that it rotates as it moves through the air, you'll see it wobble about its CG. The center of gravity itself would follow a parabolic path.
- An object's CG is its balance point; supporting the CG supports the entire object. A meter stick can be balanced by applying a force at its geometric midpoint—the location of its CG.
- Any object suspended at a single point will hang with its CG directly below the point of suspension.

11.5 Torque and Center of Gravity

☑ **If the center of gravity of an object is above the area of support, the object will remain upright.**

- If the CG extends outside the area of support, an unbalanced torque exists, and the object will topple.
- The Leaning Tower of Pisa does not topple because its CG does not extend beyond its base.
- It is difficult to balance a broom upright in the palm of your hand because the support base is very small and far beneath the CG.

11.6 Center of Gravity of People

☑ **The center of gravity of a person is not located in a fixed place, but depends on body orientation.**

- When you stand erect with your arms at your sides, your CG is within your body.
- The CG is slightly lower in women than in men because women tend to be proportionally larger in the pelvis and smaller in the shoulders.
- Raising your arms vertically over your head raises your CG by several centimeters.
- When you stand, your CG is somewhere above your support base, which is the area bounded by your feet.

11.7 Stability

☑ **When an object is toppled, the center of gravity of that object is raised, lowered, or unchanged.**

- An object balanced so that any displacement lowers its center of mass is in **unstable equilibrium.**
- An object balanced so that any displacement raises its center of mass is in **stable equilibrium.** Raising the CG of an object in stable equilibrium requires increasing the object's potential energy, which requires work.
- An object balanced so that any small movement neither raises nor lowers its center of gravity is in **neutral equilibrium.**
- An object with a low CG is usually more stable than an object with a relatively high CG.

Chapter 11   Rotational Equilibrium

Exercises

11.1 Torque (pages 189–190)

Match each term with the best description.

	Term	**Definition**
_____	**1.** rotation	**a.** distance from a turning axis to the point of contact
_____	**2.** torque	**b.** produced by a torque
_____	**3.** lever arm	**c.** produces rotational acceleration

4. Circle the letter of each statement that is true of torque.

a. tends to produce linear acceleration

b. caused by a turning force

c. caused by an applied force acting through a lever arm

d. is the same as force

5. If you apply a _____ to an object, it will likely rotate.

6. Is the following sentence true or false? The longer the handle of a claw hammer, the greater the leverage when the hammer is used to pull a nail from a piece of wood. _____

7. Look at the illustration below, which shows an arm applying a torque to a wrench.

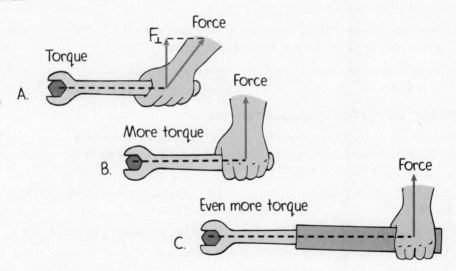

Use the definition of torque (torque = force$_\perp$ × lever arm) to explain why the applied torque increases in the illustrations A - C above.

_____

_____

8. Circle the letter of the description that would produce the greatest torque.

a. small force, short lever arm   b. small force, long lever arm

c. large force, small lever arm   d. large force, long lever arm

Chapter 11   Rotational Equilibrium

11.2 Balanced Torques (pages 191–192)

9. Two children with different weights sit on opposite sides of a seesaw. Circle the letter of the statement that must be true if the seesaw does not rotate.

  a. The children are sitting at equal distances from the pivot point.

  b. The seesaw must be broken because it is not moving.

  c. The lighter child is sitting closer to the pivot point.

  d. The torque that tends to produce a clockwise rotation equals the torque that tends to produce a counterclockwise rotation.

10. Explain how the sliding weights on a balance are used to bring the arm back to the horizontal position after a load has been placed on the pan.

   _____

   _____

11.3 Center of Mass (pages 192–194)

11. Is the following sentence true or false? When thrown end-over-end through the air, no part of a baseball bat follows a parabolic path.

   _____

12. Circle the letter of each statement that is true of an object that spins when it is thrown through the air.

  a. All parts of the object follow a parabolic path.

  b. The object spins about its center of mass.

  c. The object moves as if all its mass were concentrated at its center of mass.

  d. No part of the object follows a parabolic path.

13. If a force applied to an object does not pass through the object's center of mass, the object will _____.

11.4 Center of Gravity (pages 195–196)

14. Is the following sentence true or false? For most objects on and near Earth, the center of mass and center of gravity vary greatly.

   _____

15. Circle the letter of each statement that is true about the center of gravity of an object.

  a. It is the average position of all of the particles of weight in an object.

  b. It is often interchangeable with center of mass.

  c. It is affected by the force of gravity.

  d. For very large objects, it can be in a different location than the center of mass of that object.

16. If you throw a banana so that it rotates as it moves through the air, it will wobble about its _____.

17. Explain why the center of gravity of the solar system is not at the sun's geometric center.

   _____

   _____

   _____

Chapter 11   Rotational Equilibrium

18. An object such as a meter stick can be supported by applying a force at its _____.

19. Circle the letter that describes the location of the CG of an object that is suspended from a single point.

    a. at the point of suspension

    b. directly in line and below (or at) the point of suspension

    c. outside the object

    d. directly in line and above (or at) the point of suspension

20. Describe how to find the center of gravity of an irregularly shaped object by suspending it.

    _____

    _____

    _____

21. Is the following sentence true or false? The center of gravity of an object is always located at a point where the object physically exists.

    _____

22. Imagine a ring in the shape of a thin band. Describe the location of the ring's center of gravity.

    _____

    _____

11.5 Torque and Center of Gravity (pages 196–198)

23. Describe the conditions that are necessary so that an object will not topple.

    _____

    _____

24. Is the following sentence true or false? If a vertical line extending down from an object's CG extends outside its area of support, the object will topple. _____.

25. Circle the letter of each statement that is true.

    a. Toppling occurs when an unbalanced torque exists.

    b. Toppling occurs when a vertical line through the CG falls within the object's base.

    c. Toppling occurs whenever the CG is above the area of support.

    d. Toppling is more likely to occur in objects with small support areas.

26. Is the following sentence true or false? The four legs of a chair define a rectangular support area on the floor beneath the chair. _____

27. Circle the letter of each statement that is true.

    a. Objects with a CG high above their support are easy to balance.

    b. No object can ever truly be in balance.

    c. Objects with large support areas are easier to balance.

    d. Only a computer can balance an object like an electric scooter.

Chapter 11   Rotational Equilibrium

11.6 Center of Gravity of People (pages 199–200)

28. Is the following sentence true or false? Every person has a fixed center of gravity located somewhere in the lower body. _____

29. If a person stands with his or her arms at the sides of the body, where is the person's CG located? _____

30. The location of the CG in a woman is slightly _____ than it is in a man.

31. Is the following sentence true or false? A high jumper's CG can pass below the bar as the jumper's body passes over the bar.

_____

32. Explain why standing with your feet farther apart than normal makes it easier to stand during a bumpy bus ride.

_____

_____

11.7 Stability (pages 200–204)

Use the illustration below to answer questions 33–36.

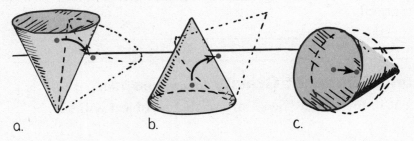

33. Describe what happens to the CG of the cone in Part a when it topples.

_____

34. Circle the letter that shows when the cone is in stable equilibrium.

   a. Part a only   b. Part b only

   c. Part c only   d. Parts b and c

35. Is the following sentence true or false? The CG of the cone shown in Part c does not change no matter which direction the cone rolls.

_____.

36. Circle the letter that shows the cone whose CG must be raised for it to topple.

   a. Part a only   b. Part b only

   c. Part c only   d. Parts b and c

37. Is the following sentence true or false? It is impossible to topple an object that is in stable equilibrium. _____

38. Is the following sentence true or false? The height of an object's CG does not affect how stable it is. _____

39. The CG of an object tends to take the _____ position available.

Chapter 11   Rotational Equilibrium

Torque

A meter stick is suspended at its midpoint and two blocks are attached along its length. A 10-N block is attached 20 cm to the left of the midpoint. Where must a 40-N block be placed in order to keep the meter stick in balance?

1. Read and Understand

What information are you given?

The 10-N block tends to rotate the meter stick in the counterclockwise direction (ccw). In order for the meter stick to remain in balance, an equal clockwise torque must be applied. Thus the 40-N block will tend to rotate the meter stick in the clockwise direction (cw). Because each weight hangs straight down, the weight of each block is equal to the perpendicular component of force.

$Force_{ccw} = F_{\perp ccw} = 10$ N

$Lever\ arm_{ccw} = d_{ccw} = 20$ cm

$Force_{cc} = F_{\perp cw} = 40$ N

2. Plan and Solve

What unknown are you trying to calculate?

Lever arm: $d_{cw} = ?$

What formula contains the given quantity and the unknown?

Counterclockwise torque = clockwise torque

$$(F_{\perp}d)_{ccw} = (F_{\perp}d)_{cw}$$

Rearrange the equation to solve for the unknown variable, d_{cw}.

$d_{cw} = (F_{\perp ccw})(d_{ccw})/(F_{\perp cw})$

Substitute the known values and solve.

$d_{cw} = (10$ N$)(20$ cm$)/(40$ N$)$

$d_{cw} = 5$ cm

3. Look Back and Check

Is your answer reasonable?

Yes, the units are correct and it makes sense that the heavier weight is located closer to the pivot point.

Math Practice

On a separate sheet of paper, solve the following problems.

1. In the question above, if the 10-N block is changed to an 80-N block, how does the location of the 40-N block change?

Chapter 11   Rotational Equilibrium

2. To remove a nut from an old rusty bolt, you apply a 100-N force to the end of a wrench perpendicular to the wrench handle. The distance from the applied force to the axis of the bolt is 25 cm. What is the torque exerted on the bolt in N·m?

3. How does torque applied to the nut in Question 2 change when the force is applied at a 45° angle to the wrench handle?

Chapter 12   Rotational Motion

Summary

THE BIG IDEA : Rotating objects tend to keep rotating while nonrotating objects tend to remain nonrotating.

12.1 Rotational Inertia

✓ **The greater the rotational inertia, the more difficult it is to change the rotational speed of an object.**

- The resistance of an object to changes in its rotational motion is called **rotational inertia,** or *moment of inertia.*

- A torque is required to change the rotational state of motion of an object.

- Rotational inertia depends on mass and how the mass is distributed. The greater the distance between an object's mass concentration and the axis of rotation, the greater the rotational inertia.

- A short pendulum has less rotational inertia and therefore swings back and forth more frequently than a long pendulum. Likewise, bent legs swing back and forth more easily than outstretched legs.

- Formulas to calculate rotational inertia for different objects vary and depend on the shape of an object and the location of the rotational axis.

12.2 Rotational Inertia and Gymnastics

✓ **The three principal axes of rotation in the human body are the longitudinal axis, the transverse axis, and the medial axis.**

- The three axes of rotation in the human body are at right angles to one another. All three axes pass through the center of gravity of the body.

- The vertical axis that passes from head to toe is the *longitudinal axis.* Rotational inertia about this axis is increased by extending a leg or the arms.

- You rotate about your *transverse axis* when you perform a somersault or a flip. Tucking in your arms and legs reduces your rotational inertia about the transverse axis; straightening your arms and legs increases your rotational inertia about this axis.

- The third axis of rotation for the human body is the front-to-back axis, or *medial axis.* You rotate about the medial axis when executing a cartwheel.

12.3 Rotational Inertia and Rolling

✓ **Objects of the same shape but different sizes accelerate equally when rolled down an incline.**

- An object with a greater rotational inertia takes more time to get rolling than an object with a smaller rotational inertia. A hollow cylinder, for example, rolls down an incline much slower than a solid cylinder.

- All objects of the same shape roll down an incline with the same acceleration, even if their masses are different.

Chapter 12   Rotational Motion

12.4 Angular Momentum

☑ **Newton's first law of inertia for rotating systems states that an object or system of objects will maintain its angular momentum unless acted upon by an unbalanced external torque.**

- All moving objects have momentum.
- **Linear momentum** is the product of the mass and velocity of an object.
- Rotating objects have angular momentum. **Angular momentum** is the product of rotational inertia, I, and rotational velocity, ω.

  angular momentum = rotational inertia × rotational velocity or

  angular momentum = $I \times \omega$

- When a direction is assigned to rotational speed, it is called **rotational velocity.**
- When an object is small compared with the radial distance to its axis of rotation, its angular momentum is equal to the magnitude of its linear momentum, mv, multiplied by the radial distance, r.

  angular momentum = mvr

- A moving bicycle is easier to balance than a bicycle at rest because of the angular momentum provided by the spinning wheels.

12.5 Conservation of Angular Momentum

☑ **Angular momentum is conserved when no external torque acts on an object.**

- The **law of conservation of angular momentum** states that if no unbalanced external torque acts on a rotating system, the angular momentum of the system is constant.
- A person who spins with arms extended obtains greater rotational speed when the arms are drawn in. In other words, whenever a rotating body contracts, its rotational speed increases.
- Zero-angular-momentum twists and turns are performed by turning one part of the body against the other.

12.6 Simulated Gravity

☑ **From within a rotating frame of reference, there seems to be an outwardly directed centrifugal force, which can simulate gravity.**

- Occupants in today's space vehicles feel weightless because they lack a support force. Future space habitats will probably spin, effectively supplying a support force that simulates gravity.
- We experience 1 g on Earth's surface due to gravity. Small-diameter space structures would have to rotate at high speeds to provide a simulated gravitational acceleration of 1 g.

Chapter 12   Rotational Motion

Exercises

12.1 Rotational Inertia (pages 213–215)

1. Is the following sentence true or false? Newton's first law does not apply to rotating objects. _____

2. Is the following sentence true or false? According to the law of inertia, rotating objects tend to keep rotating. _____

3. A _____ is required to change the rotational state of motion of an object.

4. Circle the letter of each statement that is true of rotational inertia.

   a. Rotational inertia depends on the force of gravity.

   b. Rotational inertia depends on the mass of an object.

   c. Rotational inertia depends on the distribution of mass in the object.

   d. Rotational inertia is always constant.

5. Is the following sentence true or false? As the distance between an object's mass concentration and its axis of rotation increases, its rotational inertia increases. _____

6. Explain why a tightrope walker might hold a long pole in the horizontal position while performing.

   _____

   _____

7. Circle the letter of the sequence that correctly ranks, from lowest to highest, the rotational inertia of the following: (A) a baseball bat held at its narrow end; (B) a baseball bat held at its more massive end; (C) a meter stick held at its midpoint.

   a. C, B, A   b. B, C, A

   c. C, A, B   d. A, B, C

8. A _____ pendulum swings back and forth more rapidly than a _____ pendulum because the _____ pendulum's rotational inertia is smaller.

9. Is the following sentence true or false? The rotational inertia of an object is constant and cannot change. _____

10. What happens to the rotational inertia of an object if its mass is extended farther away from the axis of rotation?

   _____

   _____

11. Circle the letter of the equation that is used to determine the rotational inertia, I, of a solid sphere spinning about its axis of rotation.

   a. $I = (1/12)mL^2$ b. $I = mr^2$

   c. $I = (2/5)mr^2$ d. $I = (1/3)mL^2$

Chapter 12   Rotational Motion

12.2 Rotational Inertia and Gymnastics (pages 216–217)

12. The major axes of rotation of the human body are the
_____ axis, the _____ axis, and the
_____ axis.

13. Is the following sentence true or false? The three major axes of rotation
of the human body are at right angles to one another and pass through
the center of gravity. _____

14. Circle the letter of each statement that is true.

   a. The human body's longitudinal axis runs from head to toe.

   b. The human body's longitudinal axis passes through the
   center of gravity.

   c. Much of the body's mass is concentrated along the
   longitudinal axis.

   d. The human body's longitudinal axis has the least rotational
   inertia of the three body axes.

Use the figure of a skater in various poses to answer questions 15 and 16.

15. The figure skater has the least amount of rotational inertia in position
_____ .

16. Circle the letter of the position that most easily allows the figure skater
to spin with a high rate of rotation.

   a. a   b. b

   c. c   d. d

17. During a somersault, a person rotates about her _____
axis.

18. Is the following sentence true or false? It is easier to spin when
your body is in a tucked position than when it is outstretched.

_____

19. When a gymnast goes from an outstretched position into a tuck, her rate
of rotation _____ .

20. Is the following sentence true or false? When doing a cartwheel, a person
rotates about his or her transverse axis. _____

Chapter 12   Rotational Motion

12.3 Rotational Inertia and Rolling (page 218)

21. Is the following sentence true or false? An object with a great rotational inertia will roll down an incline more quickly than one with a small rotational inertia. _____

22. Inertia can be thought of as a measure of _____.

23. Is the following sentence true or false? Any hollow cylinder will roll down an incline with more acceleration than any solid cylinder. _____

24. Two solid disks with the same shape but different sizes are rolled down an incline. Which disk reaches the bottom first? Explain.

_____

_____

12.4 Angular Momentum (pages 219–220)

25. Is the following sentence true or false? Any moving object has momentum. _____

26. In equation form, angular momentum is written as

_____

27. Angular momentum is a _____ quantity.

28. Is the following sentence true or false? When rotational speed is assigned a direction, it is known as rotational velocity. _____

29. Circle the letter of each true statement.

   a. Rotational velocity is a vector quantity.

   b. Rotational velocity has the same direction as angular momentum.

   c. Rotational velocity lies along the axis of rotation of an object.

   d. An object's rotational velocity is equal in magnitude to its angular momentum.

30. Is the following sentence true or false? The angular momentum of a small object rotating at a very large radial distance is equal to its linear momentum. _____

31. What happens to a rotating object that is not acted on by an external torque?

_____

_____

32. Explain how angular momentum makes a moving bicycle easier to balance than a bicycle at rest.

_____

_____

_____

12.5 Conservation of Angular Momentum (pages 221–222)

33. Does the angular momentum of a rotating system change when no unbalanced external torques act on it?

_____

34. Is the following sentence true or false? The angular momentum of a rotating system is conserved if no external torque acts on it.

_____

35. The illustration below shows a man spinning on a low-friction turntable. Explain what is happening in the two sketches. Be sure to explain how angular momentum and the quantities I and ω are involved.

_____

_____

_____

36. Is the following sentence true or false? A cat dropped upside down will twist and land on its feet while maintaining a state of zero angular momentum. _____

12.6 Simulated Gravity (pages 223–225)

37. Is the following sentence true or false? Objects in a rotating reference frame seem to experience an outwardly directed centrifugal force.

_____

38. Circle the letter of the phrase that describes the "up" direction sensed by a person in a large rotating space.

   a. radially outward

   b. tangent to the direction of rotation

   c. toward the center of rotation

   d. parallel to the direction of rotation

Chapter 12   Rotational Motion

Rotational Inertia

A 1.0-kg solid lead ball is attached to a 0.50-m string and swung in a circle. The ball's speed at the end of the string is 2.5 m/s. What is the ball's rotational inertia? Express your answer in kg · m².

1. Read and Understand

What information are you given?

Mass, $m = 1.0$ kg

Radius, $r = 0.50$ m

Speed, $v = 2.5$ m/s

2. Plan and Solve

What unknown are you trying to calculate?

Rotational inertia, I

What formula contains the given quantity and the unknown?

Use the equation for a simple pendulum from Figure 12.6.
Note that the speed of the ball, 2.5 m/s, is not needed to solve the problem.

$I = mr^2$

Substitute the known values and solve.

$I = (1.0 \text{ kg})(0.50 \text{ m})^2$

$I = 0.25$ kg · m²

3. Look Back and Check

Is your answer reasonable?

Yes, the proper equation for rotational inertia was applied and the units of the answer are correct.

Math Practice

On a separate sheet of paper, solve the following problems. Refer to Figure 12.6 for formulas.

1. A hole is drilled through the midpoint of a meter stick. The meter stick is then suspended so that it spins freely about its midpoint. If the mass of the meter stick is 0.25 kg, what is its rotational inertia about the midpoint?

2. What is its rotational inertia about the meter stick in Question 1 if it is swung in a circle about one of its ends?

3. A 2.25-kg solid sphere has a rotational inertia about its center of gravity of 1.52 kg·m². What is the radius of the sphere?

Chapter 13   Universal Gravitation

Summary

THE BIG IDEA : Everything pulls on everything else.

13.1 The Falling Apple

✔ Newton reasoned that the moon is falling toward Earth for the same reason an apple falls from a tree—they are both pulled by Earth's gravity.

- Newton understood the concept of inertia, that without an outside force, moving objects continue to move at constant speed in a straight line. He knew that if an object undergoes a change in speed or direction, then a force is responsible.

13.2 The Falling Moon

✔ The moon is actually falling toward Earth but has great enough tangential velocity to avoid hitting Earth.

- Newton reasoned that the moon must be falling *around* Earth. The moon falls in the sense that it falls beneath the straight line it would follow if no force acted on it. He hypothesized that the moon was a projectile circling Earth under the attraction of gravity.

- Newton compared the motion of the moon to a cannonball fired from the top of a high mountain. If the cannonball were fired with enough speed, its path would become a circle and the cannonball would circle indefinitely.

- Both the orbiting cannonball and the moon have a component of velocity parallel to Earth's surface. This sideways or *tangential velocity* is sufficient to ensure nearly circular motion *around* Earth rather than *into* it.

- Newton reasoned that the mass of the moon should not affect how it falls, just as mass has no effect on the acceleration of freely falling objects on Earth. How far the moon falls should relate only to its *distance* from Earth's center.

13.3 The Falling Earth

✔ Newton's theory of gravity confirmed the Copernican theory of the solar system.

- The planets don't crash into the sun because they have tangential velocities. If the tangential velocities of the planets were reduced to zero, their motion would be straight toward the sun and they would indeed crash into it. Any objects in the solar system with insufficient tangential velocities have long ago crashed into the sun.

Chapter 13   Universal Gravitation

13.4 Newton's Law of Universal Gravitation

☑ **Newton discovered that gravity is universal. Everything pulls on everything else in a way that involves only mass and distance.**

- Newton's **law of universal gravitation** states that every object attracts every other object with a force that for any two objects is directly proportional to the mass of each object.

- The law of universal gravitation can be expressed in equation form: $F = G (m_1 m_2 / d^2)$, where m_1 and m_2 are the objects' masses, and d is the distance between their centers of mass.

- The **universal gravitational constant,** G, in the equation describes the strength of gravity. In scientific notation, $G = 6.67 \times 10^{-11}$ N·m^2/kg^2. The value of G tells us that the force of gravity is a very weak force. It is the weakest of the presently known four fundamental forces.

13.5 Gravity and Distance: The Inverse-Square Law

☑ **Gravity decreases according to the inverse square law. The force of gravity weakens as the square of distance.**

- When a quantity varies as the inverse square of its distance from its source, it follows an **inverse-square law.** For example, the inverse square of 3 is $\left(\frac{1}{3}\right)^2$, or $\frac{1}{9}$.

- This law applies to all cases where the effect from a localized source spreads evenly throughout the surrounding space, such as the weakening of gravity with distance. Other examples are light, radiation, and sound.

13.6 Gravitational Field

☑ **Earth can be thought of as being surrounded by a gravitational field that interacts with objects and causes them to experience gravitational forces.**

- A **gravitational field** occupies the space surrounding a massive body. A gravitational field is an example of a *force field*, for any mass in the field space experiences a force.

- Iron filings sprinkled over a sheet of paper on top of a magnet reveal the shape of the magnet's magnetic field. The pattern of filings shows the strength and direction of the magnetic field at different locations around the magnet. Earth is a giant magnet and, like all magnets, is surrounded by a magnetic field.

- The strength of Earth's gravitational field, like the strength of its force on objects, follows the inverse-square law. Earth's gravitational field is strongest near Earth's surface and weaker at greater distances from Earth.

Chapter 13 Universal Gravitation

13.7 Gravitational Field Inside a Planet

✓ **The gravitational field of Earth at its center is zero!**

- The gravitational field of Earth exists inside Earth as well as outside.
- If you traveled through an imaginary hole drilled completely through Earth, you'd gain speed as you fell from the North Pole toward the center of Earth, and lose speed moving away from the center toward the South Pole.

13.8 Weight and Weightlessness

✓ **Pressure against Earth is the sensation we interpret as weight.**

- The force of gravity, like any force, causes acceleration. Because we are almost always in contact with Earth, we think of gravity primarily as something that presses us against Earth rather than as something that accelerates us.
- If you stand on a scale, gravity pulls you against the supporting floor and scale, and the floor and scale push upward on you. This pair of forces compresses a spring-like gauge inside the scale. The weight reading on the scale is linked to the amount of compression.
- **Weightlessness** is not the absence of gravity; rather, it is the absence of a support force. Astronauts in orbit are without a support force and experience weightlessness.

13.9 Ocean Tides

✓ **Newton showed that the ocean tides are caused by *differences* in the gravitational pull of the moon on opposite sides of Earth.**

- The moon's gravitational attraction is stronger on Earth's oceans closer to the moon, and weaker on the oceans farther from the moon. This difference causes the oceans to bulge out on opposite sides of Earth. Because Earth spins, a fixed point on Earth passes beneath both bulges each day, producing two high tides and two low tides.
- A **spring tide** is a high or low tide that occurs when the sun, Earth, and moon are all lined up. The tides due to the sun and the moon coincide, making high tides higher than average and low tides lower than average. Spring tides occur during a new or full moon.
- A **neap tide** occurs when the moon is halfway between a new moon and a full moon. The pulls of the moon and sun are perpendicular to each other. As a result, the solar and lunar tides do not overlap, so the high tides are not as high and low tides are not as low.

Chapter 13   Universal Gravitation

13.10 Black Holes

✅ **When a massive star collapses into a black hole, there is no change in the gravitational field at any point beyond the original radius of the star.**

- Two main processes occur continuously in stars like our sun: gravitation, which tends to pull solar material inward, and thermonuclear fusion, which blows material outward.

- If the fusion rate increases, the sun will get hotter and bigger; if the fusion rate decreases, the sun will get cooler and smaller.

- When the sun runs out of fusion fuel (hydrogen), gravitation will dominate and the sun will start to collapse. The collapse will cause helium to fuse into carbon, and the sun will expand into a *red giant*. When the helium is used up, the sun will collapse into a *black dwarf*.

- For stars more massive than the sun, once thermonuclear fusion ends, gravitational collapse will take over, eventually forming a **black hole.** The density of a black hole is so great that its enormous gravitational field prevents even light from escaping. The gravitational field beyond the original radius of the star is no different after the collapse than before.

13.11 Universal Gravitation

✅ **The formulation of the law of universal gravitation is one of the major reasons for the success in science that followed, for it provided hope that other phenomena of the world might also be described by equally simple and universal laws.**

- Earth is round because of gravitation. Earth attracted itself together before it became solid. Any "corners" of Earth have been pulled in so that Earth is a giant sphere.

- The solar system began when a slightly rotating ball of interstellar gas contracted due to mutual gravitation. To conserve angular momentum, the rotational speed of the ball of gas increased, causing the particles to sweep out into a disk shape.

- The deviation of an orbiting object from its path around a center of force caused by the action of an additional center of force is called a **perturbation.**

- The planet Neptune was discovered when a perturbation in the orbit of Uranus led scientists to conclude that a disturbing body beyond the orbit of Uranus was the culprit.

- According to current scientific understanding, the universe originated and grew from the explosion of a primordial fireball some 13.7 billion years ago. This is the "Big Bang" theory of the origin of the universe. All the matter of the universe was hurled outward from this event and continues in an outward expansion.

- More recent evidence suggests the universe is not only expanding, but *accelerating* outward. It is pushed by an antigravity *dark energy* that makes up an estimated 73 percent of the universe. Twenty-three percent of the universe is composed of the yet-to-be discovered particles of exotic *dark matter.* Ordinary matter makes up only 4 percent.

Chapter 13   Universal Gravitation

Exercises

13.1 The Falling Apple (page 233)

1. Describe the legend of Newton's discovery that gravity extends throughout the universe.

   _____

   _____

   _____

2. Newton understood the concept of _____, developed by Galileo, that without an outside force, moving objects continue to move at constant speed in a straight line.

3. Is the following sentence true or false? Circular motion is accelerated motion, which requires a force. _____

13.2 The Falling Moon (pages 233–235)

4. Newton realized that the moon must be falling _____ Earth.

5. Is the following sentence true or false? The moon falls beneath the straight line it would follow if no force acted on it. _____

6. Newton compared motion of the moon to a cannonball fired from the top of a high mountain. Describe the possible paths for the cannonball proposed by Newton.

   _____

   _____

   _____

   _____

7. Circle the letter of the word that best describes the tangential velocity that prevents the moon from hitting Earth.

   a. upward   b. sideways

   c. downward   d. backward

8. Is the following sentence true or false? Newton believed that the mass of the moon affects how it falls. _____

9. Explain Newton's calculation that the moon falls 1.4 millimeters each second.

   _____

   _____

   _____

Chapter 13   Universal Gravitation

13.3 The Falling Earth (page 236)

10. Is this sentence true or false? Newton's theory of gravity confirmed the Copernican theory of the solar system. _____

11. Circle the letter of the sentence that describes the motion of a planet if its tangential velocity were reduced to zero.

  a. It would drift in space.

  b. It would continue in orbit at a slower speed.

  c. It would crash into the sun.

  d. It would spin away from the solar system.

12. Why are there no large objects in the solar system today with very low tangential velocities?

_____

13.4 Newton's Law of Universal Gravitation (pages 237–239)

13. Is the following sentence true or false? Isaac Newton discovered gravity.

_____

14. State Newton's law of universal gravitation using words.

_____

_____

_____

15. What is the equation for universal gravitation?

_____

16. The constant G in this equation is called the _____ and describes the _____.

17. The English physicist _____ first measured G.

18. Is the following sentence true or false? The force of gravity is the strongest of the presently known four fundamental forces. _____

19. Is the following sentence true or false? At the top of a mountain, your weight is slightly less than at ground level. _____

13.5 Gravity and Distance: The Inverse-Square Law (pages 240–241)

20. Express the inverse square law in words.

_____

_____

21. Circle the letter of the inverse square of 9.

  a. $\frac{1}{3}$ b. $\frac{1}{81}$

  c. 3   d. 81

Chapter 13   Universal Gravitation

Match each change with the effect it would have on the force of gravity between two objects.

Change	Effect
_____ **22.** The mass of one object doubles.	a. The force is divided by 2.
_____ **23.** The mass of one object decreases by half.	b. The force is divided by 4.
	c. The force is multiplied by 2.
_____ **24.** The distance between the objects' centers of mass doubles.	d. The force is multiplied by 4.
_____ **25.** The distance between the objects' centers of mass decreases by half.	

26. Is the following sentence true or false? The gravitational influence of every object is exerted through all space. _____

13.6 Gravitational Field (pages 242–243)

27. The pulls that Earth and the moon exert on each other is action at a distance because the bodies interact without _____.

28. Define *gravitational field*.

_____

_____

29. Earth's gravitational field interacts with objects by causing them to experience _____.

30. Field lines show the _____ and _____ of a force field.

31. Field lines are closest together where a field is _____.

32. How are gravitational field lines related to the acceleration of an object around Earth?

_____

_____

13.7 Gravitational Field Inside a Planet (page 244)

33. Circle the letter that identifies the location where Earth's gravitational field is zero.

a. in a plane above Earth's surface   b. at Earth's surface

c. between Earth's surface and its center   d. at Earth's center

34. Is the following sentence true or false? The weight of a rock at Earth's center is zero. _____

13.8 Weight and Weightlessness (pages 245–246)

35. Why are people often unaware that gravity accelerates us?

_____

36. Pressure against Earth is the sensation we interpret as _____.

Chapter 13   Universal Gravitation

Match each position or movement of an elevator with your weight if you stepped on a scale in the elevator.

Elevator Position or Movement	**Weight Reading**
_____ **37.** sitting still	a. no weight
_____ **38.** accelerating downward	b. normal weight
_____ **39.** accelerating upward	c. greater weight than usual
_____ **40.** falling freely	d. less weight than usual

41. Rather than define your weight as the force of gravity that acts on you, it is more practical to define weight as

_____

42. Is the following sentence true or false? Weightlessness is the absence of gravity. _____

43. Explain why rotating giant wheels will likely be used as space habitats in the future.

_____

_____

13.9 Ocean Tides (pages 246–248)

44. How often does a high tide occur? _____

45. Is the following sentence true or false? The pull of the moon and Earth on each other causes them both to be slightly elongated rather than spherical. _____

 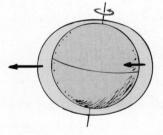

46. The figure shows the moon near the spinning Earth. Use the figure to explain the cause of ocean tides on Earth. In your explanation, describe why the arrows in the figure are different lengths.

_____

_____

_____

47. Circle the letter of the fraction that compares the sun's contribution to ocean tides to the moon's contribution.

a. one sixteenth   b. one fourth

c. one eighth   d. one half

48. The sun's pull on Earth is _____ times greater than the moon's pull on Earth.

Chapter 13   Universal Gravitation

49. Write *spring* or *neap* on each line to indicate whether the description
matches a spring tide or a neap tide.

_____ a. Occurs when the moon is halfway between a new moon and a
full moon.

_____ b. High tides are higher than usual, and low tides are lower than
usual.

_____ c. Occurs at times of a new or full moon.

_____ d. The pulls of the moon and sun are perpendicular to each other.

_____ e. Occurs when the sun, Earth, and moon are all lined up.

_____ f. The solar and lunar tides coincide.

_____ g. The solar and lunar tides do not overlap.

50. A tidal effect causes the solid surface of Earth to rise and fall as much as
_____ meter twice each day.

51. Explain why lakes have almost no tides.

_____

_____

13.10 Black Holes (pages 249–251)

52. Explain the effects that the following processes have on stars like
our sun.

a. Gravitation: _____

b. Nuclear fusion: _____

53. If the fusion rate of the sun increases, the sun will get _____
and _____.

54. If the fusion rate of the sun decreases, the sun will get _____
and _____.

55. Circle the letter that identifies the fuel for the type of fusion that
currently takes place in the sun.

a. carbon   b. hydrogen

c. nitrogen   d. oxygen

56. Explain what will cause our sun to collapse some 5 billion years
from now.

_____

_____

57. As the sun collapses, a different type of fusion will begin in which
_____ fuses into _____.

58. Fusion will eventually cause the sun to expand into a(n)
_____ which will extend beyond Earth's orbit and
swallow Earth.

59. When our sun no longer gives off heat and light, it will be a(n)
_____.

Chapter 13   Universal Gravitation

60. Explain why a star that is at least two to three times more massive than our sun will eventually collapse into a black hole.

_____

_____

61. Circle the letters of the statements that correctly describe a black hole.

   a. It has significantly more mass than the star from which it collapsed.

   b. Its gravitational field beyond the original radius of the star is unchanged.

   c. The configuration of the gravitational field around it represents a collapse of space itself.

   d. Its volume is unchanged from the star from which it collapsed.

62. Explain how a black hole that is part of a binary pair can be detected, even though it cannot be seen.

_____

_____

63. Black holes are near the centers of most galaxies. How do these black holes affect stars near them?

_____

13.11 Universal Gravitation (pages 251–254)

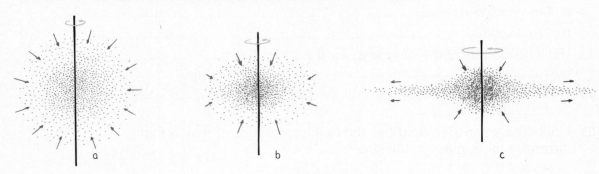

64. Refer to the figures above to describe the role that gravity played in the formation of the solar system.

_____

_____

_____

_____

Chapter 13   Universal Gravitation

65. Explain why Earth is round.

_____

_____

_____

66. Define *perturbation*.

_____

_____

_____

67. Circle the letter of the orbiting body that was discovered in just half an hour because of a perturbation in the orbit of Uranus.

    a. Jupiter

    b. Neptune

    c. Pluto

    d. Saturn

Match each type of energy or matter with its percent of the universe.

Energy or Matter	Percentage of the Universe
_____ **68.** dark energy	a. 4%
_____ **69.** dark matter	b. 23%
_____ **70.** ordinary matter	c. 73%

71. Is the following sentence true or false? The law of universal gravitation is a complicated law that only describes a few unique instances.

_____

Chapter 13   Universal Gravitation

Gravitational Force

Calculate the force of gravity between Earth (mass = 6.0×10^{24} kg) and Mars (mass = 6.4×10^{23} kg) when they are at their closest distance from each other, 5.6×10^7 km.

1. Read and Understand

What information are you given?
   Mass of Earth = $m_1 = 6.0 \times 10^{24}$ kg

   Mass of Mars = $m_2 = 6.4 \times 10^{23}$ kg

   Distance between the planets = $d = 5.6 \times 10^7$ km = 5.6×10^{10} m

2. Plan and Solve

What unknown are you trying to calculate?
   Force of gravity between the planets = F

What formula can you use to find the unknown?
   The equation for universal gravitation: $F = G(m_1 m_2/d^2)$

What other information do you need to use?
   The universal gravitational constant = $G = 6.67 \times 10^{-11}$ N·m^2/kg^2

Replace each variable and constant with its known value.
   $F = (6.67 \times 10^{-11}$ N·m^2/kg$^2)[(6.0 \times 10^{24}$ kg$)(6.4 \times 10^{23}$ kg$)/(5.6 \times 10^{10}$ m$)^2]$

   $= 8.2 \times 10^{16}$ N

3. Look Back and Check

Is your answer reasonable?
   A force this strong is reasonable between two neighboring planets.

Math Practice

On a separate sheet of paper, solve the following problems.

   1. Calculate the force of gravity between Earth (mass = 6.0×10^{24} kg) and Venus (mass = 4.9×10^{24} kg) when they are at their closest distance from each other, 3.8×10^7 km.

   2. Calculate the force of gravity between a car (mass = 2.3×10^3 kg) and a man (mass = 68 kg) when the man is standing a distance of 5.0 m from the car.

   3. Calculate the force of gravity that Saturn (mass = 5.7×10^{26} kg) exerts on a woman on Earth (mass = 61 kg) when Saturn is closest to Earth, 1.2×10^9 km.

Chapter 14   Satellite Motion

Summary

THE BIG IDEA : The path of an Earth satellite follows the curvature of Earth.

14.1 Earth Satellites

☑ A stone thrown fast enough to go a horizontal distance of 8 kilometers during the time (1 second) it takes to fall 5 meters, will orbit Earth.

- An Earth **satellite** is a projectile moving fast enough to fall continually *around* Earth rather than *into* it.

- A geometric fact about the curvature of Earth is that its surface drops a vertical distance of nearly 5 meters for every 8000 meters tangent to its surface.

- The orbital speed for close orbit about Earth is 8 km/s (29,000 km/h or 18,000 mi/h).

- A satellite must stay about 150 kilometers or more above Earth's surface to keep from burning due to the friction of the atmosphere.

14.2 Circular Orbits

☑ A satellite in circular orbit around Earth is always moving perpendicularly to gravity and parallel to Earth's surface at constant speed.

- In circular orbit the speed of a circling satellite is not changed by gravity.

- A satellite is always moving at a right angle (perpendicular) to the force of gravity, so that no change in speed occurs—only a change in direction.

- For a satellite close to Earth, the time for a complete orbit around Earth, its **period,** is about 90 minutes.

14.3 Elliptical Orbits

☑ A satellite in orbit around Earth traces an oval-shaped path called an ellipse.

- An **ellipse** is the closed path taken by a point that moves in such a way that the sum of its distances from two fixed points is constant.

- The two fixed points in an ellipse are called **foci.**

- Satellite speed, which is constant in a circular orbit, *varies* in an elliptical orbit.

14.4 Energy Conservation and Satellite Motion

☑ The sum of the KE and PE of a satellite is constant at all points along an orbit.

- In an elliptical orbit, the **apogee** is the point in a satellite's orbit farthest from the center of Earth, and the **perigee** is the point in a satellite's orbit closest to the center of Earth.

Chapter 14   Satellite Motion

- The PE is greatest when the satellite is at the apogee and least when the satellite is at the perigee.
- The KE will be least when the PE is most, and the KE will be most when the PE is least. At every point in the orbit, the sum of the KE and PE is constant.

14.5 Kepler's Laws of Planetary Motion

☑ Kepler's first law states that the path of each planet around the sun is an ellipse with the sun at one focus. Kepler's second law states that each planet moves so that an imaginary line drawn from the sun to any planet sweeps out equal areas of space in equal time intervals. Kepler's third law states that the square of the orbital period of a planet is directly proportional to the cube of the average distance of the planet from the sun.

- **Kepler's laws of planetary motion** are three important discoveries about planetary motion that were made by German astronomer Johannes Kepler in the beginning of the 1600s.
- Kepler's expectation that the planets would move in perfect circles around the sun was shattered after years of effort. He found the paths to be ellipses.
- Kepler also found that the planets do not go around the sun at uniform speed but move faster when they are nearer the sun and more slowly when they are farther from the sun.
- Kepler's laws apply not only to planets but also to moons or any satellite in orbit around any body.

14.6 Escape Speed

☑ If we give a payload any more energy than 62 MJ/kg at the surface of Earth or, equivalently, any greater speed than 11.2 km/s, then, neglecting air resistance, the payload will escape from Earth never to return.

- The **escape speed** is the minimum speed necessary for an object to escape permanently from a gravitational field that holds it.
- Different bodies in the solar system have different escape speeds.
- The first probe to escape the solar system, *Pioneer 10*, was launched from Earth in 1972 with a speed of only 15 km/s.

Chapter 14   Satellite Motion

Exercises

14.1 Earth Satellites (pages 263–265)

1. An Earth _____ is a projectile moving fast enough to fall continually around Earth rather than into it.

2. Is the following sentence true or false? A stone dropped from rest accelerates 10 m/s² and falls a vertical distance of 10 meters during the first second. _____

3. A geometric fact about the curvature of Earth is that its surface drops a vertical distance of nearly _____ meters for every _____ meters tangent to its surface.

4. a. What speed must an object have to orbit the Earth in km/s? _____

   b. In km/h? _____

   c. In mi/h? _____

5. How far above Earth's surface must an orbiting object stay to keep from burning up in the atmosphere? _____

14.2 Circular Orbits (pages 265–267)

6. Is the following sentence true or false? In circular orbit, the speed of a circling satellite is not changed by gravity. _____

7. Why are the speeds of a bowling ball rolling on a level surface and a satellite not affected by the force of gravity?

   _____

   _____

Match each value or word with the correct phrase.

_____ 8. the relationship of a circular satellite's orbit to gravity

_____ 9. the relationship of a circular satellite's orbit to Earth's surface

_____ 10. the period of a satellite close to Earth

_____ 11. period of a communications satellite

_____ 12. period of the moon

_____ 13. ISS's distance above Earth's surface

a. 24 hours

b. perpendicular

c. 360 kilometers

d. 90 minutes

e. parallel

f. 27.3 days

14.3 Elliptical Orbits (pages 267–268)

14. A satellite in orbit around Earth traces an oval-shaped path called a(n) _____.

15. Define *foci*.

   _____

16. Is the following sentence true or false? Satellite speed, which is constant in a circular orbit, varies in an elliptical orbit. _____

17. When a satellite is in an elliptical orbit around Earth, what causes the satellite to slow down and then fall back toward Earth?
_____

18. Is the following sentence true or false? The parabolic paths of projectiles are actually segments of ellipses. _____

14.4 Energy Conservation and Satellite Motion (pages 269–270)

19. The diagram below shows a satellite in a circular orbit. Explain why the KE and the PE are constant at all points in the orbit.

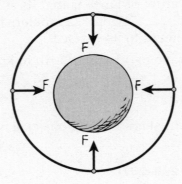

_____

_____

_____

20. Label the following on the illustration shown below: apogee, perigee, point of greatest PE, and point of greatest KE.

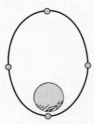

21. At all points on the orbit—except at the apogee and perigee—there is a component of _____ parallel to the direction of satellite motion.

14.5 Kepler's Laws of Planetary Motion (pages 270–272)

22. What are Kepler's laws of planetary motion?

_____

_____

23. What is the path of each planet around the sun? _____

Chapter 14   Satellite Motion

24. Is the following sentence true or false? As a planet revolves around the sun, its distance from the sun does not change. _____

25. The _____ of the orbital period of a planet is directly proportional to the _____ of the average distance of the planet from the sun.

26. Is the following sentence true or false? The triangular-shaped areas swept out during a month when a planet is orbiting far from the sun and when a planet is orbiting closer to the sun are equal.
_____

27. Isaac Newton integrated the findings of two scientists:
_____ and _____

14.6 Escape Speed (pages 272–275)

28. To achieve orbit, the payload must be launched _____ at 8 km/s, once above air resistance.

29. Neglecting air resistance, fire anything at any speed greater than _____ km/s, and it will leave Earth, going more and more slowly, but never stopping.

30. Define *escape speed*.
_____
_____

31. What is the kinetic energy per unit mass that corresponds to Earth's escape speed?
_____

32. What is the escape speed for the sun? _____

33. What is the name of the first probe to escape the solar system?
_____

34. How was the planet Jupiter used to help *Pioneer 10* escape the sun's gravitational force?
_____
_____

35. What two devices are used to correct the path of unpiloted rockets?
_____
_____

Chapter 14   Satellite Motion

Kepler's Third Law

Mars has an orbital period of 1.88 years. The average distance from Earth to the sun is 1 astronomical unit (A.U.) and Earth has an orbital period of 1 year. Use Kepler's third law to find the average distance from Mars to the sun in astronomical units (A.U.).

1. Read and Understand

What information are you given?

Orbital period of Mars = T_{Mars} = 1.88 years

Distance of Earth from the sun = r_{Earth} = 1 A.U.

Orbital period of Earth = T_{Earth} = 1 year

2. Plan and Solve

What unknown are you trying to calculate?

The average distance from Mars to the sun = r_{Mars} = ?

What formula contains the given quantities and the unknown?

$$\frac{T_{Mars}^2}{r_{Mars}^3} = \frac{T_{Earth}^2}{r_{Earth}^3}$$

Replace each variable with its known variable and known value.

$$\frac{(1.88 \text{ years})^2}{r_{Mars}^3} = \frac{(1 \text{ year})^2}{(1 \text{ A.U.})^3} \text{ ; } r_{Mars}^3 = \frac{(1.88 \text{ years})^2 \, (1 \text{ A.U.})^3}{(1 \text{ year})^2}$$

$$r_{Mars}^3 = 3.53 \text{ A.U.}^3 \text{ ; } r_{Mars} = 1.52 \text{ A.U.}$$

3. Look Back and Check

Is your answer reasonable?

Yes, the answer is less than the distance from Earth to the sun.

Math Practice

On a separate sheet of paper, solve the following problems.

1. Jupiter has an orbital period of 11.86 years, and Jupiter's average distance to the sun is 5.2 A.U. If Mercury's average distance to the sun is 0.39 A.U., what is its orbital period in years?

2. Saturn has an orbital period of 29.46 years, and its average distance to the sun is 9.54 A.U. If Venus has an orbital period of 0.62 years, what is its average distance to the sun in astronomical units (A.U.)?

Chapter 15   Special Relativity—Space and Time

Summary

THE BIG IDEA : Motion through space is related to motion in time.

15.1 Space-Time

☑ From the viewpoint of special relativity, you travel through a combination of space and time. You travel through space-time.

- Space and time are two parts of one whole called **space-time.**

- Einstein's **special theory of relativity** describes how time is affected by motion in space at constant velocity, and how mass and energy are related.

- Whenever we move through space, we to some degree alter our rate of moving into the future. This is known as *time dilation,* or the stretching of time.

- The special theory of relativity that Einstein developed rests on two fundamental assumptions, or **postulates.**

15.2 The First Postulate of Special Relativity

☑ The first postulate of special relativity states that all the laws of nature are the same in all uniformly moving frames of reference.

- Einstein reasoned that all motion is relative and all frames of reference are arbitrary. An object cannot measure its speed relative to empty space, but only relative to other objects.

- Einstein's **first postulate of special relativity** assumes our inability to detect a state of uniform motion.

- Many experiments can detect *accelerated* motion, but none can, according to Einstein, detect the state of uniform motion.

15.3 The Second Postulate of Special Relativity

☑ The second postulate of special relativity states that the speed of light in empty space will always have the same value regardless of the motion of the source or the motion of the observer.

- Einstein's **second postulate of special relativity** assumes that the speed of light is constant at 300,000 km/s.

- The ratio of space to time for light is the same for all who measure it.

Chapter 15 Special Relativity—Space and Time

15.4 Time Dilation

✓ **Time dilation occurs ever so slightly for everyday speeds but significantly for speeds approaching the speed of light.**

- Einstein proposed that time can be stretched depending on the motion between the observer and the events being observed. The stretching of time is **time dilation.**

- Einstein showed that the relation between the time t_0 (proper time) in the observer's own frame of reference and the relative time t measured in another frame of reference can be expressed in equation form:
$$t = t_0 / \sqrt{1-(v/c)^2}$$

15.5 Space and Time Travel

✓ **The amounts of energy required to propel spaceships to relativistic speeds are billions of times the energy used to put the space shuttles into orbit.**

- Because of time dilation, time for a person on Earth and time for a person in a high-speed spaceship are not the same. Therefore, prior arguments that the time necessary to reach distant stars would prevent space travel are invalid. If an astronaut traveled the speed of light to the star Procyon (11.4 light-years away), 23 years would pass on Earth but only 3 years would have passed for the astronaut.

- The practicality of space travel close to the speed of light is prohibitive, so far.

15.6 Length Contraction

✓ **When an object moves at a very high speed relative to an observer, its measured length in the direction of motion is contracted.**

- The observable shortening of objects moving at speeds approaching the speed of light is **length contraction.**

- The amount of contraction is related to the amount of time dilation. For everyday speeds, the amount of contraction is much too small to be measured. For relativistic speeds, the contraction would be noticeable.

- The contraction of speeding objects is the contraction of space itself. Space contracts in only one direction, the direction of motion.

- Relativistic length contraction is stated mathematically: $L = L_0 \sqrt{1-(v^2/c^2)}$. In this equation, v is the speed of the object relative to the observer, c is the speed of light, L is the length of the moving object as measured by the observer, and L_0 is the measured length of the object at rest.

Chapter 15   Special Relativity—Space and Time

Exercises

15.1 Space-Time (pages 283–284)

1. Einstein's _____ describes how time is affected by motion in space at constant velocity and how mass and energy are related.

2. From the viewpoint of special relativity, you travel through a combination of _____ and _____.

3. According to the special theory of relativity, how do standing still and traveling at the speed of light differ?

   _____

   _____

   _____

4. Is the following sentence true or false? Whenever we move through space, we to some degree alter our rate of moving into the future, which is called time dilation. _____

5. What is another name for a fundamental assumption?

   _____

15.2 The First Postulate of Special Relativity (pages 284–285)

6. Circle the letter of each sentence that is true about motion and frames of reference.

   a. All motion is relative.

   b. All frames of reference are arbitrary.

   c. A spaceship can measure its speed relative to empty space.

   d. A spaceship's speed must be measured relative to other objects.

7. Explain why the occupants of each of the spaceships in the figure below will be unable to determine who is moving and who is at rest.

   _____

   _____

   _____

8. What is the first postulate of special relativity?

   _____

   _____

Chapter 15   Special Relativity—Space and Time

15.3 The Second Postulate of Special Relativity (pages 285–286)

9. Einstein concluded that if an observer could travel close to the speed of light, he would measure the light as moving away from him at

   _____.

10. What is the second postulate of special relativity?

    _____

    _____

    _____

11. A person on a moving train shines a flashlight in the direction that the train is moving. Does an observer standing at rest outside of the train measure the speed of light as faster, slower, or the same speed as when the train is not moving? _____

12. What variable is used to indicate the value of the speed of light for all observers? _____

13. The ratio of _____ to _____ for light is the same for all who measure it.

15.4 Time Dilation (pages 287–291)

14. Is the following sentence true or false? Time dilation occurs ever so slightly for everyday speeds but significantly for speeds approaching the speed of light. _____

15. A moving space ship contains a light clock. How do the flashes of light from the light clock appear to move to an observer inside the spaceship?

    _____

16. A moving space ship contains a light clock. An observer is at rest with respect to the spaceship. How do the flashes of light from the light clock appear to move to the observer?

    _____

17. What is the speed of light in the light clock? _____

18. Write the equation for the relationship between the time t_0 (proper time) in the observer's own frame of reference and the relative time t measured in another frame of reference.

    _____

19. Circle the letter of each sentence that is true about the traveling twin.

   a. If the traveling twin maintains a speed of 50% the speed of light for one year (according to the clocks on the spaceship), 1 year will have lapsed on Earth.

   b. If the traveling twin maintains a speed of 87% the speed of light for one year (according to the clocks on the spaceship), 2 years will have lapsed on Earth.

   c. If the traveling twin maintains a speed of 99.5% the speed of light for one year (according to the clocks on the spaceship), 10 years will have lapsed on Earth.

   d. The traveling twin experiences three frames of reference on his round trip away from and back to Earth.

20. Explain what the graph below says about 1 second on a stationary clock as measured on a moving clock.

_____

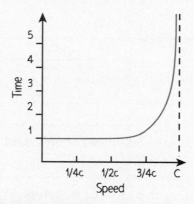

15.5 Space and Time Travel (pages 292–293)

21. Is the following statement true or false? In designing the global positioning system (GPS), which can pinpoint positions on Earth to within meters, scientists and engineers had to accommodate for relativistic time dilation. _____

22. Traveling at the speed of light, how long would it take a person to reach the center of our galaxy? _____

23. Circle the letter of each sentence that is true about space and time travel.

   a. Time for a person on Earth and time for a person in a high-speed spaceship are not the same.

   b. A person's heart beats to the rhythm of the realm of Earth time.

   c. The amount of energy required to propel spaceships to relativistic speeds are ten times the energy used to put the space shuttles into orbit.

   d. Time travels only one way—forward.

24. Why are the practicalities of long space journeys prohibitive?

_____

_____

_____

_____

15.6 Length Contraction (pages 294–295)

25. What is length contraction?

_____

_____

26. In which direction does space contract?

_____

27. A baseball is moving horizontally. Describe how the shape of the baseball changes as the relative speed between the baseball and an observer increases.

_____

_____

28. What do the variables L and L_0 represent?

_____

_____

29. Write the equation for the relationship between L and L_0.

_____

30. Consider an object with a length at rest of 6 meters. When it approaches the speed of light, an observer at rest would measure its length approaching what value?

a. 0 m   b. 7 m

c. 10 m   d. 100 m

Chapter 15   Special Relativity—Space and Time

Relativistic Length Contraction

If a meter stick is moving at 50% the speed of light, what is its contracted length?

1. Read and Understand

What information are you given?

Speed relative to observer = $v = 0.5c$

Length of object at rest = $L_0 = 1$ m

c = speed of light = 3×10^8 m/s

2. Plan and Solve

What unknown are you trying to calculate?

The contracted length = L

What formula contains the given quantities and the unknown?

$$L = L_0\sqrt{1 - \left(\frac{v^2}{c^2}\right)}$$

Replace each variable with its known variable and known value.

$$L = 1.0\sqrt{1 - \left(\frac{(0.5c)^2}{c^2}\right)} = 0.87 \text{ m}$$

3. Look Back and Check

Is your answer reasonable?

Yes, the moving meter stick has a length of less than 1.0 m.

Math Practice

On a separate sheet of paper, solve the following problems.

1. A meteor has a length of 20 meters. If the meteor is moving at 35% the speed of light, what is its contracted length?

2. A meter stick is moving at 1% the speed of light. What is its contracted length?

Chapter 16   Relativity—Momentum, Mass, Energy, and Gravity

Summary

THE BIG IDEA : According to special relativity, mass and energy are equivalent. According to general relativity, gravity causes space to become curved and time to undergo changes.

16.1 Momentum and Inertia in Relativity

✓ As an object approaches the speed of light, its momentum increases dramatically.

- Einstein showed that a new definition of momentum is required at speeds close to the speed of light. **Relativistic momentum** is the momentum at very high speeds approaching the speed of light. It can be expressed in equation form: $p = \dfrac{mv}{\sqrt{1-(v^2/c^2)}}$

- An object pushed to the speed of light would have infinite momentum and would require an infinite impulse, which is clearly impossible. Nothing that has mass can be pushed to the speed of light.

- The **rest mass** of an object is a true constant, a property of the object no matter what speed it has.

16.2 Equivalence of Mass and Energy

✓ Mass and energy are equivalent—anything with mass also has energy.

- An insight of Einstein's special theory of relativity is that mass is simply a form of energy. A piece of matter, even if at rest and even if not interacting with anything else, has an "energy of being" called its **rest energy.** Rest mass is, in effect, a kind of potential energy.

- The amount of rest energy E is related to mass m by the equation $E = mc^2$.

- The speed of light is a large quantity, and its square is even larger. Therefore, even a small amount of mass stores a large amount of energy.

16.3 The Correspondence Principle

✓ According to the correspondence principle, if the equations of special relativity (or any other new theory) are to be valid, they must correspond to those of Newtonian mechanics—classical mechanics—when speeds much less than the speed of light are considered.

- The **correspondence principle** states that a new theory and the old theory must overlap and agree in the region where the results of the old theory have been fully verified.

- Einstein's conviction that the laws of nature should be expressed in the same form in *every* frame of reference, accelerated as well as non-accelerated, was the primary motivation that led him to develop the **general theory of relativity**—a new theory of gravitation, in which gravity causes space to become curved and time to slow down.

Chapter 16   Relativity—Momentum, Mass, Energy, and Gravity

16.4 General Relativity

☑ **The principle of equivalence states that local observations made in an accelerated frame of reference cannot be distinguished from observations made in a Newtonian gravitational field.**

- There is no way you can tell whether you are being pulled by gravity or being accelerated. The effects of gravity and the effects of acceleration are equivalent.

- Einstein stated that the principle of equivalence holds for all natural phenomena, including optical, electromagnetic, and mechanical phenomena.

16.5 Gravity, Space, and a New Geometry

☑ **The presence of mass produces a curvature or warping of space-time. Conversely, a curvature of space-time reveals the presence of mass.**

- Space-time has four dimensions—three space dimensions (such as length, width, and height) and one time dimension (past to future). Einstein perceived a gravitational field as a geometrical warping of four-dimensional space-time.

- Euclidean geometry (the ordinary geometry taught in school) is no longer valid when applied to objects in the presence of strong gravitational fields.

- **Geodesics** are the lines of shortest distance between two points in curved space.

- Although space-time is curved "locally" (within a solar system or within a galaxy), recent evidence shows that the universe as a whole is "flat."

- The ripples that travel outward from the gravitational sources at the speed of light are **gravitational waves**. Any accelerating object produces a gravitational wave.

16.6 Tests of General Relativity

☑ **Upon developing the general theory of relativity, Einstein predicted that the elliptical orbits of the planets precess about the sun, starlight passing close to the sun is deflected, and gravitation causes time to slow down.**

- Using four-dimensional field questions, Einstein recalculated the orbits of the planets about the sun.

- Even after all known corrections due to possible perturbations by other planets had been applied, the calculations of scientists failed to account for the extra 43 seconds of arc on Mercury's orbit. And then came the explanation of Einstein, whose general relativity equations applied to Mercury's orbit predict the extra 43 seconds of arc per century.

- Light traveling "against gravity" is observed to have slightly lower frequency due to an effect called the **gravitational red shift**. Because red light is at the low-frequency end of the visible spectrum, a lowering of frequency shifts the color of the emitted light toward the red.

Chapter 16   Relativity—Momentum, Mass, Energy, and Gravity

Exercises

16.1 Momentum and Inertia in Relativity (pages 303–304)

1. What is Einstein's equation for momentum?

_____

2. Einstein's definition of momentum is known as _____, and it is important for speeds approaching the speed of light.

3. What is the speed limit in the universe?

_____

4. The _____ of an object, represented by m in Einstein's equation for momentum, is a true constant, a property of the object no matter what speed it has.

5. The diagram below shows an electron beam moving through a magnetic field. Explain the two possible paths of the electron beam.

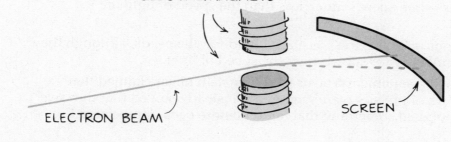

ELECTROMAGNETS

ELECTRON BEAM

SCREEN

_____

_____

_____

_____

6. Is the following statement true or false? Newton's definition of momentum is valid at low speeds. _____

16.2 Equivalence of Mass and Energy (pages 305–306)

7. A piece of matter, even if at rest and even if not interacting with anything else, has an "energy of being" called its _____.

8. Circle the letter of each statement that is true.

   a. Rest mass is a kind of potential energy.

   b. Rest mass and energy are related by the equation $E = mc$.

   c. Mass and energy are equivalent—anything with mass also has energy.

   d. The quantity c^2 is a conversion factor that converts the measurement of mass to an equivalent energy.

Chapter 16   Relativity—Momentum, Mass, Energy, and Gravity

9. What is the energy equivalent of 1 kilogram of matter? _____

10. Is the following sentence true or false? For all chemical reactions that give off energy, there is a corresponding increase in mass.

   _____

11. The sun is so massive that in a million years only _____ of the sun's rest mass will have been converted to radiant energy.

12. Is the following sentence true or false? The filament of a lightbulb has more mass when it is energized with electricity than when it is turned off. _____

13. _____ is simply congealed energy.

16.3 The Correspondence Principle (pages 307–308)

14. The _____ states that a new theory and the old theory must overlap and agree in the region where the results of the old theory have been fully verified.

15. According to the correspondence principle, the equations of special relativity must correspond to those of _____ _____ when speeds much less than the speed of light are considered.

16. The equations of _____ hold for all speeds, although they are significant only for speeds near the speed of light.

17. Is the following statement true or false? Einstein never claimed that accepted laws of physics were wrong, but instead showed that the laws of physics implied something that hadn't before been appreciated.

   _____

18. What is the general theory of relativity?

   _____

   _____

16.4 General Relativity (pages 308–311)

19. The _____ states that local observations made in an accelerated frame of reference cannot be distinguished from observations made in a Newtonian gravitational field.

20. If a wooden ball and a lead ball were dropped at the same time in an accelerating spaceship and both balls hit the floor at the same time, to what might the occupants of the spaceship attribute their observations?

   _____

   _____

21. In question 20, why did the balls hit the floor at the same time?

   _____

   _____

Chapter 16 Relativity—Momentum, Mass, Energy, and Gravity

22. Einstein stated that the correspondence principle holds for all natural phenomena, including _____, electromagnetic, and _____ phenomena.

23. Is the following sentence true or false? Just as a tossed ball curves in a gravitational field, so does a light beam. _____

24. According to Newton, tossed balls curve because of a _____.

25. According to Einstein, why is the path of a tossed ball curved?

_____

_____

_____

16.5 Gravity, Space, and a New Geometry (pages 311–314)

26. Space-time has _____ dimensions—_____ space dimensions and _____ time dimension.

Match the letters below each diagram to the correct statement.

a   b   c

_____ **27.** The sum of the angles of the triangle is greater than 180°.

_____ **28.** The sum of the angles of the triangle is less than 180°.

_____ **29.** The sum of the angles of the triangle is equal to 180°.

30. The lines of the shortest distance between two points on a curved surface are called _____.

31. Although space-time is curved within a solar system or within a galaxy, recent evidence suggests that the universe as a whole is _____.

32. A universe of zero or negative _____ is open ended and extends without limit.

33. Is the following statement true or false? The presence of mass produces a curvature or warping of space-time. Conversely, a curvature of space-time reveals the presence of mass. _____

34. Circle the letter of each statement that is true.

   a. General relativity tells us that the bumps, depressions, and warpings of geometrical space-time are gravity.

   b. It is easy to visualize four dimensions because we are four-dimensional beings.

   c. The planets that orbit the sun travel along three-dimensional geodesics in the warped space-time about the sun.

   d. Every object has mass and therefore makes a bump or depression in the surrounding space-time.

Chapter 16   Relativity—Momentum, Mass, Energy, and Gravity

35. The ripples that travel outward from the gravitational sources at the speed of light are _____.

36. Is the following statement true or false? The gravitational waves emitted by a vibrating electric charge are a trillion-trillion-trillion times weaker than the electromagnetic waves emitted by the same charge. _____

16.6 Tests of General Relativity (pages 314–316)

37. Upon developing the general theory of relativity, Einstein predicted that the elliptical orbits of the planets _____ about the sun, starlight passing close to the sun is _____, and _____ causes time to slow down.

38. Which planetary orbit is the most affected by the curvature of space? _____

39. Prior to Einstein's explanation, to what did scientists attribute the extra 43 seconds of arc per century in Mercury's orbit?

_____

_____

40. What was Einstein's second test of his general relativity theory?

_____

_____

41. When were the first measurements of the deflected starlight passing close to the sun made?

_____

_____

42. Circle the letter of each statement that is true.
   a. Einstein predicted that gravity causes clocks to run fast.
   b. Einstein predicted that clocks on the first floor of a building should tick slightly more slowly than clocks on the top floor.
   c. From the top to the bottom of the tallest skyscraper, the difference between two ticking clocks will vary only a few millionths of a second per decade.
   d. For larger differences, like those at the surface of the sun compared with the surface of Earth, the difference in two ticking clocks will be more pronounced.

43. Light traveling "against gravity" is observed to have a slightly lower frequency due to an effect called the _____.

44. Measurements of time depend not only on relative motion but also on _____.

Chapter 16   Relativity—Momentum, Mass, Energy, and Gravity

Conversion of Mass to Energy

In a nuclear reactor, 0.15 kilogram (kg) of uranium-235 is completely converted to energy. How many joules (J) of energy are produced?

1. Read and Understand

What information are you given?
Mass = m = 0.15 kg
Speed of light = c = 300,000,000 m/s = 3×10^8 m/s

2. Plan and Solve

What unknown are you trying to calculate?
The amount of energy produced = E = ?

What formula contains the given quantities and the unknown?
$E = mc^2$

Replace each variable with its known variable and known value.
$E = (0.15 \text{ kg})(3.00 \times 10^8 \text{ m/s})^2$

$E = 1.35 \times 10^{16} \text{ kg·m}^2/\text{s}^2 = 1.4 \times 10^{16} \text{ J}$

3. Look Back and Check

Is your answer reasonable?
Yes, the calculated number is quite large compared to the mass, and the units indicate energy.

Math Practice

On a separate sheet of paper, solve the following problems.

1. In a nuclear reactor, 1.5 kilograms of plutonium-239 is completely converted to energy. How many joules of energy are produced?

2. In a nuclear reactor, 0.20 kilogram of uranium-235 and 0.50 kilogram of plutonium-239 are completely converted to energy. How many joules of energy are produced?

3. A nuclear reactor produces 2.75×10^{16} joules of energy. How many kilograms of uranium-235 are completely converted to energy?

Chapter 17   The Atomic Nature of Matter

Summary

THE BIG
IDEA : Atoms are the building blocks of most matter.

17.1 Elements

☑ Every simple, complex, living, or nonliving substance in the known universe is put together from a pantry containing less than 100 elements.

- **Atoms** are the building blocks of matter.

- A material composed of only one kind of atom is called an **element.**

- There are about 115 known elements. Of these, about 90 occur in nature.

17.2 Atoms Are Small

☑ Atoms are so small that there are about 10^{23} atoms in a gram of water (a thimbleful).

- Atoms are perpetually moving. In solids the rate of migration is low, in liquids it is greater, and in gases migration is greatest.

- Atoms are too small to be seen—at least with visible light. This is because light is made up of waves, and atoms are smaller than the wavelengths of visible light.

17.3 Atoms Are Recyclable

☑ Atoms in your body have been around since long before the solar system came into existence, more than 4.6 billion years ago.

- Atoms are ageless and are much older than the materials they compose.

- People are not only made of the same *kinds* of atoms, but we are also made of the *same* atoms—atoms that cycle from person to person and creature to creature as we breathe and perspire.

17.4 Evidence for Atoms

☑ Brownian motion is evidence that atoms exist, as it results from the motion of neighboring atoms and molecules. They bump into larger particles we can see.

- The idea that matter is made of atoms goes back to the 400s B.C. This idea was revived in the early 1800s by an English meteorologist and school teacher, John Dalton.

- **Brownian motion** is the perpetual jiggling of particles that are just large enough to be seen.

- Direct evidence for the existence of atoms is provided by scanning tunneling microscopes, which allow scientists to see images of atoms.

Chapter 17   The Atomic Nature of Matter

17.5 Molecules

☑ **Molecules can be made up of atoms of the same element or of different elements.**

- A **molecule** is the smallest particle of a substance consisting of two or more atoms that are bound together by sharing electrons.

- Matter that is a gas or liquid at room temperature is usually made of molecules. But not all matter is made of molecules. Metals and crystalline minerals (including common table salt) are made of atoms that are not joined in molecules.

17.6 Compounds

☑ **Compounds have properties different from those of the elements of which they are made.**

- A **compound** is a substance that is made of atoms of different elements combined in a fixed proportion.

- The **chemical formula** of a compound tells the proportions of each kind of atom in the compound.

17.7 The Atomic Nucleus

☑ **The mass of an atom is primarily concentrated in the nucleus.**

- An atom is mostly empty space. Almost all of an atom's mass is packed into the dense central region called the **nucleus.** However, the nucleus occupies less than a trillionth of the volume of an atom.

- The principal building blocks of the nucleus are **nucleons.** Nucleons in an electrically neutral state are **neutrons.** Nucleons in an electrically charged state are **protons.**

- Atoms of the same element having different numbers of neutrons are called **isotopes** of that element.

- Atoms are classified by their **atomic number,** which is the number of protons in the nucleus.

- Electric charge comes in two kinds, positive and negative. Protons are positive and electrons are negative. Like kinds of charges repel one another and unlike kinds attract one another. Protons repel protons, but attract electrons. Electrons repel electrons, but attract protons.

Chapter 17   The Atomic Nature of Matter

17.8 Electrons in the Atom

☑ **The arrangement of electrons in the shells about the atomic nucleus dictates the atom's chemical properties.**

- Electrons that orbit the atomic nucleus are identical to the electrons that flow in the wires of electric circuits.

- In an electrically neutral atom, the number of negatively charged electrons always equals the number of positively charged protons in the nucleus.

- When the number of electrons in an atom differs from the number of protons, the atom is no longer neutral and has a net charge. An atom with a net charge is an **ion.**

- Attraction between a proton and an electron can cause a *bond* between atoms to form a molecule.

- Scientists use a model to explain how atoms of different elements interact to form compounds. In the **shell model of the atom,** electrons are pictured as orbiting in spherical shells around the nucleus.

- The **periodic table** is a chart that lists atoms by their atomic number and by their electron arrangements. Elements in the same column have similar chemical properties, and are said to belong to the same *group* or family of elements.

17.9 The Phases of Matter

☑ **Matter exists in four phases: solid, liquid, gaseous, and plasma.**

- In the **plasma** phase, matter consists of positive ions and free electrons. The plasma phase exists only at high temperatures.

- In all phases of matter, the atoms are constantly in motion.

- In the solid phase, the atoms and molecules vibrate about fixed positions.

- All substances can be transformed from one phase to another.

Chapter 17   The Atomic Nature of Matter

Exercises

17.1 Elements (pages 325–326)

Match each phrase with the correct word or words.

_____	**1.** the building blocks of matter	a. elements
_____	**2.** materials composed of only one kind of atom	b. about 115
_____	**3.** number of known elements	c. atoms
_____	**4.** number of naturally occurring elements	d. about 90

5. Every simple, complex, living, or nonliving substance in the known universe is put together from a pantry containing less than _____ elements.

6. Which five elements make up most living things?

_____

_____

7. Which element is the most abundant element in the universe?

_____

8. Where are most of the natural elements formed?

_____

9. Research has confirmed that about 23 percent of the matter in the universe is composed of unseen _____.

17.2 Atoms Are Small (page 327)

10. Atoms are so small that there are about _____ atoms in a gram of water.

11. Is the following sentence true or false? In solids, the rate of migration of atoms is lower than it is in liquids. _____

12. Is the following sentence true or false? In gases, the rate of migration of atoms is lower than it is in liquids. _____

13. Why are atoms too small to be seen with visible light?

_____

_____

17.3 Atoms Are Recyclable (page 328)

14. Is the following sentence true or false? Most atoms are about 6 million years old. _____

15. Atoms in your body have been around since long before the solar system came into existence, more than _____ years ago.

16. Is the following sentence true or false? People are made of the same atoms—atoms that cycle from person to person and creature to creature as we breathe and perspire. _____

Chapter 17   The Atomic Nature of Matter

17.4 Evidence for Atoms (pages 328–329)

17. Circle the letter of each statement that is true.

   a. The idea that matter is made of atoms goes back to the Romans in 4 B.C.

   b. English meteorologist and school teacher John Dalton demonstrated that atoms do not exist.

   c. The first fairly direct evidence for the existence of atoms was unknowingly discovered by the Scottish botanist, Robert Brown.

   d. Looking through a microscope, Robert Brown observed dust particles and grains of soot in a constant state of agitation.

18. _____ is the perpetual jiggling of particles that are just large enough to be seen.

19. Provide two kinds of evidence that atoms exist.

   _____

   _____

   _____

   _____

   _____

17.5 Molecules (page 330)

20. A(n) _____ is the smallest particle of a substance consisting of two or more atoms that bond together by sharing electrons.

21. Is the following sentence true or false? Molecules are made only of atoms of the same element. _____

22. What elements combine to form water?

   _____

23. Matter that is a _____ or _____ at room temperature is usually made of molecules.

24. _____ and _____ are made of atoms that are not joined in molecules.

25. Which sense can humans use to detect the presence of molecules such as sulfur dioxide, ammonia, or ether?

   _____

17.6 Compounds (page 331)

26. A _____ is a substance that is made of atoms of different elements combined in a fixed proportion.

27. The _____ of a compound tells the proportions of each kind of atom in the compound.

Name _____ Class _____ Date _____

Chapter 17   The Atomic Nature of Matter

Use the figure below to answer Questions 28 and 29.

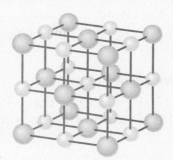

28. The atoms in the compound shown above differ from those found in water. What kinds of atoms make up NaCl? _____

29. How many sodium atoms surround each chlorine atom in NaCl? _____

30. Is the following sentence true or false? Compounds have properties that are the same as the elements that compose them. _____

17.7 The Atomic Nucleus (pages 331–333)

31. Where is most of the mass of an atom located?

_____

_____

32. Describe how Ernest Rutherford discovered that an atom is composed mostly of empty space.

_____

_____

_____

_____

_____

_____

Match each phrase with the correct word or words.

_____ 33. principal building blocks of an atom's nucleus

_____ 34. nucleons in an electrically neutral state

_____ 35. nucleons in an electrically charged state

_____ 36. atoms of the same element having different numbers of neutrons

_____ 37. the number of protons in an atom's nucleus

a. protons

b. atomic number

c. nucleons

d. neutrons

e. isotopes

38. Is the following sentence true or false? Like kinds of charges attract one another and unlike kinds repel one another. _____

Chapter 17   The Atomic Nature of Matter

39. Protons repel _____ but attract _____.

40. Electrons repel _____ but attract _____.

41. Is the following sentence true or false? Inside the nucleus, protons are held together by an electromagnetic force. _____.

17.8 Electrons in the Atom (pages 334–335)

42. Is the following sentence true or false? Electrons that orbit the atomic nucleus are identical to the electrons that flow in the wires of electric circuits. _____

43. How does the mass of an electron compare to the mass of a proton and a neutron?

_____

_____

44. Is the following sentence true or false? In an electrically neutral atom, the number of negatively charged electrons is greater than the number of positively charged protons. _____

45. An atom with a net charge is a(n) _____.

Use the figure below to answer Questions 46 and 47.

46. Which atomic model is illustrated? _____

47. Where are the electrons located?

_____

48. The _____ is a chart that lists atoms by their atomic number and by their electron arrangements.

17.9 The Phases of Matter (page 337)

49. Is the following sentence true or false? Matter exists in four phases: solid, liquid, gaseous, and plasma. _____

50. In the _____ phase, matter consists of positive ions and free electrons.

51. The plasma phase exists only at _____.

52. Is the following sentence true or false? In all phases of matter, atoms are rarely in motion. _____

Chapter 17   The Atomic Nature of Matter

Calculating Mass

A unit called an atomic mass unit (amu) is used to measure the mass of atoms and compounds. One hydrogen atom has a mass of 1.008 amu. One oxygen atom has a mass of 15.999 amu. What is the mass of one molecule of water (H_2O) in atomic mass units?

1. Read and Understand

What information are you given?

mass of one hydrogen atom = m_H = 1.008 amu

mass of one oxygen atom = m_O = 15.999 amu

2. Plan and Solve

What unknown are you trying to calculate?

The mass of one molecule of water, which is composed of two hydrogen atoms and one oxygen atom

What mathematical equation can you use to calculate the unknown?

$2m_H + m_O = m_{water}$

2(1.008 amu) + 15.999 amu = 18.015 amu

3. Look Back and Check

Is your answer reasonable?

Yes, the answer is closer in value to oxygen's mass than hydrogen's mass, because oxygen has a greater mass than hydrogen does. Also, the units in the answer are correct.

Math Practice

On a separate sheet of paper, solve the following problems.

1. Carbon has a mass of 12.011 amu and hydrogen has a mass of 1.008 amu. What is the mass of methane (CH_4) in atomic mass units?

2. Carbon has a mass of 12.011 amu and chlorine has a mass of 35.453 amu. What is the mass of carbon tetrachloride (CCl_4) in atomic mass units?

3. Sodium has a mass of 22.990 amu and chlorine has a mass of 35.453 amu. What is the mass of common table salt, NaCl, in atomic mass units?

Chapter 18 Solids

Summary

THE BIG IDEA : Solids can be described in terms of crystal structure, density, and elasticity.

18.1 Crystal Structure

✔ The shape of a crystal mirrors the geometric arrangement of atoms within the crystal.

- Minerals are made of **crystals,** or regular geometric shapes whose component particles are arranged in an orderly, repeating pattern. The shape of a crystal mirrors the geometric arrangement of atoms within the crystal.

- The existence of crystals in many solids was not discovered until X-rays became a tool of research early in the twentieth century. Every crystalline structure has its own unique X-ray pattern.

18.2 Density

✔ The density of a material depends upon the masses of the individual atoms that make it up, and the spacing between those atoms.

- **Density** is a measure of how much matter occupies a given space; it is the amount of mass per unit volume: density = mass/volume.

- Density is a property of a material. Density doesn't depend on how much of the material you have.

- The density of solids and liquids varies somewhat with temperature and pressure.

- A quantity known as **weight density** can be expressed by the amount of weight a body has per unit volume: weight density = weight/volume. Weight density is commonly used when discussing liquid pressure.

- A standard measure of density is **specific gravity**—the ratio of the mass (or weight) of a substance to the mass (or weight) of an equal volume of water. Because specific gravity is a ratio of the density of a material to the density of water, it has no units.

18.3 Elasticity

✔ A body's elasticity describes how much it changes shape when a deforming force acts on it, and how well it returns to its original shape when the deforming force is removed.

- A material that returns to its original shape after it has been stretched or compressed is said to be **elastic.**

- Materials that do not resume their original shape after being distorted are said to be **inelastic.**

- According to **Hooke's law,** the amount of stretch (or compression), x, is directly proportional to the applied force F. In equation form, $F \sim \Delta x$.

Chapter 18   Solids

- The distance at which permanent distortion occurs is called the **elastic limit.** Hooke's law holds only as long as the force does not stretch or compress the material beyond its elastic limit.

18.4 Compression and Tension

☑ **A horizontal beam supported at one or both ends is under stress from the load it supports, including its own weight. It undergoes a stress of both compression and tension (stretching).**

- A horizontal beam supported at one end sags because of its own weight and the load it carries. The top part of the beam is stretched. The bottom part of the beam is compressed. A region between the top and bottom is neither stretched nor compressed. This is the *neutral layer.*

- A horizontal beam that is supported at both ends and carries a load in the middle will experience compression at the top of the beam and tension at the bottom. A neutral layer exists in the middle portion of the beam.

- Most of the material in an I-beam is concentrated in the top and bottom parts, called the *flanges*. The piece joining the bars, called the *web*, is thinner.

- An I-beam is nearly as strong as a solid bar, and its weight is considerably less.

18.5 Scaling

☑ **When linear dimensions are enlarged, the cross-sectional area (as well as the total surface area) grows as the square of the enlargement, whereas volume and weight grow as the cube of the enlargement. As the linear size of an object increases, the volume grows faster than the total surface area.**

- The study of how size affects the relationship between weight, strength, and surface area is known as **scaling.** As the size of a thing increases, it grows heavier much faster than it grows stronger.

- Weight depends on volume, and strength comes from the area of the cross section of the limbs (for example, tree limbs or animal limbs).

- The fact that volume (and weight) grows as the cube of linear enlargement, while strength (and surface area) grows as the square of linear enlargement, is evident in the disproportionately thick legs of large animals compared with those of small animals.

- Volume grows as the cube of the enlargement, and both cross-sectional area and total surface area grow as the square of the enlargement. So as an object grows, the surface area to volume ratio *decreases*.

- Smaller objects have more surface area per unit mass than larger objects.

- Scaling affects living organisms. In the case of mammals, for example, size affects the life span of an organism. Small mammals live fast and die young; larger mammals live at a leisurely pace and live longer.

Chapter 18   Solids

Exercises

18.1 Crystal Structure (page 345)

1. Minerals are made of _____, which are regular geometric shapes whose component particles are arranged in an orderly, repeating pattern.

2. What determines the shape of a crystal?

   _____

   _____

3. Is the following sentence true or false? Every crystalline structure shows several different X-ray patterns. _____

4. Metals such as iron, copper, and gold have relatively _____ crystal structures.

18.2 Density (pages 346–347)

5. Is the following sentence true or false? Density is the amount of mass per unit length: density = mass/length. _____

6. Circle the letter of each statement that is true.

   a. Density is not mass; it is volume.

   b. Density is a ratio; it is the amount of mass per unit volume.

   c. Density depends on how much of a material you have.

   d. A pure iron nail has the same density as a pure iron frying pan.

7. The density of a material depends upon the _____ of the individual atoms that make it up, and the _____ between those atoms.

8. Is the following sentence true or false? A common unit of density is grams per cubic centimeter, or g/cm^3. _____

9. What is the density of water at 4°C? _____

10. A quantity known as weight volume can be expressed by the amount of _____ a body has per unit _____.

11. Define specific gravity.

    _____

    _____

    _____

12. Copper has a specific gravity of 8.9. What is the density of copper?

    _____

Chapter 18   Solids

18.3 Elasticity (pages 348–349)

Match each phrase with the correct word or words.

a. Hooke's law   b. elastic   c. elastic limit

d. inelastic   e. elasticity

_____ **13.** describes a material that returns to its original shape after it has been stretched or compressed

_____ **14.** a property that describes how much a body changes shape when a deforming force acts on it, and how well it returns to its original shape when the deforming force is removed

_____ **15.** describes a material that does not resume its original shape after being distorted

_____ **16.** states that the amount of stretch (or compression), x, is directly proportional to the applied force F

_____ **17.** the distance at which permanent distortion occurs in a body

18. Is the following statement true or false? Hooke's law holds only as long as the force does not stretch or compress the material beyond its elastic limit. _____

18.4 Compression and Tension (pages 350–352)

19. What properties of steel make it an excellent material for springs and construction girders?

_____

_____

20. A horizontal beam supported at one or both ends undergoes both _____ and _____.

21. What is the neutral layer in a steel beam?

_____

_____

_____

Use the diagram of an I-beam below to answer Questions 22–23.

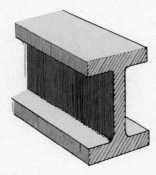

22. Label the *flanges* and the *web* of the I-beam on the diagram.

Chapter 18 Solids

23. Where is most of the stress in an I-beam when it is used horizontally in construction?

_____

18.5 Scaling (pages 353–356)

24. The study of how size affects the relationship between weight, strength, and surface area is known as _____

25. Is the following sentence true or false? As the size of an object or living thing increases, it grows heavier much slower than it grows stronger.

_____

26. Circle the letter of each statement that is true.

    a. Weight depends on size, and strength comes from weight.

    b. When linear dimensions are enlarged, the cross-sectional area (as well as the total surface area) grows as the square of the enlargement.

    c. When linear dimensions are enlarged, volume and weight grow as the cube of the enlargement.

    d. If the linear dimensions of an object double, the cross-sectional area grows by a factor of 8.

27. Calculate the surface area and volume of the big cube shown at right if the dimensions of each component cube are 1 cm × 1 cm × 1 cm. What is the ratio of surface area to volume for the big cube? How does this ratio compare to that of one of the component cubes?

28. As the linear size of an object _____, the volume grows faster than the total surface area.

29. Explain why big ears are important for elephants.

_____

_____

_____

Chapter 18   Solids

Calculating Density

Suppose you find an elaborate silver thimble at a flea market. You are not sure if the thimble is solid silver or silver plate. The thimble has a mass of 223 grams, and you determine that it has a volume of 21.2 cm^3. Pure silver has a density of 10.5 g/cm^3. Is the thimble solid silver?

1. Read and Understand

What information are you given?

  mass of object = 223 grams

  volume of object = 21.2 cm^3

  density of pure silver = 10.5 g/cm^3

2. Plan and Solve

What unknown are you trying to calculate?
  density of object

What mathematical expression can you use to calculate the unknown?

  $$density = \frac{mass}{volume}$$

  $$density = \frac{223 \text{ g}}{21.2 \text{ cm}^3} = 10.5 \text{ g/cm}^3$$

Since the density of the object equals the density of pure silver, the object is likely pure silver.

3. Look Back and Check

Is your answer reasonable?
  Yes, the units (g/cm^3) indicate density.

Math Practice

On a separate sheet of paper, solve the following problems.

1. A nugget appears to be copper. It has a mass of 335 grams and a volume of 27.5 cm^3. Pure copper has a density of 8.96 g/cm^3. Is the nugget pure copper?

2. A piece of metal is found in the laboratory. One student says that it is a piece of aluminum and another student says that it is a piece of magnesium. The piece of metal has a mass of 425 grams and a volume of 244.5 cm^3. Magnesium has a density of 1.738 g/cm^3, and aluminum has a density of 2.699 g/cm^3. What is the composition of the piece of metal?

Chapter 19   Liquids

Summary

**THE BIG
IDEA** : In the liquid phase, molecules can flow freely from position to position by sliding over one another. A liquid takes the shape of its container.

19.1 Liquid Pressure

☑ The pressure of a liquid at rest depends only on gravity and the density and depth of the liquid.

- Pressure is defined as the force per unit area on which the force acts; pressure = force/area.

- The pressure created by a liquid, in equation form, is pressure due to liquid = density × g × depth.

- At a given depth, a given liquid exerts the same pressure against any surface—the bottom or sides of its container, or even the surface of an object submerged in the liquid to that depth.

- Pressure of a liquid does not depend on the amount, volume, or weight of the liquid.

- At any point within a liquid, the forces that produce pressure are exerted equally in all directions.

19.2 Buoyancy

☑ When the weight of a submerged object is greater than the buoyant force, the object will sink. When the weight is less than the buoyant force, the object will rise to the surface and float.

- **Buoyancy** is the apparent loss of weight of objects when submerged in a liquid.

- The **buoyant force** is the net upward force exerted by a fluid on a submerged or immersed object.

- When the weight of a submerged object is equal to the buoyant force, the submerged object will remain at any level, like a fish.

- A completely submerged object always displaces a volume of liquid equal to its own volume.

19.3 Archimedes' Principle

☑ Archimedes' principle states that the buoyant force on an immersed object is equal to the weight of the fluid it displaces.

- **Archimedes' principle** describes the relationship between buoyancy and displaced liquid. This principle is true for liquids and gases, which are both fluids.

- *Immersed* means "either completely or partially submerged."

- Whatever the shape of a submerged object, the buoyant force equals the weight of liquid displaced.

Chapter 19   Liquids

19.4 Does It Sink, or Does It Float?

✔ Sinking and floating can be summed up in three simple rules.

  1. An object more dense than the fluid in which it is immersed sinks.
  2. An object less dense than the fluid in which it is immersed floats.
  3. An object with density equal to the density of the fluid in which it is immersed neither sinks nor floats.

- When a buoyant force exactly equals the weight of a completely submerged object, the object's weight is equal to the weight of displaced fluid. Since the volumes of the object and of the displaced fluid are the same, the density of the object must equal the density of the fluid.

- The density of a submarine is controlled by the flow of water into and out of its ballast tanks. A fish changes its density by increasing or contracting its volume. A crocodile changes its density by swallowing stones.

19.5 Flotation

✔ The principle of flotation states that a floating object displaces a weight of fluid equal to its own weight.

- A solid iron block sinks, while the same block shaped to occupy at least eight times as much volume floats.

- Every ship must be designed to displace a weight of water equal to its own weight.

- A canoe and a ship float lower in the water when they are loaded.

- If a submarine displaces a weight of water greater than its own weight, it will rise. If it displaces less, it will go down. If it displaces exactly its weight, it will remain at constant depth.

19.6 Pascal's Principle

✔ Pascal's principle states that changes in pressure at any point in an enclosed fluid at rest are transmitted undiminished to all points in the fluid and act in all directions.

- **Pascal's principle** describes how changes in a pressure are transmitted in a fluid.

- Pascal's principle was discovered in the seventeenth century by Blaise Pascal, for whom the SI unit of pressure is named.

- Pascal's principle is employed in a hydraulic press. In a hydraulic press in which one side is larger, any additional pressure of 1 N/cm^2 is exerted against every square centimeter of the larger piston. If the larger piston has an area of 50 cm^2, then total force exerted by the larger piston is 50 newtons.

Chapter 19 Liquids

Exercises

19.1 Liquid Pressure (pages 363–365)

1. Define pressure in words.

   _____

   _____

2. What is the equation for pressure?_____

3. What three factors determine the pressure of a liquid?

   _____

4. Is the following sentence true or false? How much a liquid weighs, and thus how much pressure it exerts, depends on its density. _____

5. Consider two identical containers, one filled with a dense liquid and the other filled to the same depth with a less dense liquid. Which container exerts more pressure?

   _____

   _____

6. Circle the letter of each statement that is true.

   a. The pressure of a liquid at rest does not depend on the shape of the container or the size of its bottom.

   b. The pressure due to liquid = density $\times g \times$ depth.

   c. At a given depth, a liquid exerts more pressure on the bottom of its container.

   d. The total pressure of a liquid is: density $\times g \times$ depth *plus* the pressure of the atmosphere.

7. Is the following sentence true or false? The pressure of a liquid depends on the amount of liquid._____

8. One dam holds back the water from a large, but shallow lake. Another dam holds back the water from a small, but deep lake. Which dam must withstand the greater pressure?

   _____

   _____

9. What principle about liquid and pressure do Pascal's vases demonstrate?

   _____

   _____

   _____

Chapter 19   Liquids

19.2 Buoyancy (pages 366–367)

10. The _____ is the net upward force exerted by a fluid on a submerged or immersed object.

Match each sentence with the correct result.

_____ 11. The weight of a submerged object is greater than the buoyant force.

_____ 12. The weight of a submerged object is less than the buoyant force.

_____ 13. The weight of a submerged object is equal to the buoyant force.

a. The object will remain at any level.

b. The object will sink.

c. The object will float on the surface.

14. How much liquid does a completely submerged object displace?

_____

15. Describe a method of determining the volume of an irregularly shaped object.

_____

_____

_____

19.3 Archimedes' Principle (pages 367–368)

16. What does Archimedes' principle state?

_____

_____

17. What does *immersed* mean?

_____

_____

18. Is the following sentence true or false? An immersed container will displace the same volume of water and the same weight of water at any depth._____

19. Explain the relationship between the upward force due to water pressure on the bottom of a submerged block and the downward force due to water pressure on the top of the submerged block.

_____

_____

19.4 Does It Sink, or Does It Float? (pages 369–370)

20. A submerged object's _____ determines the buoyant force.

21. When the buoyant force equals the weight of an object completely submerged in water, then the object's weight must equal

_____.

Chapter 19   Liquids

Match each phrase with the correct word or words.

_____ **22.** An object will sink.

_____ **23.** An object will float.

_____ **24.** An object neither sinks nor floats.

a. An object has a density equal to the density of the fluid in which it is immersed.

b. An object is more dense than the fluid in which it is immersed.

c. An object is less dense than the fluid in which it is immersed.

25. Why does a submarine take in or release water from its ballast tanks?

_____

26. How do fish and crocodiles control their density?

_____

_____

_____

19.5 Flotation (pages 371–372)

27. Explain why in the figure below, the iron block on the left sinks, while the reshaped piece of iron on the right floats.

_____

_____

28. Is the following statement true or false? The principle of flotation states that a floating object displaces a weight of fluid equal to its own volume. _____

29. Every ship must be designed to displace a weight of water equal to

_____

19.6 Pascal's Principle (pages 373–374)

30. What does Pascal's principle state?

_____

_____

_____

Chapter 19   Liquids

31. Circle the letter of each statement that is true.

   a. Pascal's principle was discovered in the seventeenth century.

   b. The SI unit for pressure is named after Pascal.

   c. The SI unit for force is named after Pascal.

   d. Pascal's principle is employed in a hydraulic press.

Use the figure below to answer Questions 32–34.

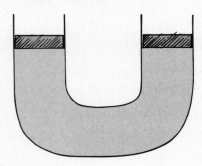

32. If pressure is applied to the left piston, what happens to the pressure on the right piston?

_____

33. If pressure is applied to the left piston, is there any point in the enclosed fluid where the pressure is greater?

_____

_____

34. In a hydraulic press, the surface area of the smaller piston is 1 cm^2 and the surface area of the large piston is 50 cm^2. What is the force on the larger piston if 1 N/cm^2 of pressure is applied to the smaller piston?

_____

35. Explain why energy is conserved in a hydraulic press even though force is multiplied.

_____

_____

_____

36. Is the following statement true or false? Pascal's principle applies to liquids and gases._____

37. Explain how an automobile lift works.

_____

_____

Chapter 19   Liquids

Calculating Pressure

In a hydraulic lift, a small piston with an area of 2.50 m² exerts a force of 4.00 N. If the large piston has an area of 7.00 m², what force does the large piston exert?

1. Read and Understand

What information are you given?

force of small piston = F_1 = 4.00 N

area of small piston = A_1 = 2.50 m²

area of large piston = A_2 = 7.00 m²

2. Plan and Solve

What unknown are you trying to calculate?

force exerted by large piston = F_2

What mathematical expression can you use to calculate the unknown?

$$\frac{F_1}{A_1} = \frac{F_2}{A_2}$$

$$\frac{4.00 \text{ N}}{2.50 \text{ m}^2} = \frac{F_2}{7.00 \text{ m}^2}$$

$$F_2 = \frac{(4.00 \text{ N})(7.00 \text{ m}^2)}{2.50 \text{ m}^2} = 11.2 \text{ N}$$

3. Look Back and Check

Is your answer reasonable?

Yes, the force exerted by the larger piston is greater than the force exerted by the smaller piston and the units indicate a force.

Math Practice

On a separate sheet of paper, solve the following problems.

1. A small piston with an area of 1.75 m² exerts a force of 6.25 N. What force does the larger piston exert if it has an area of 5.25 m²?

2. A small piston with an area of 5.50 m² exerts a force of 325 N. What force does the large piston exert if it has an area of 10.25 m²?

3. A large piston with an area of 9.75 m² exerts a force of 525 N. What force does the small piston exert if it has an area of 2.75 m²?

Chapter 20 Gases

Summary

THE BIG IDEA : Gas molecules are far apart and can move freely between collisions.

20.1 The Atmosphere

☑ **Earth's atmosphere consists of molecules that occupy space and extends many kilometers above Earth's surface.**

- The molecules that make up Earth's atmosphere are energized by sunlight and kept in continual motion. Without Earth's gravity, the molecules would fly off into outer space.

- Earth's atmosphere has no definite surface. Its density decreases with altitude.

- In interplanetary space, there is a gas density of about one molecule per cubic centimeter. This is primarily hydrogen, the most plentiful element in the universe.

- Ninety nine percent of the atmosphere is below an altitude of about 30 kilometers. Compared with Earth's radius, Earth's atmosphere is just a thin shell.

20.2 Atmospheric Pressure

☑ **Atmospheric pressure is caused by the weight of air, just as water pressure is caused by the weight of water.**

- The density of air changes with temperature. At sea level, 1 cubic meter of air at 20°C has a mass of about 1.2 kg.

- The weight of air that bears down on a 1-square-meter surface at sea level is about 100,000 newtons.

- Aside from variations with altitude, there are variations in atmospheric pressure at any one locality due to moving air currents and storms.

20.3 The Simple Barometer

☑ **The height of the mercury in the tube of a simple barometer is a measure of the atmospheric pressure.**

- An instrument for measuring the pressure of the atmosphere is called a **barometer.** In a simple mercury barometer, changes in the atmospheric pressure result in a change in the height of the mercury in the tube.

- The operation of a barometer is similar to liquid rising through a straw. Atmospheric pressure on the liquid's surface pushes liquid up into the reduced-pressure region.

Chapter 20   Gases

20.4 The Aneroid Barometer

✓ **An aneroid barometer uses a small metal box that is partially exhausted of air. The box has a slightly flexible lid that bends in or out as atmospheric pressure changes.**

- An **aneroid barometer** is an instrument that measures variations in atmospheric pressure without a liquid. The barometer's lid bends in or out as atmospheric pressure changes.

- Since atmospheric pressure decreases with increasing altitude, a barometer can be used to determine elevation. An aneroid barometer calibrated for altitude is called an *altimeter*.

20.5 Boyle's Law

✓ **Boyle's law states that the product of pressure and volume for a given mass of gas is a constant as long as the temperature does not change.**

- When the number of air molecules in a given volume doubles, air density is doubled. If the molecules have the same temperature, the number of collisions will double. This means the air pressure is doubled. So, air pressure is proportional to density.

- The density of the air can also be doubled by simply compressing the air to half its volume.

- **Boyle's law** describes the relationship between the pressure and volume of a gas. "Pressure × volume" for a sample of gas at one time is equal to any "different pressure × different volume" of the same sample of gas at any other time. In equation form, $P_1 V_1 = P_2 V_2$.

20.6 Buoyancy of Air

✓ **Any object less dense than the air around it will rise.**

- Archimedes' principle for air states that an object surrounded by air is buoyed up by a force equal to the weight of the air displaced.

- Any object that has a mass less than the mass of an equal volume of surrounding air will rise. A gas-filled balloon rises in air because it is less dense than the surrounding air.

Chapter 20   Gases

20.7 Bernoulli's Principle

☑ **Bernoulli's principle in its simplest form states that when the speed of a fluid increases, pressure in the fluid decreases.**

- The amount of water that flows continually past all sections of a pipe is the same. Water in the wider parts will slow down, and water in narrower parts will speed up.

- **Bernoulli's principle** describes the relationship between the speed of a fluid and the pressure in the fluid. Bernoulli found that the greater the speed of water flow in a pipe, the less is the force of the water at right angles (sideways) to the direction of flow.

- In steady flow, one small bit of fluid follows the same path as a bit of fluid in front of it. **Streamlines** are the smooth paths of small regions of fluid in steady flow. The paths are closer together in narrower regions, where the flow is faster and pressure is less.

- Bernoulli's principle holds only for steady flow. If the flow speed is too great, the flow may become turbulent and follow a changing, curling path known as an **eddy**. In that case Bernoulli's principle doesn't hold.

20.8 Applications of Bernoulli's Principle

☑ **When lift equals weight, horizontal flight is possible.**

- **Lift** is the upward force created by the difference between the air pressure above and below a surface. Lift is greater for higher speeds and larger surface areas.

- Unequal air pressures on opposite sides of a moving ball curve the path of the ball.

- Passing ships risk sideways collisions when water flowing between the ships travels faster than water flowing past their outer sides because water pressure acting against the hulls is reduced between the ships.

- In a shower, a greater atmospheric pressure outside the shower curtain pushes the curtain inward.

Chapter 20   Gases

Exercises

20.1 The Atmosphere (page 383)

1. The _____ energizes the molecules in Earth's atmosphere.

2. Why is gravity important to Earth's atmosphere?

   _____

   _____

3. What would happen to Earth's atmosphere without the sun?

   _____

   _____

4. Is the following sentence true or false? Like the ocean, Earth's atmosphere has a definite surface. _____

5. The density of the atmosphere _____ with altitude.

6. How are the molecules that make up Earth's atmosphere like a huge pile of feathers?

   _____

   _____

7. What is the density of gas in interplanetary space?

   _____

   _____

8. Circle the letter of the most plentiful element in the universe.
   a. oxygen   b. nitrogen
   c. hydrogen   d. carbon

9. Circle the letter of the level below which 99% of the atmosphere is found.
   a. 3 kilometers   b. 30 kilometers
   c. 300 kilometers   d. 3,000 kilometers

10. Compare the thickness of Earth's atmosphere to Earth's radius.

    _____

    _____

11. Describe how the temperature of the atmosphere changes with increasing altitude.

    _____

    _____

20.2 Atmospheric Pressure (pages 384–385)

12. Atmospheric pressure is caused by the _____ of air.

13. What is the mass of air in a room that has a volume of 50 m^3? The temperature of the room is 20°C. _____

14. Is the following sentence true or false? Air doesn't weigh very much, no matter how much you have of it. _____

Chapter 20   Gases

15. Consider a 1-square-meter column of air that extends up through the atmosphere.

   a. What is the mass of the air in the column? _____

   b. What is the weight of the air in the column?
      _____

   c. What pressure does the air in the column produce?
      _____

16. The average atmospheric pressure at sea level is _____.

17. Name three things that can cause variations in atmospheric pressure.

   a. _____

   b. _____

   c. _____

18. Measurement of changing _____ is important to meteorologists in predicting weather.

20.3 The Simple Barometer (pages 386–387)

19. What does a barometer measure?
    _____

20. Circle the letter of the word or phrase that completes the statement. The tube of a mercury barometer must be _____ 76 cm tall.

   a. exactly   b. less than

   c. approximately   d. greater than

21. Under what conditions would the mercury in a barometer completely fill the tube?
    _____
    _____

22. How would a barometer differ if water were used in the tube instead of mercury?
    _____
    _____

23. Circle the letter of each statement that is true.

   a. The liquid in a barometer is pushed up by pressure.

   b. The liquid in a straw is sucked up by pressure.

   c. Sucking on a straw increases the air pressure in the straw.

   d. In an old-fashioned pump, the atmosphere pushes water from below into a pipe at the surface.

Chapter 20   Gases

20.4 The Aneroid Barometer (page 388)

24. An aneroid barometer is an instrument that measures variations in atmospheric pressure without a _____.

25. How does an aneroid barometer measure atmospheric pressure?

_____

_____

26. A(n) _____ is an aneroid barometer calibrated to determine elevation.

20.5 Boyle's Law (pages 389–390)

27. The _____ and the _____ are greater inside an inflated tire than outside.

28. Describe what causes the pressure exerted by air inside an inflated tire.

_____

_____

29. Is the following sentence true or false? If the density of air in a tire increases, the air pressure increases. _____.

30. The figure below shows how the movement of a piston in a cylinder can affect the air inside the cylinder. Use the figure to complete the table below.

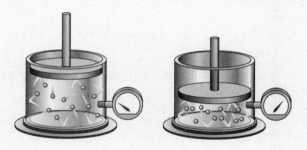

Movement of Piston	Change in the Air's Volume	Change in the Air's Density	Change in the Air's Pressure
Downward	decreases by half	_____	_____
Upward	_____	decreases by half	_____
_____	decreases to a third of its original value	_____	three times its original value
_____	_____	a third of its original value	a third of its original value

Chapter 20   Gases

31. State Boyle's law in words and in an equation.

a. in words:

_____

_____

b. as an equation: _____

32. Why is Boyle's law important to a scuba diver who is ascending?

_____

_____

_____

20.6 Buoyancy of Air (page 391)

33. The rules for buoyancy hold for both _____ and

_____.

34. State Archimedes' principle for air.

_____

_____

35. Any object that is _____ than the air around it will rise.

20.7 Bernoulli's Principle (pages 392–393)

36. Is the following sentence true or false? Atmospheric pressure increases in a hurricane. _____

37. Consider a continuous flow of water through a pipe. Circle the letter of each statement that is true.

a. The amount of water that flows past any section of the pipe changes with pipe width.

b. The water will slow down in a wider part of the pipe.

c. The water will speed up in a narrower part of the pipe.

d. The amount and speed of the water in the pipe does not change.

38. State Bernoulli's principle.

_____

_____

39. Is the following statement true or false? The pressure within a fluid is different from the pressure it can exert on anything in its path that slows it down. _____

40. Define streamlines.

_____

_____

41. Streamlines that are closer together indicate a(n) _____ in fluid speed and a(n) _____ in the fluid's internal pressure.

Chapter 20   Gases

42. Explain how air bubbles in a fluid are related to the fluid's pressure and speed.

_____

_____

_____

43. What is an eddy?

_____

20.8 Applications of Bernoulli's Principle (pages 394–395)

44. What happens to a sheet of paper if you hold one end and blow air across the top of it? _____

45. Define lift.

_____

_____

46. Use the figure below to explain how lift makes horizontal flight possible.

_____

_____

_____

47. Is the following sentence true or false? During a strong wind, such as a tornado, the air inside a building may push the roof off.

_____

48. Explain why passing ships run the risk of sideways collisions.

_____

_____

_____

49. Is the following sentence true or false? A shower curtain billows inward when the shower is turned on full blast because air pressure inside the shower increases. _____

Chapter 20   Gases

Boyle's Law

A movable piston encloses 0.78 m^3 of gas in a cylinder. The piston is then pushed downward, changing the volume of the gas to 0.36 m^3 and the pressure to 2.8 kPa. What was the original pressure of the gas?

1. Read and Understand

What information are you given?
initial volume of the piston = V_1 = 0.78 m^3
final volume of the piston = V_2 = 0.36 m^3
final pressure of the piston = P_2 = 2.8 kPa

2. Plan and Solve

What unknown are you trying to calculate?
original pressure of the piston = P_1

What mathematical equation can you use to calculate the unknown?
Boyle's law: $P_1 V_1 = P_2 V_2$

Rearrange the equation to solve for the unknown variable.

$$P_1 = \frac{P_2 V_2}{V_1}$$

Substitute the values you know into the equation.

$$P_1 = \frac{(2.8 \text{ kPa})(0.36 \text{ m}^3)}{0.78 \text{ m}^3} = 1.3 \text{ kPa}$$

3. Look Back and Check

Is your answer reasonable?
Yes, the final pressure, 2.8 kPa, is about twice the original pressure, 1.3 kPa.

Math Practice

On a separate sheet of paper, solve the following problems.

1. A cylinder contains 850 mL of gas at a pressure of 130 kPa. A piston compresses the gas until its pressure is 170 kPa. What is the new volume of the gas?

2. A container holds 4.2 L of a gas. The volume of the gas is reduced to 2.8 L with a pressure of 240 kPa. What was the original pressure of the gas?

3. A movable piston encloses 4.5 L of a gas in a cylinder with a pressure of 280 kPa. The piston is pulled upward, reducing the pressure to 160 kPa. What is the new volume of the gas?

Chapter 21 Temperature, Heat, and Expansion

Summary

THE BIG IDEA : When matter gets warmer, the atoms or molecules in the matter move faster.

21.1 Temperature

✓ The higher the temperature of a substance, the faster is the motion of its molecules.

- **Temperature** tells how hot or cold something is compared with a standard.

- On the **Celsius scale,** the number 0 is the temperature at which water freezes, and the number 100 is the temperature at which water boils (at standard atmospheric pressure).

- On the **Fahrenheit scale,** the number 32 designates the temperature at which water freezes, and the number 212 is the temperature at which water boils (at 1 atm).

- On the **Kelvin scale,** the number 0 is **absolute zero,** the temperature at which a substance has no kinetic energy to give up. Absolute zero corresponds to –273°C.

- Temperature is proportional to the *average* kinetic energy of molecular translational motion (that is, motion along a straight or curved path).

21.2 Heat

✓ When two substances of different temperatures are in thermal contact, heat flows from the higher-temperature substance into the lower-temperature substance.

- The energy that transfers from one object to another because of a temperature difference between them is called **heat.**

- Matter does not contain heat. Heat is energy *in transit.* Energy resulting from heat flow is sometimes called *thermal energy.* Scientists prefer the name *internal energy.*

- When heat flows from one object or substance to another it is in contact with, the objects or substances are said to be in **thermal contact.**

21.3 Thermal Equilibrium

✓ When a thermometer is in contact with a substance, heat flows between them until they have the same temperature.

- After objects in thermal contact with each other reach the same temperature, so that no heat flows between them, the objects are in **thermal equilibrium**.

- We read a thermometer after it reaches thermal equilibrium with the substance being measured. The temperature of the thermometer is also the temperature of the substance.

Chapter 21 Temperature, Heat, and Expansion

21.4 Internal Energy

✓ **When a substance takes in or gives off heat, its internal energy changes.**

- The total of all energies inside a substance is called **internal energy.**

- Absorbed heat may make the molecules of a substance jostle faster, or may make the substance undergo a phase change.

21.5 Measurement of Heat

✓ **The amount of heat transferred can be determined by measuring the temperature change of a known mass of a substance that absorbs the heat.**

- The **calorie** is the amount of heat required to raise the temperature of 1 gram of water by 1°C.

- The **kilocalorie** is 1000 calories (the heat required to raise the temperature of 1 kilogram of water by 1°C). The heat unit used in rating foods is actually a kilocalorie, although it's often referred to as the calorie. The food unit is sometimes called a Calorie (written with a capital C).

- The SI unit for heat and other forms of energy is the joule; 1 calorie equals 4.186 J.

21.6 Specific Heat Capacity

✓ **The capacity of a substance to store heat depends on its chemical composition.**

- Different substances have different capacities for storing internal energy.
- The **specific heat capacity** of a material is the quantity of heat required to raise the temperature of a unit mass of the material by 1 degree. Specific heat capacity is like thermal inertia since it signifies the resistance of a substance to change in its temperature.

- Absorbed energy that increases the translational speed of molecules is responsible for increases in temperature. Absorbed energy may also increase the rotation of molecules, increase the internal vibrations within molecules, or stretch intermolecular bonds and be stored as potential energy.

21.7 The High Specific Heat Capacity of Water

✓ **The property of water to resist changes in temperature improves the climate in many places.**

- Water has a much higher capacity for storing energy than most common materials. A relatively small amount of water absorbs a greater deal of heat for a correspondingly small temperature rise. Because of this, water is a very useful cooling agent.

- Water's capacity to store heat also affects the global climate. Water takes more energy to heat up than land does.

Chapter 21   Temperature, Heat, and Expansion

- If water did not have a high heat capacity, the countries of Europe would be as cold as the northeastern regions of Canada. The Atlantic current known as the Gulf Stream brings warm water northeast from the Caribbean to the coast of Europe, where it then cools. The energy released is carried by prevailing westerly winds over the European continent.

- The climates differ on the east and west coasts of North America. Because of water's high heat capacity, ocean temperature does not vary much from summer to winter. The water warms the air near western coastal regions in winter and cools it in summer.

- Land, with a lower specific heat capacity, gets hot in summer but cools rapidly in winter, so the east coast is generally hotter in summer and cooler in winter than the west coast.

21.8 Thermal Expansion

☑ **Most forms of matter—solids, liquids, and gases—expand when they are heated and contract when they are cooled.**

- When the temperature of a substance is increased, its molecules jiggle faster and normally tend to move farther apart, resulting in expansion.

- For comparable pressures and comparable changes in temperature, gases generally expand or contract much more than liquids, and liquids expand or contract more than solids.

- Concrete sidewalks and highway paving are laid in sections separated by small gaps to allow for expansion and contraction due to differences in summer and winter temperatures. The expansion of materials must be allowed for in the construction of structures and devices of all kinds, such as dental filling materials, automobile engine pistons, and bridges.

- In a **bimetallic strip,** two strips of different metals, say one of brass and the other of iron, are welded or riveted together. Because the two substances expand at different rates, the strip bends when heated or cooled.

- A **thermostat** is a device that uses a bimetallic strip to control temperature. As the temperature of a room changes, the back-and-forth bending of the bimetallic coil opens and closes an electric circuit, turning the heat on or off.

21.9 Expansion of Water

☑ **At 0°C, ice is less dense than water, and so ice floats on water.**

- Unlike almost all other liquids, water at the temperature of melting ice, 0°C, contracts when the temperature is increased. As the water is heated, it continues to contract until it reaches a temperature of 4°C. Then it begins to expand.

- A given amount of water has its smallest volume—and its greatest density—at 4°C. The same amount of water has its largest volume—and smallest density—as ice.

Chapter 21 Temperature, Heat, and Expansion

- Ice has open-structured crystals. These crystals result from the angular shape of the water molecules, plus the fact that the forces binding water molecules together are strongest at certain angles. Water molecules in this open structure occupy a greater volume than they do in the liquid state.

- When ice melts, not all the crystals collapse right away. Ice water is therefore less dense than slightly warmer water. The collapsing of ice crystals plus increased molecular motion with increasing temperature combine to make water most dense at 4°C.

- The behavior of water is of great importance in nature. If the greatest density of water were at its freezing point, ponds would freeze from the bottom up, and pond organisms would be destroyed in winter months. Instead, water at the freezing point, 0°C, is less dense and floats, so ice forms at the surface while the pond remains liquid below the ice.

- As pond water cools from higher temperatures to freezing, it must first cool to 4°C. If the water below the surface is any temperature other than 4°C, it will sink before cooling. Because of water's high specific heat and poor ability to conduct heat, the bottom of deep lakes in cold regions is a constant 4°C the year round.

Chapter 21   Temperature, Heat, and Expansion

Exercises

21.1 Temperature (pages 407–408)

1. Define temperature.

   _____

   _____

2. Explain how a common liquid thermometer works.

   _____

   _____

   _____

Match each number with the corresponding description.

Temperature	Description
_____ **3.** –273	a. Water freezes on the Celsius scale.
_____ **4.** 0	b. Water freezes on the Fahrenheit scale.
_____ **5.** 32	c. Water boils on the Celsius scale.
_____ **6.** 100	d. Water boils on the Fahrenheit scale.
_____ **7.** 212	e. Absolute zero on the Celsius scale.

8. Define absolute zero.

   _____

   _____

9. Identify where each temperature scale is primarily used.

   a. Celsius:_____

   b. Fahrenheit:_____

   c. Kelvin:_____

10. Divisions on the Celsius and Fahrenheit scales are called
    _____, but divisions on the Kelvin scale are called
    _____.

11. For an ideal gas, temperature is _____ to the average
    kinetic energy of molecular translational motion.

12. Define translational motion.

    _____

    _____

13. Is the following sentence true or false? For solids and liquids,
    temperature is unrelated to the average kinetic energy of molecular
    translational motion._____

14. What is the relationship between the temperature of a substance and the
    rate of motion of its molecules?

    _____

    _____

Chapter 21   Temperature, Heat, and Expansion

15. Suppose you have a 2-liter pot of boiling water, and you pour out 1 liter of the water. Explain whether the average kinetic energy and temperature of the water in the pot has changed.

_____

_____

21.2 Heat (page 409)

16. Define heat.

_____

_____

17. Describe the spontaneous energy transfer that occurs when you touch a cube of ice.

_____

_____

18. Is the following sentence true or false? A cup of hot water contains more heat than a cup of cold water._____

19. Explain the meanings of the terms *thermal energy* and *internal energy*.

_____

_____

_____

_____

20. Define thermal contact.

_____

_____

21. When two substances of different temperature are in thermal contact, heat flows from the _____ substance into the _____ substance.

22. Is the following sentence true or false? Heat always flows from a substance with more total molecular kinetic energy to a substance with less._____

23. Is the following sentence true or false? Heat never flows on its own from a cooler substance into a hotter substance._____

21.3 Thermal Equilibrium (page 410)

24. After objects in thermal contact with each other reach the same temperature, the objects are in _____.

25. When a thermometer is in contact with a substance, heat flows between them until _____.

26. Why is it important for a thermometer to be small in comparison to the substance it is measuring?

_____

Chapter 21   Temperature, Heat, and Expansion

21.4 Internal Energy (page 411)

27. Name four types of energy within substances.

a. _____

b. _____

c. _____

d. _____

28. _____ is the grand total of all energies inside a substance.

29. What are two ways the internal energy of a substance can change?

_____

_____

30. Describe two ways a substance can change when it absorbs heat.

a. _____

_____

b. _____

_____

21.5 Measurement of Heat (pages 411–412)

31. How can you determine the amount of heat transferred from one substance to another?

_____

_____

32. In order to quantify heat, we must specify the _____ and _____ of substance affected.

33. Suppose you place a pot with 1 cup of water and an identical pot with 2 cups of water on a hot stove for the same amount of time. Circle the letters beside the sentences that correctly describe what happens.

a. More heat is added to the pot with 2 cups of water.

b. The same amount of heat is added to both pots.

c. The temperature of the pot with 1 cup of water increases more.

d. The temperature increase of both pots is the same.

34. Define calorie.

_____

_____

35. Circle the letter beside the number of kilocalories that equals 50,000 calories.

a. 5   b. 50

c. 500   d. 5000

Chapter 21   Temperature, Heat, and Expansion

36. A Calorie, used to describe the energy of _____, is equivalent to one _____.

37. One calorie is equivalent to _____ joules, the SI unit for all forms of energy.

21.6 Specific Heat Capacity (pages 413–414)

38. The capacity of a substance to store heat depends on its _____.

39. What is specific heat capacity?

_____

_____

Specific Heat Capacities		
Material	**(J/g°C)**	**(cal/g°C)**
Aluminum	0.900	0.215
Copper	0.386	0.092
Lead	0.128	0.031

40. Use the table above to complete these statements.

a. _____ calorie(s) of heat are needed to raise the temperature of 1 gram of aluminum by 1 Celsius degree.

b. _____ joule(s) of heat are needed to raise the temperature of 2 grams of copper by 1 Celsius degree.

c. _____ joule(s) of heat are needed to raise the temperature of 1 gram of lead by 2 Celsius degrees.

41. Explain this statement: We can think of specific heat capacity as thermal inertia.

_____

_____

_____

42. Why does water have a higher specific heat capacity than iron?

_____

_____

_____

Chapter 21 Temperature, Heat, and Expansion

21.7 The High Specific Heat Capacity of Water (pages 415–416)

43. Is the following sentence true or false? Water takes longer to heat to a certain temperature than most substances, and it takes longer to cool. _____

44. Explain why Europe is much warmer than northeastern Canada, even though they are at similar latitudes.

_____

_____

_____

45. The high specific heat of ocean water near the west coast of North America causes the winters there to be _____ and the summers to be _____ than near the east coast.

21.8 Thermal Expansion (pages 416–419)

46. Why do most forms of matter expand when they are heated?

_____

_____

47. If concrete sidewalks and highway paving were laid down in one continuous piece, cracks would appear as the materials _____ on hot summer days and _____ on cold winter days.

48. Describe one way that each of the following handles the different rates of thermal expansion in materials.

a. Dentist: _____

_____

b. Automobile engines: _____

_____

c. Civil engineer: _____

_____

49. Roadways on bridges often have tongue-and-groove-type gaps called _____ to allow for thermal expansion.

Chapter 21   Temperature, Heat, and Expansion

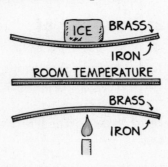

50. Explain how the bimetallic strip in the figure above is affected in each case.

a. Heated by a flame:

_____

_____

_____

b. Cooled by ice:

_____

_____

_____

51. Describe how a thermostat uses a bimetallic strip.

_____

_____

_____

21.9 Expansion of Water (pages 419–422)

52. Water is most dense at a temperature of _____.

53. Complete the table by writing *increase* or *decrease* to describe how the volume and density of water changes during each temperature change.

Temperature Change	Change in Volume	Change in Density
0°C to 4°C		
4°C to 10°C		

54. Describe how the thermal expansion and contraction of water is different from most other materials.

_____

_____

55. Explain why water has such an unusual thermal expansion and contraction behavior.

_____

_____

_____

Chapter 21 Temperature, Heat, and Expansion

Use the figure below to answer questions 56–60.

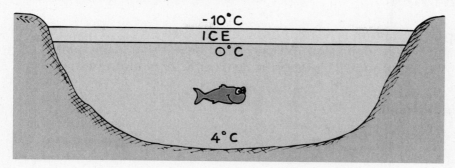

56. Where does most of the cooling in the pond take place?

_____

57. What determines whether the water will float at the surface?

_____

_____

58. What must be true in order for water at 4°C to remain at the surface?

_____

_____

_____

59. What must be true in order for ice to begin forming at the surface of the pond?

_____

_____

60. If only some of the water in a deep pond is 4°C, where will it be?

_____

Chapter 21   Temperature, Heat, and Expansion

Heat Transfer

A 50-gram strip of aluminum is heated to 100°C. It is then dropped into a container of water where it gives off 753 calories of heat. What is the final temperature of the aluminum? (The specific heat capacity of aluminum is 0.215 cal/g°C.)

1. Read and Understand

What information are you given?

mass = m = 50 g

specific heat capacity = c = 0.215 cal/g°C

initial temperature = T_i = 100°C

heat = Q = –753 cal

2. Plan and Solve

What unknown are you trying to calculate?

final temperature = T_f

What equation can you use to find the unknown?

$Q = mc\Delta T = mc(T_f - T_i)$

Rearrange the equation to solve for the unknown.

$$T_f = \frac{Q}{mc} + T_i$$

Replace each variable with its known value.

$$T_f = \frac{-753 \text{ cal}}{(50 \text{ g})(0.215 \text{ cal/g°C})} + 100°C = 30°C$$

3. Look Back and Check

Is your answer reasonable?

Because heat is given off (Q is a negative value), the final temperature should be less than the original temperature, which it is. The answer is reasonable.

Math Practice

On a separate sheet of paper, solve the following problems.

1. A 35-gram piece of silver is dropped into a container of water. As it cools, the silver gives off 180 calories of heat. What is the silver's temperature change? (The specific heat capacity of silver is 0.056 cal/g°C.)

2. What mass of copper will give up 240 calories when its temperature drops from 90.0°C to 30.0°C? (The specific heat capacity of copper is 0.092 cal/g°C.)

Chapter 22   Heat Transfer

Summary

THE BIG IDEA Heat can be transferred by conduction, by convection, and by radiation.

22.1 Conduction

☑ **In conduction, collisions between particles transfer thermal energy, without any overall transfer of matter.**

- **Conduction** of heat is the transfer of energy within materials and between different materials that are in direct contact.

- Materials that conduct heat well are known as **conductors.** Metals—such as silver, copper, aluminum, and iron—are the best conductors.

- Conduction occurs within a heated material when atoms vibrate against neighboring atoms, which in turn do the same. In metals, free electrons that can drift through the metal jostle and transfer energy by colliding with atoms and other free electrons.

- An **insulator** is any material that is a poor conductor of heat and that delays the transfer of heat. Liquids and gases are generally good insulators. Porous materials, such as wood, wool, straw, paper, cork, and polystyrene, are also good insulators.

22.2 Convection

☑ **In convection, heat is transferred by movement of the hotter substance from one place to another.**

- **Convection** is heat transfer by movement of the heated substance itself. Heat is transferred by movement of the hotter substance from one place to another.

- Convection occurs in all fluids, whether liquid or gas. When the fluid is heated, it expands, becomes less dense, and rises. Cooler fluid then moves to the bottom, and the process continues. In this way, convection currents keep a fluid stirred up as it heats.

- Convection currents stirring the atmosphere produce winds. This is evident at the seashore. Uneven heating of air over land and water causes a sea breeze that blows toward the land in the daytime and toward the sea at night.

22.3 Radiation

☑ **In radiation, heat is transmitted in the form of radiant energy, or electromagnetic waves.**

- **Radiation** is energy transmitted by *electromagnetic waves.*

- **Radiant energy** is any energy that is transmitted by radiation. Radiant energy includes radio waves, microwaves, infrared radiation, visible light, ultraviolet radiation, X-rays, and gamma rays.

Chapter 22   Heat Transfer

22.4 Emission of Radiant Energy

☑ **All substances continuously emit radiant energy in a mixture of wavelengths.**

- Objects at low temperatures emit long waves. High-temperature objects emit waves of shorter wavelengths. The average frequency of radiant energy is directly proportional to the Kelvin temperature T of the emitter.

- The radiant energy emitted by stars is called **stellar radiation.** A blue-hot star is hotter than a white-hot star, and a red-hot star is less hot.

- Radiant energy emitted by Earth is called **terrestrial radiation,** which is in the form of infrared waves—below our threshold of sight.

22.5 Absorption of Radiant Energy

☑ **Good emitters of radiant energy are also good absorbers; poor emitters are poor absorbers.**

- If the temperature of an object doesn't change, the object absorbs and radiates energy at the same rate. It is in thermal equilibrium with its environment.

- If you warm or cool an object that is in thermal equilibrium, it will radiate more or less energy, eventually reaching a new thermal equilibrium.

- A good absorber reflects little radiant energy and appears dark. Good reflectors are poor absorbers. Light-colored objects reflect more light and heat than dark-colored ones.

22.6 Newton's Law of Cooling

☑ **The colder an object's surroundings, the faster the object will cool.**

- An object hotter than its surroundings cools to match the surrounding temperature.

- **Newton's law of cooling** states that the rate of cooling of an object is approximately proportional to the temperature difference between the object and its surroundings. Newton's law of cooling also holds for heating.

22.7 Global Warming and the Greenhouse Effect

☑ **The near unanimous view of climate scientists is that human activity is a main driver of global warming and climate change.**

- The **greenhouse effect** is the warming of a planet's surface due to the trapping of radiation by the planet's atmosphere.

- The transparency of things depends on the wavelength of radiation. Air is transparent to both infrared (long) waves and visible (short) waves, unless the air contains excess carbon dioxide and water vapor, in which case it absorbs infrared waves.

Chapter 22   Heat Transfer

Exercises

22.1 Conduction (pages 431–432)

1. Define conduction.

   _____

   _____

2. What is a conductor?

   _____

   _____

3. _____ are the best conductors.

4. In conduction, _____ between particles transfer thermal energy.

5. Is the following sentence true or false? Conduction occurs without any overall transfer of matter. _____

6. Is the following sentence true or false? Materials that are good conductors of heat are usually poor conductors of electricity. _____

7. Imagine stepping with one bare foot onto metal and with the other bare foot onto wood. Explain why the metal feels cool and the wood feels warm, even though they have the same temperature.

   _____

   _____

   _____

   _____

8. Define insulator.

   _____

   _____

9. How do birds vary their insulation?

   _____

   _____

10. Classify each of the following materials by writing *C* beside each conductor and *I* beside each insulator.

    _____ a. wood

    _____ b. aluminum

    _____ c. straw

    _____ d. silver

    _____ e. air

    _____ f. cork

    _____ g. iron

    _____ h. wool

    _____ i. paper

    _____ j. copper

    _____ k. polystyrene

Chapter 22   Heat Transfer

11. Explain why snow is sometimes used to construct dwellings in cold climates.

_____

_____

_____

12. Is the following sentence true or false? Both heat and cold are forms of energy. _____

13. Is the following sentence true or false? An insulator cannot totally prevent heat from getting through, but instead just reduces the rate at which heat penetrates. _____

22.2 Convection (pages 433–435)

14. In convection, heat is transferred by movement of the _____ substance from one place to another.

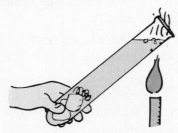

15. The figure above shows ice at the bottom of a test tube and boiling water at the top. Explain why the heat that boils the water doesn't melt the ice.

_____

_____

_____

16. Suppose a heater is placed near the floor of a room. Describe the steps in which convection currents keep the air stirred up in the room.

_____

_____

_____

17. Convection currents stirring the atmosphere produce _____.

18. Explain the two ways convection currents produced by uneven heating of Earth's surface produce sea breezes.

a. During the day:

_____

_____

_____

b. At night:

_____

_____

_____

Chapter 22   Heat Transfer

19. Is the following sentence true or false? As air rises, it expands because more atmospheric pressure squeezes on it at higher altitudes. _____

20. When a molecule collides with a molecule that is receding, its rebound speed after the collision is _____ than it was before the collision.

21. Is the following sentence true or false? As air rises and expands, it collides with more molecules that are receding than are approaching. _____

22. In expanding air, the average speed of the molecules _____, and the air cools.

22.3 Radiation (page 436)

23. Why can't energy move from the sun to Earth by conduction or convection?

_____

_____

_____

_____

24. Radiation is energy transmitted by _____.

25. Define radiant energy. _____

26. Order the different types of radiant energy from longest to shortest wavelength by placing a number from 1 to 7 beside each.

_____ a. gamma rays   _____ e. ultraviolet radiation

_____ b. infrared radiation   _____ f. visible light

_____ c. microwaves   _____ g. X-rays

_____ d. radio waves

27. Circle the letter of the type of radiant energy you feel as heat if you sit near a fireplace.

a. infrared radiation   b. microwaves

c. ultraviolet radiation   d. X-rays

22.4 Emission of Radiant Energy (pages 437–438)

28. Is the following sentence true or false? All substances continuously emit only one specific wavelength of radiant energy. _____

29. Do objects at low temperatures emit waves with a longer or shorter wavelength than objects with higher temperatures? _____

30. Objects of everyday temperatures emit waves mostly in the _____ end of the infrared region.

31. An infrared thermometer measures the infrared radiant energy emitted by a body and converts it to _____.

32. The average _____ of radiant energy is directly proportional to the Kelvin temperature of the emitter.

Chapter 22   Heat Transfer

33. Order the star colors white, red, and blue from coolest to hottest.

_____

34. The radiant energy emitted by stars is called _____.

35. The radiant energy emitted by Earth is called _____.

36. The part of radiant energy that is absorbed by objects increases the
_____ energy of the objects.

22.5 Absorption of Radiant Energy (pages 438–440)

37. An object in thermal equilibrium is both _____ and
_____ energy at the same rate.

38. The _____ of an object doesn't change if it is in thermal
equilibrium.

39. Good emitters of radiant energy are also good _____.

40. You notice that a blacktop pavement becomes hotter than other nearby
surfaces on a hot day. What will you notice about the temperature of the
blacktop pavement at night?

_____

_____

41. A good absorber of radiant energy appears _____.

42. Suppose you have a box, painted white inside, which is closed except
for a hole 2 centimeters wide. Circle the letter beside the sentence that
explains why the hole appears black.

   a. The white paint inside the box absorbs almost all of the radiant
energy that strikes it.

   b. The hole in the box is much too small to allow wavelengths of light
to pass through.

   c. Light that enters is reflected and partly absorbed so many times that
little is left to come out.

   d. The light that enters leaks out through the walls of the box.

43. Is the following sentence true or false? Light-colored objects reflect more
light than dark-colored ones. _____

44. On a sunny day, Earth's surface is a net _____, and at
night it is a net _____.

45. Record-breaking cold nights occur when the skies are _____.

22.6 Newton's Law of Cooling (pages 440–441)

46. An object hotter than its surroundings eventually _____
to match the surrounding temperature.

47. A hot apple pie will cool faster in a freezer than on a kitchen table
because _____

_____

Chapter 22   Heat Transfer

48. State Newton's law of cooling.

_____

_____

49. Is the following sentence true or false? Newton's law of cooling also holds for heating. _____

22.7 Global Warming and the Greenhouse Effect (pages 441–443)

50. What is the greenhouse effect?

_____

_____

51. Air is transparent to both infrared (long) waves and visible (short) waves, unless the air contains excess _____ and

_____.

52. Glass is _____ to visible light waves, but _____ infrared waves.

53. Explain why the inside of a car becomes so much hotter than its surroundings on a hot day.

_____

_____

_____

_____

SOLAR SHORT WAVES

TERRESTRIAL LONG WAVES

EARTH

54. Use the figure above to explain Earth's global warming.

_____

_____

_____

_____

55. _____ is the main greenhouse gas.

56. _____ is the gas most rapidly increasing in the atmosphere.

Summary

THE BIG IDEA : Changes of phase involve a transfer of energy.

23.1 Evaporation

☑ **Evaporation is a process that cools the liquid left behind.**

- The four possible forms of matter—solid, liquid, gas, and plasma—are called **phases.**
- **Evaporation** is a change of phase from a liquid to a gas that takes place at the surface of a liquid.
- Molecules at the surface of a liquid that gain kinetic energy by being bumped from below may have enough energy to break free of the liquid. They then comprise a *vapor*, molecules in the gaseous phase.

23.2 Condensation

☑ **Condensation warms the area where the liquid forms.**

- **Condensation** is the changing of a gas to a liquid.
- When any substance contains the maximum amount of another substance, the first substance is said to be **saturated.**
- The ratio between how much water vapor is in the air and the maximum amount that *could* be in the air at the same temperature is called the **relative humidity.**
- The faster water molecules move, the less able they are to condense to form droplets. A key feature of fog and cloud formation is a slowing down of water vapor molecules in the air.

23.3 Evaporation and Condensation Rates

☑ **The molecules and energy leaving a liquid's surface by evaporation can be counteracted by as many molecules and as much energy returning by condensation.**

- Evaporation and condensation normally take place at the same time.
- If evaporation exceeds condensation, the liquid is cooled; if condensation exceeds evaporation, the liquid is warmed.

23.4 Boiling

☑ **Increasing the pressure on the surface of a liquid raises the boiling point of the liquid.**

- The change of phase from liquid to gas beneath a liquid's surface is called **boiling.**
- The pressure of the vapor within the bubbles in a boiling liquid must be great enough to resist the pressure of the surrounding water. Bubbles do not form until the boiling point is reached.

Chapter 23   Change of Phase

23.5 Freezing

✓ **In general, dissolving anything in a liquid lowers the liquid's freezing temperature.**

- When energy is extracted from water at a temperature of 0°C and at atmospheric pressure, ice is formed.
- The change in phase from liquid to solid is called **freezing.**
- If sugar or salt is dissolved in water, the freezing point will be lowered.

23.6 Boiling and Freezing at the Same Time

✓ **Lowering the atmospheric pressure can cause water to boil and freeze at the same time!**

- If drops of coffee are sprayed into a vacuum chamber, they will boil until they freeze. After they are frozen, the water molecules evaporate until crystals of coffee are left—this is how freeze-dried coffee is made.

23.7 Regelation

✓ **Regelation can occur only in substances that expand when they freeze.**

- The phenomenon of melting under pressure and freezing again when the pressure is reduced is called **regelation.**
- When you make a snowball you use regelation; you compress the snow with your hands, causing a slight melting that helps the bind the snow into a ball.

23.8 Energy and Changes of Phase

✓ **Energy must be put into a substance to change its phase from solid to liquid to gas. Conversely, energy must be extracted from a substance to change its phase from gas to liquid to solid.**

- If a piece of ice is heated, its temperature will rise steadily until it reaches 0°C. The temperature will then remain at 0°C until all of the ice melts. After all of the ice melts to form water, the water's temperature will rise steadily until it reaches 100°C. The temperature will then remain constant at 100°C until all of the water becomes steam. After all of the water is changed to steam, the temperature will continue to rise.
- The phase change process is reversible. The energy required to vaporize a gram of water is a relatively large amount of energy—much more than is required to change a gram of ice at absolute zero to boiling water at 100°C.
- A refrigerator's cooling cycle is a good example of the energy interchanges that occur with the changes of phase of the refrigeration fluid.
- A device that moves heat is called a **heat pump.**

Chapter 23   Change of Phase

Exercises

23.1 Evaporation (page 451)

1. The four forms in which matter exists—solid, liquid, gas, and plasma—are called _____.

2. Water that is left out in an open container will eventually _____.

3. Is the following sentence true or false? Evaporation is a change from liquid to gas. _____

4. Is the following sentence true or false? Evaporation takes place throughout a liquid. _____

5. Circle the letter that best describes the particle most likely to break free from the surface of a liquid.
   a. slow-moving
   b. low kinetic energy
   c. solid
   d. high kinetic energy

6. A group of molecules in the gas phase is also known as a _____.

7. How does evaporation change the temperature of the liquid that is left behind?

   _____

8. Describe how sweat helps cool the body.

   _____

   _____

23.2 Condensation (pages 452–453)

9. Is the following sentence true or false? Condensation is the process opposite to evaporation. _____

10. Circle the letter that best describes condensation.
    a. change from solid to liquid
    b. change from liquid to solid
    c. change from gas to liquid
    d. change from solid to gas

11. Is the following sentence true or false? Condensation occurs when gas particles are captured by liquids. _____

12. Describe how condensation affects the temperature of the area where liquid forms.

    _____

13. Is the following sentence true or false? A substance that contains any amount of another substance is said to be saturated. _____

14. The ratio between how much water vapor is in the air and the maximum that could be in the air is the _____.

15. Is the following sentence true or false? When air is saturated with water vapor, the relative humidity is 100%. _____

16. What must happen to the speed of water vapor molecules in air in order for clouds or fog to form?

    _____

Chapter 23 Change of Phase

23.3 Evaporation and Condensation Rates (page 454)

17. Explain why you feel cold after stepping out of a hot shower into a dry room.

   _____

   _____

18. Is the following sentence true or false? Condensation and evaporation can occur at the same time. _____

19. Is the following sentence true or false? Condensation and evaporation can occur at the same rate. _____

23.4 Boiling (pages 454–455)

20. Is the following sentence true or false? Boiling only takes place at the surface of a liquid. _____

21. Boiling is a change of phase from a(n) _____ to a(n) _____.

22. Is the following sentence true or false? Bubbles do not form in a liquid until the boiling point is reached. _____

23. Circle the letter that describes how increased atmospheric pressure affects the boiling point of a liquid.

   a. the boiling point decreases   b. the boiling point does not change

   c. the boiling point increases   d. boiling cannot occur

PRESSURE OF ATMOSPHERE

24. The arrows pushing outward from the inside of the bubble shown above represent _____.

25. Boiling depends on _____ and _____.

26. Explain why a pressure cooker cooks food faster than an ordinary pan.

   _____

   _____

27. How does boiling affect the temperature of the liquid left behind?

   _____

Chapter 23   Change of Phase

23.5 Freezing (page 456)

28. As energy is removed from a liquid, its particles move more _____.

29. Is the following sentence true or false? As the energy of a liquid decreases, molecular forces pull the particles closer together. _____

30. Circle the letter that best describes the conditions at which ice forms.

    a. energy added to water at 0°C and atmospheric pressure

    b. energy removed from water at 100°C and atmospheric pressure

    c. energy removed from water at 0°C and atmospheric pressure

    d. energy added to water at 100°C and atmospheric pressure

31. Freezing is a phase change from a(n) _____ to a(n) _____.

32. Circle the letter that describes how dissolving a substance in a liquid affects the freezing point of the liquid.

    a. The freezing point decreases.

    b. The freezing point does not change.

    c. The freezing point increases.

    d. The freezing point matches the boiling point.

23.6 Boiling and Freezing at the Same Time (pages 456–457)

33. Is the following sentence true or false? Boiling and freezing can occur at the same time in high-pressure conditions. _____

34. Describe what happens to a container of water in a vacuum chamber as the pressure is gradually decreased.

    _____

    _____

    _____

35. A _____ is used to produce freeze-dried coffee.

Chapter 23   Change of Phase

23.7 Regelation (page 457)

36. Is the following sentence true or false? When pressure is applied to ice, the ice will melt at a lower temperature. _____

37. Circle the letter that best describes regelation.

    a. melting under zero pressure then freezing under pressure

    b. melting and freezing at the same temperature

    c. melting under pressure and then refreezing after the pressure is removed

    d. melting and freezing at the same pressure

38. Circle the letter of the property a substance must have in order for regelation to occur.

    a. high density

    b. low melting point

    c. expands as it freezes

    d. soft at low temperatures

39. Describe how regelation plays a role in forming a snowball.

    _____

    _____

23.8 Energy and Changes of Phase (pages 458–461)

40. Circle the letter that shows the phases in the order they occur when a piece of ice is continually heated.

    a. solid → liquid → gas

    b. gas → liquid → solid

    c. liquid → solid → gas

    d. gas → solid → liquid

41. Describe the flow of energy when a substance changes from gas to liquid to solid.

    _____

42. Is the following sentence true or false? The phase change process for a substance is reversible. _____

43. Explain why a burn from condensing steam is so dangerous.

    _____

    _____

44. A(n) _____ is a device that moves heat.

Name _____ Class _____ Date _____

Chapter 23   Change of Phase

The graph below shows the energy involved in the heating and the change of phase of 1 gram of H₂O. Use the graph to answer Questions 45–48.

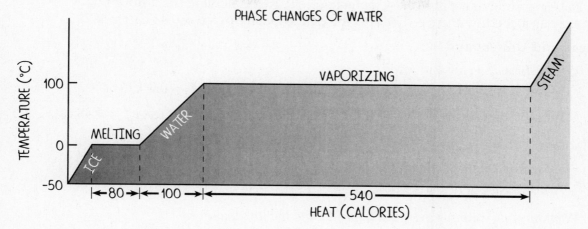

PHASE CHANGES OF WATER

45. Circle the letter of the statement that is true.

  a. The same amount of energy is required to melt and to vaporize 1 gram of water.

  b. The temperature is constant during melting and vaporizing.

  c. It takes more energy to melt 1 gram of water than it does to vaporize it.

  d. 100 calories are needed to melt 1 gram of ice.

46. Explain why the portion of the line that represents vaporizing is longer than the portion of the line that represents melting.

  _____

  _____

47. Circle the letter of the amount of energy given off when 1 gram of water condenses.

  a. 80 calories   b. 100 calories

  c. 540 calories   d. 720 calories

48. Circle the letter of the temperature at which vaporization occurs.

  a. –50°C   b. 0°C

  c. 100°C   d. from 0°C to 100°C

Chapter 23 Change of Phase

Phase Change of Water

A 25.0-g sample of ice at –10.0°C is heated to 0.0°C. Calculate the amount of energy absorbed by the ice. The specific heat capacity of ice is 0.48 cal/g·°C.

Read and Understand

What information are you given?

Mass, m = 25.0 g   Final temperature, T_f = 0.0°C

Initial temperature, T_i = –10.0°C   Specific heat capacity of ice, c_{ice} = 0.48 cal/g·°C

Plan and Solve

What unknown are you trying to calculate?

Amount of energy absorbed, Q

What formula contains the given quantity and the unknown?

$Q = mc\Delta T = mc(T_f - T_i)$

Substitute the known values and solve.

$Q = (25.0 \text{ g})(0.48 \text{ cal/g·°C})(0.0°C - (–10.0°C)) = 120 \text{ cal}$

Look Back and Check

Is your answer reasonable?

Yes, the sign shows that heat was absorbed and the unit, calories, is a proper unit for energy.

Math Practice

On a separate sheet of paper, solve the following problems. Note that quantity of heat energy required to change the phase of a substance is given by the following equation: $Q = mL$, where Q is the heat required, m is the mass, and L is the heat of fusion or vaporization.

1. How much energy is absorbed when 25.0 g of ice at 0.0°C melts to form water at 0.0°C? The heat of fusion of ice is 80 cal/g.

2. How much energy is absorbed when the water at 0.0°C in Question 1 is heated to 100.0°C? The specific heat of water is 1.0 cal/g·°C.

3. How much energy is absorbed when the water at 100.0°C in Question 2 vaporizes to 100.0°C? The heat of vaporization of water is 540 cal/g.

4. The steam in Question 3 is used to melt ice. How much ice will be melted by the energy released by the condensation of the steam at 100.0°C?

Chapter 24   Thermodynamics

Summary

THE BIG IDEA : Heat normally flows from hot to cold.

24.1 Absolute Zero

☑ As the thermal motion of atoms in a substance approaches zero, the kinetic energy of the atoms approaches zero, and the temperature of the substance approaches a lower limit.

- The study of heat and its transformation into mechanical energy is called **thermodynamics.**

- **Absolute zero** is the temperature at which no more energy can be extracted from a substance and no further lowering of its temperature is possible.

- Absolute zero corresponds to zero on the Kelvin scale and is written 0 K.

- Degrees on the Kelvin scale are the same size as those on the Celsius scale.

- Ice melts at 0°C, or 273 K, and water boils at 100°C, or 373 K.

24.2 First Law of Thermodynamics

☑ The first law of thermodynamics states that whenever heat is added to a system, it transforms to an equal amount of some other form of energy.

- The **first law of thermodynamics** is the law of conservation of energy applied to thermal systems. A system is any group of atoms, particles, or objects.

- The flow of heat is nothing more than the flow of energy itself.

- Energy added to a system does one or both of two things: (1) increases the internal energy of the system if it remains in the system and (2) does external work if it leaves the system. So, the first law of thermodynamics states:

$$\text{Heat added} = \text{increase in internal energy}$$
$$+ \text{ external work done by system}$$

- If work is done *on* a system, the system's internal energy will increase. If work is done *by* the system, the system's internal energy will decrease.

24.3 Adiabatic Processes

☑ When work is done on a gas by adiabatically compressing it, the gas gains internal energy and becomes warmer.

- When a gas is compressed or expanded so that no heat enters or leaves a system, the process is said to be **adiabatic.**

- Adiabatic changes of volume can be achieved by performing the process rapidly or by thermally insulating a system from its surroundings.

Chapter 24 Thermodynamics

- When a gas adiabatically expands, it does work on its surroundings, gives up internal energy, and becomes cooler.
- Air temperature may be changed by adding or subtracting heat, by changing the pressure of the air, or by both.
- The adiabatic form of the first law of thermodynamics is as follows:

    Change in air temperature ~ pressure change

- The temperature of a mass of dry air drops by 10°C for each 1-kilometer increase in altitude.

24.4 Second and Third Laws of Thermodynamics

Ⓥ **The second law of thermodynamics states that heat will never of itself flow from a cold object to a hot object.**

- Without external effort, the direction of heat flow is from hot to cold.
- The third law of thermodynamics states that no system can reach absolute zero.
- Physicists have been able to record temperatures that are less than a millionth of 1 Kelvin—but never as low as 0 K.

24.5 Heat Engines and the Second Law

Ⓥ **According to the second law of thermodynamics, no heat engine can convert all heat input to mechanical energy output.**

- A **heat engine** is any device that changes internal energy into mechanical work.
- The basic idea behind a heat engine is that mechanical work can be obtained only when heat flows from a high temperature to a low temperature.
- A high-temperature reservoir is something from which we can extract heat without cooling it down. Likewise, a low-temperature reservoir is something that can absorb heat without itself warming up.
- Every heat engine will (1) increase its internal energy by absorbing heat from a high-temperature reservoir, (2) convert some of this energy to mechanical work, and (3) expel the remaining energy as heat to a low-temperature reservoir.
- Only some of the heat can be transformed into work, with the remainder expelled in the process.
- The **Carnot efficiency,** or ideal efficiency, of a heat engine is the ideal maximum percentage of input heat energy that the engine can convert to work. The equation for ideal efficiency is as follows:

$$\text{Ideal efficiency} = \frac{T_{hot} - T_{cold}}{T_{hot}}$$

where T_{hot} is the temperature of the hot reservoir and T_{cold} is the temperature of the cold reservoir. Ideal efficiency depends only on the temperature difference between input and output.

Chapter 24   Thermodynamics

- Whenever ratios of temperatures are involved, the absolute temperature scale must be used.
- In the case of heat engines, the overriding concept is the second law of thermodynamics; only some of the heat input can be converted to work—even without friction.

24.6 Order Tends to Disorder

☑ **Natural systems tend to proceed toward a state of greater disorder.**

- Whenever energy transforms, some of the useful energy degenerates to nonuseful forms and is unavailable for doing the same work again.
- Organized energy in the form of electricity that goes into electric lights in home and office buildings degenerates to heat energy.
- Disordered energy can be changed into ordered energy only at the expense of work input.
- The message of the second law of thermodynamics is that the tendency of the universe, and all that is in it, tends to disorder.

24.7 Entropy

☑ **According to the second law of thermodynamics, in the long run, the entropy of a system always increases for natural processes.**

- **Entropy** is the measure of the amount of disorder in a system.
- When disorder increases, entropy increases.
- When there is work input, as in living organisms, entropy decreases. All livings things, from bacteria to trees to human beings, extract energy from their surroundings and use it to increase their own organization. This order in life forms is maintained by increasing entropy elsewhere.
- Disordered states are much more probable than ordered states.

Chapter 24   Thermodynamics

Exercises

24.1 Absolute Zero (page 469)

1. Is the following sentence true or false? There is no limit to how cold an object can get. _____

2. Define absolute zero.

   _____

   _____

   _____

3. Circle the letter of each statement about a substance near absolute zero that is true.

   a. The thermal motion of its atoms approaches zero.

   b. The kinetic energy of its atoms approaches zero.

   c. A considerable amount of energy can still be removed from the substance.

   d. Its temperature can still be significantly lowered.

4. Is the following sentence true or false? Negative Kelvin temperature values do not exist. _____

5. Circle the letter that describes how the size of one Celsius degree and one Kelvin are related.

   a. They are equal.

   b. Celsius degrees are smaller.

   c. Celsius degrees are larger.

   d. They have no consistent relationship.

Match each term or description to its Kelvin temperature.

Term	Definition
_____ 6. absolute zero	a. 373 K
_____ 7. melting point of ice	b. 0 K
_____ 8. boiling point of water	c. 273 K

24.2 First Law of Thermodynamics (pages 470–471)

9. Is the following sentence true or false? The flow of heat is not directly related to the flow of energy. _____

10. The law of conservation of energy when applied to thermal systems is known as the _____.

11. Circle the letter that best describes what happens when heat is added to a system.

   a. Much of it is destroyed immediately.

   b. It transforms to an equal amount of some other form of energy.

   c. Much of it is lost.

   d. It is used to overcome friction.

Chapter 24   Thermodynamics

12. A group of particles or objects that you want to analyze is called a(n) _____.

13. Describe two things energy added to a system can do.

_____

_____

14. Is the following sentence true or false? The first law of thermodynamics states that the heat added to a system is equal to the system's increase in internal energy and the external work done by the system.

_____

15. Is the following sentence true or false? The internal energy of a system increases when the system does external work. _____

24.3 Adiabatic Processes (pages 472–474)

16. Circle the letter that describes the compression or expansion of a gas such that no heat enters or leaves a system.

   a. ideal   b. equibaric

   c. constant   d. adiabatic

17. Is the following sentence true or false? Adiabatic processes often occur very quickly. _____

18. Is the following sentence true or false? The compression and expansion of gases within the cylinders of an automobile engine is nearly adiabatic.

_____

19. Circle the letter that describes what happens to a gas that undergoes an adiabatic compression.

   a. It gains internal energy and its temperature increases.

   b. It is compressed into a liquid by adiabatic liquefaction.

   c. It loses internal energy and condenses.

   d. Its volume decreases but its temperature remains constant.

20. What happens to a gas when it adiabatically expands and does work on its surroundings?

_____

_____

21. What are two ways the temperature of air can be increased?

_____

_____

22. Circle the letter that describes the adiabatic form of the first law of thermodynamics.

   a. pressure = constant

   b. energy out > energy in

   c. change in air temperature ~ pressure change

   d. energy in = energy out + work

Chapter 24   Thermodynamics

23. Is the following sentence true or false? Adiabatic processes occur in large air masses in the atmosphere. _____

24. Describe what happens to a large warm air blob as it gains several kilometers in altitude.

    _____

Use the illustration below to answer questions 25 and 26.

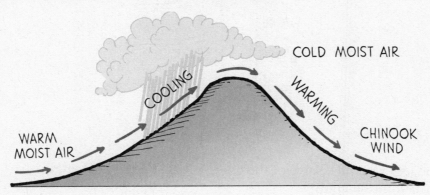

25. Circle the letter that describes the process that occurs to create the warm wind.

    a. adiabatic expansion   b. adiabatic compression

    c. isobaric contraction   d. thermal gain from landmass

26. What type of weather do communities in the path of chinooks experience in mid-winter? _____

24.4 Second and Third Laws of Thermodynamics (pages 474–475)

27. Circle the letter of the thermodynamic law that states heat will never of itself flow from a cold object to a hot object.

    a. first law of thermodynamics   b. second law of thermodynamics

    c. third law of thermodynamics   d. fourth law of thermodynamics

28. Heat flows one way, from _____ to _____.

29. Describe how heat can be made to flow the other way—from cold to hot.

    _____

30. What is the third law of thermodynamics?

    _____

24.5 Heat Engines and the Second Law (pages 475–478)

31. A device that changes internal energy into mechanical energy is called a(n) _____.

32. Is the following sentence true or false? For a heat engine to do mechanical work, heat must flow from a high temperature to a low temperature. _____

Chapter 24   Thermodynamics

Use the illustration below of a heat engine to answer Questions 33–34.

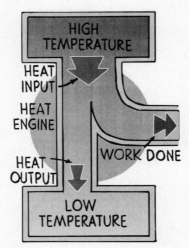

33. Circle the letter of the source of the energy used by the heat engine to increase its internal energy.

   a. work output
   b. the sun
   c. low-temperature reservoir
   d. high-temperature reservoir

34. The energy that is not converted to usable mechanical energy is expelled at the _____.

35. Is the following sentence true or false? Many heat engines are able to convert all heat input into mechanical energy output.

   _____

36. The ideal efficiency of a heat engine is known as its _____ efficiency.

37. Is the following sentence true or false? No heat engine can have an ideal efficiency of 100%. _____

38. What determines the ideal efficiency of a heat engine?

   _____

39. When performing a calculation involving temperature ratios, the temperatures must be expressed using the _____ temperature scale.

24.6 Order Tends to Disorder (page 479)

40. Is the following sentence true or false? Usable energy tends to become disorganized and unusable. _____

41. Is the following sentence true or false? Once energy in an engine degenerates into nonuseful forms, it is unavailable to do the same work again. _____

Chapter 24 Thermodynamics

42. Circle the letter that best describes how the second law of thermodynamics applies to order and disorder.

    a. For all systems, overall order is constant.

    b. Natural systems tend toward a state of greater disorder.

    c. Natural systems are equally likely to become more ordered or more disordered.

    d. All natural systems tend toward increasing order.

43. A sample of gas is contained in a sealed flask. Circle the letter with the greatest disorder.

    a. the sample at 25°C in the sealed flask

    b. the sample at 50°C in the sealed flask

    c. the sample immediately after opening the flask

    d. the sample after it expands to fill the room

44. Is the following sentence true or false? Even if work is done on disordered energy, it cannot become more ordered. _____

24.7 Entropy (pages 480–481)

45. Define entropy.

_____

46. Does disorder increase or decrease when entropy increases?

_____

47. Circle the letter that best describes the entropy of natural systems.

    a. Most natural systems will have a constant level of entropy.

    b. In the long run, the entropy will always increase.

    c. In all but a few cases, entropy in the long run will decrease.

    d. All natural systems have constant levels of entropy.

48. Circle the letter of each example of increasing entropy.

    a. gas molecules escaping from a bottle

    b. an unattended house breaking down

    c. a plant using energy from the sun to form new cells

    d. a breeze blowing papers off of your desk

49. Is the following sentence true or false? It is impossible for a natural system to change in a way such that its entropy decreases.

_____

Chapter 24   Thermodynamics

Carnot Efficiency

A 25-kW heat engine operates between a 3200-K hot reservoir and a 450-K cold reservoir. What is the engine's Carnot, or ideal, efficiency?

Read and Understand

What information are you given?

Power of engine = 25 kW

High-temperature reservoir, T_{hot} = 3200 K

Low-temperature reservoir, T_{cold} = 450 K

Plan and Solve

What unknown are you trying to calculate?

Carnot efficiency = ?

What formula contains the given quantity and the unknown?

Carnot efficiency = $\dfrac{T_{hot} - T_{cold}}{T_{hot}}$

Substitute the known values and solve.

Note that because the hot and cold reservoir temperatures are given in kelvins, they can be directly substituted into the equation.

Carnot efficiency = $\dfrac{T_{hot} - T_{cold}}{T_{hot}} = \dfrac{3200 \text{ K} - 450 \text{ K}}{3200 \text{ K}} = 0.86$ or 86%

Look back and check

Is your answer reasonable?

Yes, a high efficiency is expected due to the large difference between the reservoir temperatures.

Math Practice

On a separate sheet of paper, solve the following problems.

1. A heat engine has a hot-reservoir temperature of 1200°C. Its cold-reservoir temperature is room temperature air. What is the Carnot efficiency of the engine? (Note that room temperature air is about 25°C.)

2. A heat engine has an efficiency of 52% when it runs with a hot-reservoir temperature of 400°C and cold-reservoir temperature of 50°C. What is the efficiency if the hot-reservoir temperature is raised to 800°C?

Chapter 25 Vibrations and Waves

Summary

THE BIG IDEA Waves transmit energy through space and time.

25.1 Vibration of a Pendulum

☑ **The period of a pendulum depends on only the length of the pendulum and the acceleration of gravity.**

- A repeating back-and-forth motion about an equilibrium position is a **vibration.**

- The time a pendulum takes to swing back and forth through small angles depends on the length of the pendulum—the mass has no effect.

- The time of a back-and-forth swing of a pendulum is called the **period.**

- A long pendulum has a longer period than a shorter pendulum. The longer pendulum swings back and forth more slowly—less frequently—than a short pendulum.

25.2 Wave Description

☑ **The source of all waves is something that vibrates.**

- A disturbance that is transmitted progressively from one place to the next with no actual transport of matter is a **wave.**

- The back-and-forth vibratory motion (often called oscillatory motion) of a swinging pendulum is called **simple harmonic motion.**

- A **sine curve** is a pictorial representation of a wave.

- The high points on a wave are called **crests.**

- Low points on a wave are called **troughs.**

- The term **amplitude** refers to the distance from the midpoint to the crest (or trough) of the wave.

- The **wavelength** of a wave is the distance from the top of one crest to the top of the next one. Or, equivalently, the wavelength is the distance between successive identical parts of the wave.

- The number of vibrations an object makes in a unit of time is an object's **frequency.**

- The unit of frequency is called the **hertz** (Hz). A frequency of one cycle per second is 1 hertz.

- Frequency and period are inverses of each other:

$$\text{Frequency} = \frac{1}{\text{period}} \quad \text{or} \quad \text{Period} = \frac{1}{\text{frequency}}$$

Chapter 25   Vibrations and Waves

25.3 Wave Motion

✔ **The energy transferred by a wave from a vibrating source to a receiver is carried by a disturbance in a medium.**

- When energy is transferred by a wave from a vibrating source to a distant receiver, there is no transfer of matter between the two points.
- When someone talks to you from across the room, the sound wave is a disturbance in the air that travels across the room.

25.4 Wave Speed

✔ **You can calculate the speed of a wave by multiplying the wavelength by the frequency.**

- The speed of a wave depends on the medium through which the wave moves.
- Sound waves move at speeds of about 330 m/s to 350 m/s in air.
- Whatever the medium, the speed, wavelength, and frequency of the wave are related.
- In equation form, the relationship for wave speed is as follows:

$$v = \lambda f$$

  where v is wave speed, λ (Greek letter lambda) is the wavelength, and f is wave frequency.

- Wavelength and frequency vary inversely to produce the same wave speed for all sounds.

25.5 Transverse Waves

✔ **Waves in the stretched strings of musical instruments and the electromagnetic waves that make up radio waves and light are transverse.**

- Whenever the motion of the medium is at right angles to the direction in which a wave travels, the wave is a **transverse wave.**

25.6 Longitudinal Waves

✔ **Sound waves are longitudinal waves.**

- When the particles in the medium oscillate parallel to or *along* the direction of the wave rather than at right angles to it, the wave is a **longitudinal wave.**

25.7 Interference

✔ **Interference patterns occur when waves from different sources arrive at the same point—at the same time.**

- An **interference pattern** is a regular arrangement of places where wave effects are increased, decreased, or neutralized.
- In **constructive interference,** the crest of one wave overlaps the crest of another and their individual effects add together.

Chapter 25   Vibrations and Waves

- The result of constructive interference is a wave of increased amplitude.
- In **destructive interference,** the crest of one wave overlaps the trough of another and their individual effects are reduced.
- Destructive interference is also called cancellation.
- When waves are **out of phase,** the crests of one wave overlap the troughs of another to produce regions of zero amplitude.
- When waves are **in phase,** the crests of one wave overlap the crests of another, and the troughs overlap as well.
- Interference is characteristic of all wave motion, whether the waves are water waves, sound waves, or light waves.

25.8 Standing Waves

✓ **A standing wave forms only if half a wavelength or a multiple of half a wavelength fits exactly into the length of the vibrating medium.**

- A **standing wave** is a wave that appears to stay in one place—it does not seem to move through the medium.
- **Nodes** are the stationary points on a standing wave.
- The positions on a standing wave with the largest amplitudes are known as **antinodes.**
- Standing waves are the result of interference. Standing waves can be produced in either transverse or longitudinal waves.

25.9 The Doppler Effect

✓ **As a wave source approaches, an observer encounters waves at a higher frequency. As the wave source moves away, an observer encounters waves with a lower frequency.**

- The apparent change in frequency due to the motion of the source (or receiver) is called the **Doppler effect.** The greater the speed of the source, the greater the Doppler effect.
- The Doppler effect is evident when you hear the changing pitch of a siren as a firetruck passes you. Police make use of the Doppler effect of radar waves in measuring the speeds of cars on the highway.
- The Doppler effect also occurs for light.
- An increase in the frequency of light is called a **blue shift,** because the increase is toward the high-frequency, or blue, end of the color spectrum.
- A decrease in the frequency of light is called a **red shift,** referring to the low-frequency, or red, end of the color spectrum.

Chapter 25   Vibrations and Waves

25.10 Bow Waves

☑ **A bow wave occurs when a wave source moves faster than the wave it produces.**

- When wave crests overlap at the edges and the pattern made by these overlapping crests is a V shape, the wave is called a **bow wave.**

- The familiar bow wave generated by a speedboat knifing through the water is produced by the overlapping of many circular wave crests.

- After the speed of the source exceeds the wave speed, increased speed produces a bow wave with a narrower V shape.

25.11 Shock Waves

☑ **A shock wave occurs when an object moves faster than the speed of sound.**

- A **shock wave** is a three-dimensional wave that consists of overlapping spheres that form a cone.

- The sharp crack heard when the shock wave that sweeps behind a supersonic aircraft reaches the listener is called a **sonic boom.**

- It is not necessary that the moving source emit sound for it to produce a shock wave.

Chapter 25 Vibrations and Waves

Exercises

25.1 Vibration of a Pendulum (page 491)

1. The time it takes for one back-and-forth motion of a pendulum is called the _____.

2. List the two things that determine the period of a pendulum.

   _____

3. Circle the letter of each statement about a pendulum that is true.

   a. A longer pendulum has a longer period.

   b. A shorter pendulum swings with a greater frequency.

   c. Mass does not affect the period of the pendulum.

   d. All pendulums swing at the same rate.

25.2 Wave Description (pages 491–493)

4. What is simple harmonic motion?

   _____

5. Is the following sentence true or false? A sine curve is a pictorial representation of a wave. _____

6. Circle the letter that describes the source of all waves.

   a. a temperature change   b. a change in pressure

   c. something that vibrates   d. an electrical current

Match each phrase with the correct word or words.

Term		Definition
_____	7. crest	a. distance between successive identical parts of a wave
_____	8. trough	b. low point on a wave
_____	9. amplitude	c. vibrations per unit of time
_____	10. wavelength	d. high point on a wave
_____	11. frequency	e. distance from a midpoint to a crest
_____	12. hertz	f. unit of frequency

13. Is the following sentence true or false? As the frequency of a vibrating source increases, the period increases. _____

25.3 Wave Motion (pages 493–494)

14. Describe the wave that forms and what is transmitted when a stone is dropped in a pond.

    _____

    _____

15. Sounds waves are a(n) _____ that travels through the air.

Chapter 25   Vibrations and Waves

16. Circle the letter of each statement about sound waves in air that is true.

a. They carry energy.

b. Air is the medium they travel through.

c. They are a disturbance that moves through the air.

d. Air molecules are carried along with the wave.

25.4 Wave Speed (pages 495–496)

17. Is the following sentence true or false? The speed of a wave depends on the medium through which it travels. _____

18. The speed of sound in air is about _____ m/s to _____ m/s.

19. Is the following sentence true or false? Sound travels faster in air than in water. _____

20. Circle the letter of each wave property that is related.

a. speed   b. frequency

c. direction   d. wavelength

21. Describe how to calculate the speed of a wave.

_____

_____

22. Circle the letter of the equation used to calculate a wave's speed.

a. $v = \lambda p$ b. $v = \lambda t$

c. $v = \lambda f$ d. $v = \lambda a$

23. The Greek letter _____ is often used to represent wavelength.

24. Is the following sentence true or false? The equation for calculating the speed of a wave does not apply to light waves. _____

25. Describe how wavelength and frequency are related for sound waves.

_____

25.5 Transverse Waves (pages 497)

26. Circle the letter that best describes a transverse wave.

a. The medium does not vibrate.

b. The medium vibrates at right angles to the direction the wave travels.

c. The medium vibrates in the same direction the wave travels.

d. A sound wave.

27. Circle the letter of each example of a transverse wave.

a. waves in the strings of instruments

b. radio waves

c. light waves

d. sound waves

Chapter 25   Vibrations and Waves

25.6 Longitudinal Waves (page 497)

28. Describe the motion of the particles in a medium when a longitudinal wave passes through it.

_____

_____

29. What is an example of a longitudinal wave? _____

30. Identify the types of waves formed in part (a) and part (b) of the illustration below.

a. _____   b. _____

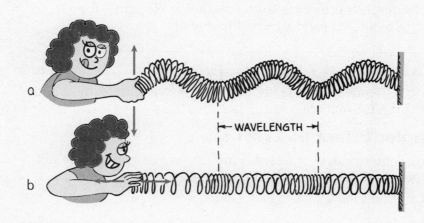

25.7 Interference (pages 498–499)

31. A(n) _____ is a regular arrangement of places where wave effects are increased, decreased, or neutralized.

Match each term to its definition.

Term	**Definition**
_____ **32.** constructive interference	a. when crests overlap troughs and effects are reduced
_____ **33.** destructive interference	b. when crests of one wave overlap the crests of another wave
_____ **34.** out of phase	c. when crests overlap and effects add together
_____ **35.** in phase	d. when crests and troughs overlap to produce zero amplitude

36. Describe when wave interference occurs.

_____

_____

37. Is the following sentence true or false? Wave interference only occurs with transverse waves. _____

Chapter 25   Vibrations and Waves

25.8 Standing Waves (pages 500–501)

38. Is the following sentence true or false? A wave that appears not to move is likely to be a standing wave. _____

39. The points on a standing wave where no motion occurs are called

_____.

40. Circle the letter of each statement about antinodes that is true.

   a. They seem not to move.   b. They occur midway between nodes.

   c. location of largest amplitude d. location of zero amplitude

41. Standing waves occur because of _____.

42. Describe the conditions necessary—in terms of wavelength—for a standing wave to form in a rope attached to a wall.

_____

_____

43. Is the following sentence true or false? Standing waves can form in both transverse and longitudinal waves. _____

25.9 The Doppler Effect (pages 501–503)

44. Is the following sentence true or false? A moving wave source does not affect the frequency of the wave encountered by an observer. _____

45. Describe the Doppler effect.

_____

_____

46. Circle the letter of each statement about the Doppler effect that is true.

   a. it occurs when a wave source moves toward an observer

   b. it occurs when an observer moves toward a wave source

   c. it occurs when a wave source moves away an observer

   d. it occurs when an observer moves away from a wave source

47. Is the following sentence true or false? A higher frequency results when a wave source moves toward an observer. _____

48. Two fire trucks with sirens on speed toward and away from an observer as shown below. Identify which truck produces a higher than normal siren frequency and which produces a lower than normal siren frequency.

_____

_____

Chapter 25 Vibrations and Waves

49. The blue shift and red shift refer to how the Doppler effect affects _____ waves.

50. A(n) _____ in frequency is called a blue shift, while a(n) _____ is called a red shift.

25.10 Bow Waves (pages 504–505)

51. Is the following sentence true or false? Bow waves form a V-shaped wake in back of the moving source. _____

52. Bow waves form when the wave source moves _____ than the wave speed.

53. Is the following sentence true or false? The crests of bow waves overlap at their edges. _____

54. Circle the letter that describes how increasing the speed of the wave source above the wave speed affects the shape of the bow wave that is formed.

    a. The bow wave is unchanged.

    b. The bow wave has a narrower V shape.

    c. The bow wave has a wider V shape.

    d. The bow wave forms a straight line.

25.11 Shock Waves (pages 505–506)

55. A shock wave has the shape of a _____.

56. Circle the letter that describes the conditions needed for a shock wave to form.

    a. An object moves at the speed of sound.

    b. The wave speed exceeds the object's speed.

    c. The wave speed equals the object's speed.

    d. An object moves faster than the speed of sound.

57. What is a sonic boom?

_____

_____

58. Why don't we hear a sonic boom from a subsonic aircraft?

_____

_____

59. Is the following sentence true or false? A sonic boom is formed only at the moment an object breaks through the sound barrier. _____

Chapter 25   Vibrations and Waves

Wave Speed

While watching the ocean surf roll in at the beach, you estimate the ocean wave frequency is about one wave every 10 s. You also estimate the average wavelength is about 25 m. What is the speed of the ocean waves?

Read and Understand

What information are you given?

   Period = 10 s

   Wavelength, λ = 25 m

Plan and Solve

What unknown are you trying to calculate?
   Wave speed, v = ?

What formulas contains the given quantity and the unknown?

   $F = \dfrac{1}{T}$ and $v = \lambda f$

Substitute the known values and solve.

   $f = \dfrac{1}{10 \text{ s}} = 0.1 \text{ s}^{-1}$

   $v = \lambda f = (25 \text{ m})(0.1 \text{ s}^{-1}) = 2.5 \text{ m/s}$

Look Back and Check

Is your answer reasonable?
   Yes, the calculated speed of 2.5 m/s seems reasonable for an ocean wave.

Math Practice

On a separate sheet of paper, solve the following problems.

 1. One wave passes by a pier every 5 s. If the wavelength of the wave is 12 m, what is the wave speed?

 2. A sound wave has a speed of 340 m/s in air. If the wave has a frequency of 185 Hz, what is its wavelength?

 3. A sound wave travels at 345 m/s in air and has a wavelength of 1.9 m. What is the period of the wave?

Chapter 26   Sound

Summary

THE BIG IDEA : Sound is a form of energy that spreads out through space.

26.1 The Origin of Sound

☑ **All sounds originate in the vibrations of material objects.**

- Sound is produced when a vibration stimulates the vibration of something larger or more massive. This vibrating material then sends a disturbance through a surrounding medium, usually air, in the form of longitudinal waves. Under ordinary conditions, the frequency of the sound waves produced equals the frequency of the vibrating source.

- We describe our subjective impression about the frequency of sound by the word **pitch.** A high-pitched sound has a high vibration frequency, while the low-pitched sound has a low vibration frequency.

- A young person can normally hear pitches with frequencies from 20 to 20,000 hertz. As we grow older, our hearing range shrinks, especially at the high-frequency end.

- Sound waves with frequencies below 20 hertz are called **infrasonic,** and those with frequencies above 20,000 hertz are called **ultrasonic.** We cannot hear infrasonic or ultrasonic sound waves.

26.2 Sound in Air

☑ **As a source of sound vibrates, a series of compressions and rarefactions travels outward from the source.**

- A sound pulse goes out in all directions from the source.

- When sound moves away from its source, each particle of air moves back and forth along the direction of motion of the expanding wave. A pulse of compressed air is called a **compression.** A pulse of low-pressure air is called a **rarefaction.**

- For all wave motion, it is not the medium that travels, but a *pulse* that travels.

- As a source of sound vibrates, a series of compressions and rarefactions is produced.

26.3 Media That Transmit Sound

☑ **Sound travels in solids, liquids, and gases.**

- The speed of sound differs in different materials. In general, sound is transmitted faster in liquids than in gases, and still faster in solids.

- Sound cannot travel in a vacuum. The transmission of sound requires a medium. If there is nothing to compress and expand, there can be no sound. There may still be vibrations, but without a medium there is no sound.

Chapter 26   Sound

26.4 Speed of Sound

☑ **The speed of sound in a gas depends on the temperature of the gas and the mass of the particles in the gas. The speed of sound in a material depends on the material's elasticity.**

- During a thunderstorm, you hear thunder *after* you see the lightning. This is evidence that sound is much slower than light.

- The speed of sound in dry air at 0°C is about 330 meters per second, or about 1200 kilometers per hour.

- Water vapor in the air and increased temperatures increase the speed of sound in air slightly. For each degree increase in air temperature above 0°C, the speed of sound in air increases by about 0.60 m/s. In air at a normal room temperature of about 20°C, sound travels at about 340 m/s.

- The speed of sound in a gas also depends on the mass of its particles. Lighter gas particles move faster and transmit sound much more quickly than heavier gas particles.

- The speed of sound in a solid material depends not on the material's density, but on its elasticity. Elasticity is the ability of a material to change shape in response to an applied force, and then resume its initial shape once the distorting force is removed. Steel is very elastic; putty is inelastic.

26.5 Loudness

☑ **Sound intensity is objective and is measured by instruments. Loudness, on the other hand, is a physiological sensation sensed in the brain.**

- The intensity of a sound is proportional to the square of the amplitude of a sound wave. The unit of intensity for sound is the decibel (dB).

- Starting with zero at the threshold of hearing for a normal ear, an increase of each 10 dB means that sound intensity increases by a factor of 10. A sound of 10 dB is 10 times as intense as sound of 0 dB. Likewise, 20 dB is not twice but 10 times as tense as 10 dB, or 100 times as intense as the threshold of hearing.

- Physiological hearing damage begins at exposure to 85 decibels. The extent of damage depends on the length of exposure and on frequency characteristics.

26.6 Natural Frequency

☑ **When any object composed of an elastic material is disturbed, it vibrates at its own special set of frequencies, which together form its special sound.**

- An object's **natural frequency** is the frequency at which the object vibrates when it is disturbed. Natural frequency depends on the elasticity and shape of the object.

- Most things—from planets to atoms and almost everything else in between—have a springiness to them and vibrate at one or more natural frequencies.

Chapter 26   Sound

- A natural frequency is one at which minimum energy is required to produce forced vibrations. It is also the frequency that requires the least amount of energy to continue this vibration.

26.7 Forced Vibration

☑ **Sounding boards are an important part of all stringed musical instruments because they are forced into vibration and produce the sound.**

- A **forced vibration** occurs when an object is made to vibrate by another vibrating object that is nearby.

- The vibration of guitar strings in an acoustical guitar would be faint if they weren't transmitted to the guitar's wooden body. The mechanism in a music box is mounted on a sounding board. Without the sounding board, the sound would be barely audible.

26.8 Resonance

☑ **An object resonates when there is a force to pull it back to its starting position and enough energy to keep it vibrating.**

- **Resonance** occurs when the frequency of a vibration forced on an object matches the object's natural frequency, causing a dramatic increase in amplitude.

- A common experience illustrating resonance occurs on a swing. Even small pumps or pushes, if delivered in rhythm with the natural frequency of the swinging motion, produce large amplitudes.

- When you tune a radio set, you are adjusting the natural frequency of the electronics in the set to match one of the many incoming signals. The set then resonates to one station at a time, instead of playing all the stations at once.

26.9 Interference

☑ **When constructive interference occurs with sound waves, the listener hears a louder sound. When destructive interference occurs, the listener hears a fainter sound or no sound at all.**

- The crest of a transverse wave corresponds to a compression of a sound wave, and the trough of a transverse wave corresponds to a rarefaction of a sound wave.

- When the crests of one wave overlap the crests of another wave, there is constructive interference and an increase in amplitude. When the crests of one wave overlap the troughs of another wave, there is destructive interference and a decrease in amplitude.

- Destructive sound interference is a useful property in antinoise technology.

Chapter 26   Sound

26.10 Beats

☑ **When two tones of slightly different frequency are sounded together, a regular fluctuation in the loudness of the combined sounds is heard.**

- The periodic variation in the loudness of sound is called **beats.**

- Beats can be heard when two slightly mismatched tuning forks are sounded together. When the combined waves reach your ears in step, the sound is a maximum. When the forks are out of step, in the sound is a minimum.

- Beats can occur with any kind of wave and are a practical way to compare frequencies. When wave frequencies are identical, beats disappear.

Chapter 26 Sound

Exercises

26.1 The Origin of Sound (page 515)

Match each sound source with the part that vibrates.

	Sound Source	**Vibrating Part**
_____	**1.** violin	a. strings
_____	**2.** your voice	b. reed
_____	**3.** saxophone	c. column of air at the mouthpiece
_____	**4.** flute	d. vocal chords

5. Sound waves are a type of _____ wave.

6. What normally determines the frequency of sound waves?

_____

_____

7. Define pitch.

_____

8. As people grow older, they often have more trouble hearing sounds at the _____ end of the range of frequencies.

9. Sound waves with frequencies below the normal range are _____ waves.

10. Sound waves with frequencies above the normal range are _____ waves.

26.2 Sound in Air (pages 515–517)

11. Is the following sentence true or false? Sound vibrates the air much like particles move back and forth along a stretched spring. _____

12. A pulse of compressed air is called a _____, and a pulse of low-pressure air is called a _____.

13. For all wave motion, it is not the _____ that travels, but a _____ that travels.

14. Explain what happens when a tuning fork is struck against one end of an open tube.

_____

_____

_____

26.3 Media That Transmit Sound (page 517)

15. What did Native Americans learn long ago when they put their ears to the ground?

_____

_____

Chapter 26   Sound

16. Suppose a friend far away taps a metal fence. Circle the letter of the true statement.

    a. The sound is softer and travels slower through the metal than through air.

    b. The sound is louder and travels slower through the metal than through air.

    c. The sound is softer and travels faster through the metal than through air.

    d. The sound is louder and travels faster through the metal than through air.

17. Circle the letter of the best conductor of sound.

    a. a gas   b.   a liquid

    c. a solid   d.   a vacuum

18. Suppose a ringing bell is placed inside a sealed jar filled with air. The air is then removed from the jar, creating a vacuum. Describe the difference in what a person nearby hears before and after the air is removed from the jar.

    _____

    _____

    _____

26.4 Speed of Sound (page 518)

19. Is the following sentence true or false? During a thunderstorm, you hear the thunder before you see the lightning. _____

20. The speed of sound in a gas depends primarily on _____ and _____.

21. Circle the letter of the speed of sound in dry air at 0°C.

    a. 20 m/s   b.   330 m/s

    c. 60 m/s   d.   1200 m/s

22. _____ in the air increases the speed of sound in air.

23. For each degree increase in air temperature above 0°C, the speed of sound in air increases about _____ m/s.

24. The speed of sound at normal room temperature is about _____.

25. Do lighter gas particles transmit sound faster or slower than heavier gases found in air? _____

26. Is the following sentence true or false? The speed of sound in a solid material depends not on the material's density, but on its elasticity.

    _____

26.5 Loudness (page 519)

27. What is the intensity of sound proportional to?

    _____

Chapter 26   Sound

28. Is the following sentence true or false? Sound intensity is a physiological sensation, but loudness can be measured by instruments. _____

Sound Levels	
Source of Sound	**Level (dB)**
Jet engine, at 30 m	140
Old subway train	100
Average factory	90
Normal speech	60
Library	40

29. Study the table above. Circle the letter beside the source of sound that is 100 times as intense as the normal sound of a library.

a. Jet engine, at 30 m   b. Old subway train

c. Average factory   d. Normal speech

30. Physiological hearing damage begins at exposure to _____ decibels.

31. Is the following sentence true or false? The cells of the receptor organ in the inner ear do not regenerate. _____

26.6 Natural Frequency (page 520)

32. Define natural frequency.

_____

33. Circle the letter of the properties upon which an object's natural frequency depends.

a. elasticity and shape   b. mass and shape

c. volume and elasticity   d. volume and mass

34. Is the following sentence true or false? A natural frequency is one at which maximum energy is required to produce forced vibrations.

_____

26.7 Forced Vibration (page 520)

35. Why is the sound made by an unmounted tuning fork faint when compared to the sound of the fork when its base is on a tabletop?

_____

_____

36. Define forced vibration.

_____

_____

37. The part of any stringed musical instrument that undergoes forced vibration and makes the sound you hear is a _____.

Chapter 26   Sound

26.8 Resonance (pages 521–522)

38. Define resonance.

_____

_____

_____

39. Describe how a child's swing illustrates resonance.

_____

_____

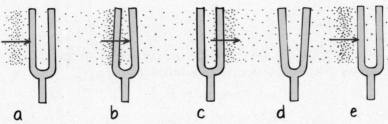

a   b   c   d   e

40. Describe what is happening to the tuning fork shown in the figure above.

a. _____

b. _____

c. _____

d. _____

e. _____

41. Describe how resonance affects the way you listen to a radio.

_____

_____

26.9 Interference (pages 522–523)

42. A _____ of a sound wave corresponds to a crest of a transverse wave.

43. A _____ of a sound wave corresponds to a trough of a transverse wave.

44. When the crests of one wave overlap the crests of another wave, there is _____ interference and an increase in _____.

45. When the crests of one wave overlap the troughs of another wave, there is _____ interference and a decrease in _____.

46. Is the following sentence true or false? Constructive sound interference is a useful property in antinoise technology. _____

47. Describe how antinoise technology is used to protect the hearing of jackhammer users.

_____

_____

_____

Chapter 26 Sound

26.10 Beats (pages 524–525)

Use the figure below to answer Questions 48 and 49.

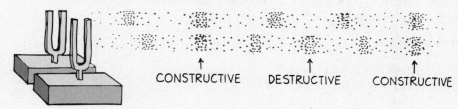

CONSTRUCTIVE   DESTRUCTIVE   CONSTRUCTIVE

48. Use the figure to explain how beats are formed.

_____

_____

_____

_____

_____

49. Suppose one tuning fork in the figure vibrates 264 times per second, and the other vibrates 262 times per second.

   a. How often are the forks in step? _____

   b. What is the frequency of beats? _____

50. Is the following sentence true or false? If a piano tuner hears beats, the piano is out of tune. _____

Chapter 26   Sound

Relating Properties of Sound

A musical note has a frequency of 264 Hz. What is the wavelength of the sound if it moves with a speed of 345 m/s?

1. Read and Understand

What information are you given?

speed of the sound wave = v = 345 m/s

frequency of the sound wave = f = 264 Hz

2. Plan and Solve

What unknown are you trying to calculate?

wavelength = λ

What relationship can you use to find the unknown?

wave speed = wavelength × frequency: $v = \lambda f$

Rearrange the equation to solve for the unknown variable.

$\lambda = \dfrac{v}{f}$

Replace each variable with its known value.

$\lambda = \dfrac{345 \text{ m/s}}{264 \text{ Hz}} = 1.3 \text{ m}$

3. Look Back and Check

Is your answer reasonable?

A speed of 345 m/s indicates that the medium through which the sound is traveling is probably air. A sound with a frequency of 264 Hz is an audible sound. The wavelength of 1.3 m is reasonable for an audible sound traveling through air.

Math Practice

On a separate sheet of paper, solve the following problems.

1. A dolphin emits a sound with a frequency of 1.2×10^5 Hz. What is the wavelength of this sound as it moves through seawater with a speed of 1530 m/s?

2. Sound with a wavelength of 5.8 m moves through a material at a speed of 1508 m/s. What is the frequency of the sound?

3. Sound with a frequency of 468 Hz and a wavelength of 4.7 m moves through a material. What is the speed of the sound?

Chapter 27   Light

Summary

THE BIG IDEA : Light is the ONLY thing you see! All visible objects either emit or reflect light.

27.1 Early Concepts of Light

✅ **Scientists now agree that light has a dual nature, part particle and part wave.**

- Until Einstein, some scientists believed light consisted of particles. Other scientists argued that light was a wave.

- Einstein published a theory to explain the *photoelectric effect*. His theory stated that light consists of particles called photons. **Photons** are massless bundles of concentrated electromagnetic energy.

27.2 The Speed of Light

✅ **Michelson's experimental value for the speed of light was 299,920 km/s, which is usually rounded to 300,000 km/s.**

- The first demonstration that light travels at a finite speed was supplied by Olaus Roemer when he measured discrepancies in the periods of Jupiter's moons. Christian Huygens was able to explain the discrepancies.

- Albert Michelson used a mirror arrangement to measure the speed of light.

- The distance light travels in one year is called a **light-year.**

27.3 Electromagnetic Waves

✅ **The electromagnetic spectrum consists of radio waves, microwaves, infrared, light, ultraviolet rays, X-rays, and gamma rays.**

- Light is energy that is emitted by accelerating electric charges. This energy travels as an **electromagnetic wave** that is partly electric and partly magnetic.

- The range of electromagnetic waves is the **electromagnetic spectrum.**

- Electromagnetic waves of frequencies lower than the red of visible light are called **infrared** waves, and those with frequencies higher than violet are called **ultraviolet** waves.

27.4 Light and Transparent Materials

✅ **Light passes through materials whose atoms absorb the energy and immediately reemit it as light.**

- When light strikes matter, electrons in the matter are forced into vibration that depends on the frequency of the light and the natural frequency of electrons in the material.

Chapter 27   Light

- Materials that transmit light are **transparent.** Glass and water are transparent.
- Electrons in glass have a natural frequency in the ultraviolet range. Ultraviolet light increases the amplitude of the atoms' vibrations. This energy is in the form of heat.
- When electromagnetic waves with lower frequency than ultraviolet shine on glass, the atoms are forced into vibration with smaller amplitudes. The atoms then hold the energy for only a short time before reemitting it as transmitted light.
- Infrared waves vibrate not only the electrons, but the entire structure of glass. This vibration increases the internal energy of the glass and makes it warmer.

27.5 Opaque Materials

☑ **In opaque materials, any coordinated vibrations given by light to the atoms and molecules are turned into random kinetic energy—that is, into internal energy.**

- Materials that absorb light without reemission and thus allow no light through them are **opaque.** Opaque materials become slightly warmer as light strikes them.
- Light that shines on metal sets free electrons into vibration, and this energy is reemitted as visible light in the form of a reflection. That's why metals are shiny.
- Our atmosphere is transparent to visible light and some infrared, but fortunately, almost opaque to high-frequency ultraviolet waves.

27.6 Shadows

☑ **When light shines on an object, some of the rays may be stopped while others pass on in a straight-line path.**

- A thin beam of light is often called a **ray.** Any beam of light can be thought of as made of a bundle of rays.
- A **shadow** forms where light rays cannot reach. Shadows usually have a dark part on the inside and a lighter part around the edges. A total shadow is called an **umbra.** A partial shadow is called a **penumbra.** A penumbra appears where some of the light is blocked but where other light fills in.
- Both an umbra and a penumbra form during a solar eclipse, when the moon's shadow falls on Earth, and during a lunar eclipse, when Earth's shadow falls on the moon.
- Shadows also occur when light is bent in passing through a transparent material such as water.

Chapter 27   Light

27.7 Polarization

☑ **Light that reflects at glancing angles from nonmetallic surfaces, such as glass, water, or roads, vibrates mainly in the plane of the reflecting surface.**

- **Polarization** is the alignment of vibrations in a transverse wave, usually by filtering out waves traveling in other directions.

- If you shake the end of a rope up and down, the vibrations are back and forth in the vertical direction. So, the wave is vertically polarized. If you shake the rope from side to side, a horizontally polarized wave is produced.

- A single vibrating electron emits an electromagnetic wave that is polarized. Common light sources, such as light bulbs or the sun, emit light that is not polarized.

- A special filter can polarize light. Such filters eliminate glare from a horizontal surface.

27.8 Polarized Light and 3-D Viewing

☑ **A pair of photographs or movie frames, taken a short distance apart (about average eye spacing), can be seen in 3-D when the left eye sees only the left view and the right eye sees only the right view.**

- Vision in three dimensions depends on the fact that both eyes give impressions simultaneously (or nearly so), with each eye viewing a scene from a slightly different angle.

- A 3-D slide show or movie has one horizontally polarized view and another vertically polarized view. The viewer wears polarizing eyeglasses with the lens axes also at right angles. The views merge in the brain to produce an image with depth—a 3-D image.

Chapter 27 Light

Exercises

27.1 Early Concepts of Light (page 533)

Match the scientist with his idea about the nature of light. An idea may be used more than once.

Scientist

_____ **1.** Einstein

_____ **2.** Empedocles

_____ **3.** Euclid

_____ **4.** Huygens

_____ **5.** Plato

_____ **6.** Socrates

Idea About Light

a. Light is a wave.

b. Light consists of tiny particles.

c. Vision results from streamers or filaments emitted by the eye making contact with an object.

7. Is the following sentence true or false? The idea that light consists of tiny particles was first proposed in the early 1900s. _____

8. What characteristic of light did Huygens provide evidence of?

_____

_____

9. What phenomena did Einstein explain in the theory he published in 1905? _____

10. _____ are massless bundles of concentrated electromagnetic energy.

11. What is the modern theory of light?

_____

_____

27.2 The Speed of Light (pages 534–535)

12. Is the following sentence true or false? Roemer's measurement of discrepancies in the position of Jupiter's moon Io was the first demonstration showing that light travels at a finite speed. _____

13. How did Huygens interpret the discrepancy in Roemer's measurement?

_____

_____

14. Circle the letter beside the correct speed of light.

    a. 300,000 m/s   b. 300,000,000 m/s

    c. 300,000 km/s   d. 300,000,000 km/s

15. Albert Michelson received the Nobel Prize for using a system of mirrors to measure _____.

16. How much time does it take light to travel from the sun to Earth?

_____

17. What is a light-year? _____

Chapter 27   Light

27.3 Electromagnetic Waves (page 536)

18. What is the source of the energy in light?

_____

19. The energy in an electromagnetic wave is part _____ and
part _____.

20. Name the different waves that make up the electromagnetic spectrum.

a. _____   e. _____

b. _____   f. _____

c. _____   g. _____

d. _____

21. Electromagnetic waves of frequencies slightly lower than the red waves
of visible light are called _____.

22. Electromagnetic waves of frequencies slightly higher than the violet
waves of visible light are called _____.

27.4 Light and Transparent Materials (pages 537–538)

23. Is the following sentence true or false? How a receiving material
responds when light is incident upon it depends only on the frequency
of the light. _____

24. Is the following sentence true or false? Electrons are able to respond to
the ultrafast vibrations of visible light because the electrons have a small
enough mass to vibrate that fast. _____

25. How do the atoms in a transparent material interact with light?

_____

26. The natural vibration frequencies of an electron depend on how strongly
it is attached to _____.

27. What two things can happen to the energy received by an atom in glass
when ultraviolet light shines on the glass?

a. _____

b. _____

28. Why does resonance occur when ultraviolet light shines on glass?

_____

29. What happens when electromagnetic waves with frequencies lower than
ultraviolet light shine on glass?

_____

_____

30. Is the following sentence true or false? Infrared waves vibrate only the
electrons in glass. _____

Chapter 27   Light

27.5 Opaque Materials (page 539)

31. What are opaque materials?

_____

_____

32. Is the following sentence true or false? In opaque materials, any coordinated vibrations given by light to the atoms and molecules are turned into random kinetic energy, or internal energy. _____

33. Explain why metals reflect light and appear shiny.

_____

_____

_____

34. Our atmosphere is transparent to _____ light and _____ light, but almost opaque to _____ light.

35. Why is it possible to get a sunburn on a cloudy day?

_____

27.6 Shadows (pages 540–541)

36. What is a light ray? _____

37. Generally, shadows form where _____.

38. Would you position a light source close or far from an object in order to produce a sharp shadow?_____

39. Is the following sentence true or false? Most shadows have clearly defined edges. _____

40. A total shadow is called a(n) _____.

41. Where are two places a penumbra can form?

_____

_____

42. During a solar eclipse, the shadow of _____ falls on _____.

43. What will you observe if you stand in an umbra during a solar eclipse?

_____

44. What will you observe if you stand in a penumbra during a solar eclipse?

_____

45. What is a lunar eclipse?

_____

46. Is the following sentence true or false? Shadows cannot occur when light is bent while passing through a transparent material. _____

Chapter 27 Light

27.7 Polarization (pages 542–543)

47. Is the following sentence true or false? Polarization is a characteristic of transverse waves and not longitudinal waves. _____

48. Define polarization.

_____

_____

49. If you shake a rope up and down, it becomes _____ polarized.

50. If you shake a rope from side to side, it becomes _____ polarized.

51. Write *P* if the source emits polarized light or *NP* if the source emits unpolarized light.

_____ a. vibrating electron   _____ c. the sun

_____ b. incandescent bulb   _____ d. a candle flame

52. Describe what happens to light from an unpolarized source that falls on a polarizing filter.

_____

_____

53. Each of the figures below is an analogy for the effect of crossed sheets of polarizing material. Explain what happens if the ropes are light and the picket fences are polarizing filters.

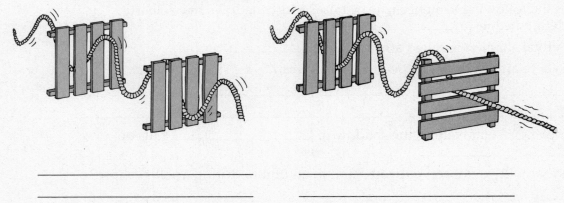

_____   _____

_____   _____

_____   _____

54. How are the axes of polarized sunglasses aligned in order to eliminate glare from horizontal surfaces? _____

Chapter 27   Light

27.8 Polarized Light and 3-D Viewing (pages 544–546)

55. How do your eyes perceive vision in three dimensions?

_____

_____

56. Is the following sentence true or false? The combination of views you see from both eyes gives depth to what you see. _____

57. Explain the effect that allows you to see a hidden message in a stereogram.

_____

_____

_____

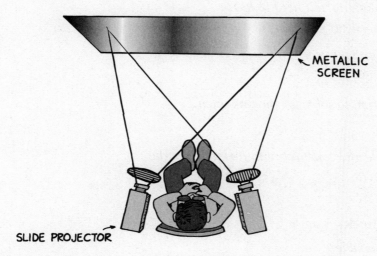

METALLIC SCREEN

SLIDE PROJECTOR

58. The figure above shows a person watching a 3-D slide show.

a. How are the photographs taken in order to be used in the 3-D slide show?

_____

_____

b. How are the photographs used in the slide show projected?

_____

_____

c. How is the viewer able to see the 3-D effect in the show?

_____

_____

Chapter 27   Light

Relating Properties of Light

Assume the visible yellow light emitted by the sun has a wavelength of 5.8×10^{-7} m. What is the frequency of this light?

1. Read and Understand

What information are you given?
wavelength = $\lambda = 5.8 \times 10^{-7}$ m

2. Plan and Solve

What unknown are you trying to calculate?
frequency = f

What other information do you need to use?
speed of light = $c = 3.0 \times 10^{8}$ m/s

What relationship can you use?
speed of light = $c = \lambda f$

Rearrange the equation to solve for the unknown.
$$f = \frac{c}{\lambda}$$

Replace each variable and constant with its known value.
$$f = \frac{3.0 \times 10^{8}\ \text{m/s}}{5.8 \times 10^{-7}\ \text{m}} = 5.2 \times 10^{14}\ \text{Hz}$$

3. Look Back and Check

Is your answer reasonable?
A frequency around 10^{14} Hz is reasonable for visible light. The units of meters cancel, leaving 1/s or Hz, as it should.

Math Practice

On a separate sheet of paper, solve the following problems.

1. Ultraviolet rays from the sun can cause sunburn and skin damage. What is the wavelength of ultraviolet rays that have a frequency of 8.6×10^{14} Hz?

2. Green light from a laser has a wavelength of 5.3×10^{-7} m. What is the frequency of this light?

3. A microwave oven cooks food by emitting electromagnetic waves with a frequency of about 2.45×10^{9} Hz. What is the wavelength, in centimeters, of these waves?

Chapter 28   Color

Summary

THE BIG IDEA : The colors of the objects depend on the color of the light that illuminates them.

28.1 The Color Spectrum

☑ **By passing a narrow beam of sunlight through a triangular-shaped glass prism, Newton showed that sunlight is composed of a mixture of all the colors of the rainbow.**

- A prism casts sunlight into a **spectrum**—a spread of colors formed in the order red, orange, yellow, green, blue, and violet.

- Under white light, white objects appear white and colored objects appear in their individual colors.

- **White light** is not a color, but a combination of all of the colors. Black is also not a color, but the absence of light. Objects appear black when they absorb light of all visible frequencies.

28.2 Color by Reflection

☑ **The color of an opaque object is the color of the light it reflects.**

- Different materials have different natural frequencies for absorbing and emitting radiation. At resonant frequencies where the amplitudes of oscillation are large, light is absorbed.

- At frequencies above and below resonant frequencies, light is reemitted. If a material is transparent, the remitted light passes through it. If a material is opaque, the reemitted light passes back into the medium from which it came. This is reflection.

- Cells that contain chlorophyll absorb most frequencies incident upon them and reflect the green part, so they appear green.

- A candle flame emits light that is deficient in the higher frequencies; thus, it emits a yellowish light.

- An incandescent lamp emits light of all the visible frequencies, but is richer toward the lower frequencies, enhancing the reds. A fluorescent lamp is richer in the higher frequencies, so the blues are enhanced.

28.3 Color by Transmission

☑ **The color of a transparent object is the color of light it transmits.**

- A piece of blue glass appears blue because it transmits primarily blue light and absorbs the other colors that illuminate it.

- The material in glass that selectively absorbs colored light is known as a **pigment.**

- The energy of the light absorbed by glass increases the kinetic energy of the atoms, and the glass is warmed.

- Ordinary window glass is colorless because it transmits light of all visible frequencies equally well.

Chapter 28   Color

28.4 Sunlight

☑ **Yellow-green light is the brightest part of sunlight.**

- The brightness of solar frequencies is uneven. The lowest frequencies are in the red region.

- The graphical distribution of the sun's brightness versus frequency is called the *radiation curve* of sunlight.

28.5 Mixing Colored Light

☑ **You can make almost any color at all by overlapping red, green, and blue light and adjusting the brightness of each color of light.**

- Light of all the visible frequencies mixed together produces white. White also results from the combination of only red, green, and blue light.

- When only red and green light overlap, yellow is produced. When red and blue light overlap, the bluish red color called *magenta* is produced. Green and blue light alone produce the greenish blue color called *cyan*.

- Red, green, and blue are called the **additive primary colors.**

- Color television is based on the ability of the human eye to see combinations of the three additive primary colors as a variety of different colors.

28.6 Complementary Colors

☑ **Every color has some complementary color that when added to it will produce white.**

- When two colors are added together to produce white, they are called **complementary colors.**

- Yellow and blue are complementary colors. Magenta and green are complementary colors, as are cyan and red.

- Whenever you subtract some color from white light, you end up with the complementary color of the subtracted color.

28.7 Mixing Colored Pigments

☑ **When paints and dyes are mixed, the mixture absorbs all the frequencies each paint or dye absorbs.**

- The mixing of paints and dyes is an entirely different process from the mixing of colored light.

- The mixing of pigments is called *color mixing by subtraction*, to distinguish it from the effect of mixing colored light, which is called *color mixing by addition*.

- Magenta, yellow, and cyan are the **subtractive primary colors,** and are the most useful in color mixing by subtraction.

- Color printing is done on a press that prints each page with four differently colored inks (magenta, yellow, cyan, and black) in succession.

Chapter 28   Color

28.8 Why the Sky Is Blue

☑ **The sky is blue because its component particles scatter high-frequency light.**

- **Scattering** is a process in which sound or light is absorbed and reemitted in all directions. Atoms and molecules behave like tiny optical tuning forks and reemit light waves that shine on them. The reemitted light is sent in all directions; it is scattered.

- Of the visible frequencies, violet light is scattered the most, followed by blue, green, yellow, orange, and red, in that order. Although violet light is scattered more than blue, our eyes are more sensitive to blue, so we see a blue sky.

- In places where there are a lot of particles of dust and other particles larger than oxygen and nitrogen molecules, the lower frequencies of light are scattered more and the sky takes on a whitish appearance.

28.9 Why Sunsets Are Red

☑ **By the time a beam of light gets to the ground at sunset, all of the high-frequency light has already been scattered. Only the lower frequencies remain, resulting in a red sunset.**

- Red light, which is scattered the least, passes through more of the atmosphere without interacting with matter than light of any other color.

- The relative amounts of scattering depend on atmospheric conditions, which change from day to day and give us a variety of sunsets.

28.10 Why Water Is Greenish Blue

☑ **Water is greenish blue because water molecules absorb red.**

- Water molecules resonate somewhat to the visible-red frequencies, causing a gradual absorption of red light by water.

28.11 The Atomic Color Code—Atomic Spectra

☑ **After an excited atom emits light, it returns to its normal state.**

- The **excited state** of an atom is a state with greater energy than the atom's lowest energy state. When an electron transitions from an excited state to its original state, it emits a pulse of light—a photon.

- The frequency of an emitted photon, or its color, is directly proportional to the energy transition of the electron.

- The light from glowing elements can be analysed with an instrument called a **spectroscope.**

- The spectrum of an element appears not as a continuous band of color, but as a series of lines. This spectrum is known as a **line spectrum.** Each line corresponds to a distinct frequency of light.

Chapter 28   Color

Exercises

28.1 The Color Spectrum (pages 555–556)

1. _____ was the first person to do a systematic study of color.

2. Circle the letter of each statement that is true about Newton's study of color.

   a. He studied sunlight.

   b. He passed sunlight through triangular-shaped pieces of glass.

   c. He observed that sunlight was broken into a rainbow-like pattern of colors.

   d. He showed that sunlight is yellow light.

3. A spread of colors is called a _____.

4. List the colors of the visible spectrum in the correct order.

   _____

5. Is the following sentence true or false? Sunlight is a combination of all colors. _____

6. A white object appears _____ when illuminated by white light.

7. Explain this statement: White and black are not actually colors.

   _____

   _____

8. Is the following sentence true or false? Black objects that you can see absorb all light that falls on them. _____

28.2 Color by Reflection (pages 556–558)

9. Circle the letter that best describes the color of an opaque object.

   a. An opaque object is the color it absorbs.

   b. An opaque object is the color of the light that shines on it.

   c. An opaque object is the color it reflects.

   d. An opaque object is the color of white light.

10. Different materials have different _____ for absorbing and emitting radiation.

11. Describe what happens when the frequency of the light shining on an object resonates with the object's natural frequency.

    _____

12. Describe what happens when the frequency of the light shining on an object is higher or lower than the object's natural frequency.

    _____

13. Is the following sentence true or false? When an object reemits the light that shines on it, absorption occurs. _____

Chapter 28 Color

14. Circle the letter that best explains why cells containing chlorophyll are green.

    a. They absorb green light.

    b. They produce food.

    c. They reflect green light.

    d. They are very small.

15. Is the following sentence true or false? Different sources of light produce light made up of different frequencies. _____

28.3 Color by Transmission (page 558)

16. What determines the color of a transparent object?

    _____

17. The illustration below shows what happens when sunlight shines on a piece of blue glass. Describe what happens to the sunlight as it passes through the glass.

    _____

    _____

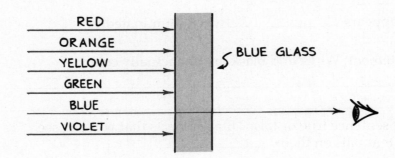

18. A _____ is a material in glass that selectively absorbs colored light.

19. Circle the letter that explains what the energy from the light absorbed by a piece of glass does to the glass.

    a. The energy hardens the glass.

    b. The energy warms the glass.

    c. The energy darkens the glass.

    d. The energy has no effect on the glass.

28.4 Sunlight (page 559)

20. Is the following sentence true or false? Human vision is most sensitive to colors in the red-orange part of the visible spectrum. _____

21. The graphical distribution of brightness versus frequency in sunlight is called the _____.

Chapter 28 Color

Use the graph of brightness versus frequency of sunlight to answer Questions 22 and 23.

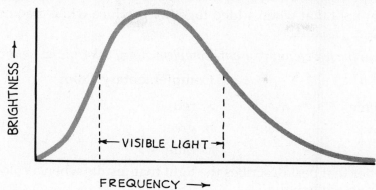

22. Is the following sentence true or false? The brightness of sunlight is directly proportional to frequency. _____

23. What is the brightest portion of the spectrum of sunlight?

_____

28.5 Mixing Colored Light (pages 560–561)

24. What color of light is produced when red, blue, and green light of equal brightness overlap? _____.

Match the name of each color of light to the mixture of colors that produces it.

Color of Light	**Mixtures That Produce the Color**
_____ **25.** magenta	a. mixture of green and blue
_____ **26.** yellow	b. mixture of red and blue
_____ **27.** cyan	c. mixture of red and green

28. Is the following sentence true or false? By mixing red, blue, and green light and adjusting the brightness of each, virtually any color can be formed. _____

29. Red, blue, and green light are known as the _____ colors.

30. Explain how a color television produces a wide range of colors on its screen.

_____

_____

_____

Chapter 28   Color

28.6 Complementary Colors (pages 562–563)

31. Two colors of light that when added together produce white are known as _____.

Match each color in the left column with its complementary color in the right column.

Color	Complementary Color
_____ **32.** magenta	a. red
_____ **33.** yellow	b. green
_____ **34.** cyan	c. blue

35. Circle the letter that best describes the light that results when a color is subtracted from white light.

   a. black

   b. magenta

   c. muddy brown

   d. the complementary color to the subtracted color

28.7 Mixing Colored Pigments (pages 564–565)

36. Is the following sentence true or false? The mixing of colored paints yields similar results as mixing the same colors of light. _____

37. Explain what happens when paints or dyes are mixed.

_____

_____

38. What color(s) are absorbed by blue paint?

_____

39. What color(s) are absorbed by yellow paint?

_____

40. If white light shines on a mixture of blue and yellow paint, what color is not absorbed? _____

41. The mixing of pigments, paints, or dyes is known as color mixing by _____.

42. Magenta, yellow, and cyan are the _____ colors used in printing illustrations in full color.

43. Describe the process used to print a color image in a book.

_____

_____

_____

Chapter 28   Color

28.8 Why the Sky Is Blue (pages 566–567)

44. Circle the letter of the process in which sound or light is absorbed and reemitted in all directions.

a. reflection
b. resonance
c. scattering
d. stimulated emission

45. Is the following sentence true or false? Atoms and molecules can behave like optical tuning forks, reemitting light waves that shine on them.
_____

46. Describe the relationship between the size of a particle in the atmosphere and the frequency of the light it scatters.

_____

_____

47. Is the following sentence true or false? The sky appears blue because particles in the atmosphere scatter low-frequency light. _____

48. Although violet light is scattered more than blue light, our eyes see the sky as blue. Explain.

_____

_____

49. Circle the letter that describes what occurs when many particles larger than oxygen and nitrogen molecules are in the atmosphere.

a. The sky appears darker blue.

b. The sky appears black.

c. The sky appears whitish.

d. The sky appears green.

50. Is the following sentence true or false? The presence of water droplets in the atmosphere does not affect how much light is scattered or what frequencies of light are scattered. _____

51. Explain why many clouds appear white.

_____

_____

52. A cloud containing many large water droplets appears _____.

28.9 Why Sunsets Are Red (pages 568–569)

53. Circle the letter of the color of light that is scattered the least as it passes through the atmosphere.

a. red
b. orange
c. yellow
d. blue

54. Is the following sentence true or false? At sunset, light reaches Earth's surface through a shorter path than at noon. _____

55. As the path of sunlight through the atmosphere increases, what color of light is scattered more? _____

Chapter 28   Color

56. Describe how the color of the sky changes as more and more high frequency light is scattered.

_____

57. Is the following sentence true or false? At sunset, only lower-frequency light strikes Earth. _____

58. Is the following sentence true or false? The amount of scattering that occurs at sunset varies very little from day to day. _____

28.10 Why Water Is Greenish Blue (pages 570–571)

59. Is the following sentence true or false? The deep-blue color of a pond or an ocean is due to the color of the water itself. _____

60. Is the following sentence true or false? Water is transparent to nearly all the frequencies of white light. _____

61. Circle the letter of the color(s) that water molecules absorb.

    a. red   b. green

    c. blue   d. all

62. Water molecules absorb certain frequencies of colored light. Circle the letter of the complementary color to the color that is absorbed.

    a. magenta   b. yellow

    c. cyan   d. white

28.11 The Atomic Color Code—Atomic Spectra (pages 571–573)

63. Is the following sentence true or false? When made to emit light, each element has its own unique color. _____

64. What determines the colors emitted by an atom?

_____

65. An energy level greater than an atom's lowest energy state is known as an _____.

66. After reaching an excited state, an atom emits a(n) _____ and then returns to its normal state.

67. How is the frequency of a photon related to the energy change in an atom?

_____

68. What is a spectroscope?

_____

69. Is the following sentence true or false? The spectrum emitted by an excited atom is continuous. _____

70. What does each line in a line spectrum represent?

_____

Chapter 29   Reflection and Refraction

Summary

THE BIG IDEA When waves interact with matter, they can be reflected, transmitted, or a combination of both. Waves that are transmitted can be refracted.

29.1 Reflection

☑ **When a wave reaches a boundary between two media, usually some or all of the wave bounces back into the first medium.**

- The return of a wave back to its original medium is called **reflection.**

- If you fasten a spring to a wall and send a pulse along the spring's length, all of the wave energy is reflected back along the spring rather than transmitted into the wall. Waves that travel along the spring are almost *totally reflected* at the wall.

- If the wall is replaced with a less rigid medium, such as a heavy spring, some energy is transmitted into the new medium. Some of the wave energy is still reflected and the incoming wave is *partially reflected.*

- Metals reflect almost all the frequencies of visible light.

- When light shines perpendicularly on the surface of still water or glass, only a very small percentage of its energy is reflected; the rest is transmitted.

29.2 The Law of Reflection

☑ **The law of reflection states that the angle of incidence and the angle of reflection are equal to each other.**

- Incident rays and reflected rays make equal angles with a line perpendicular to the surface, called the **normal.**

- The angle between the incident ray and the normal is called the **angle of incidence.** It is equal to the **angle of reflection,** which is the angle between the reflected ray and the normal.

- The **law of reflection** is the relationship between the angle of incidence and angle of reflection. The law of reflection applies to both partially reflected and totally reflected waves.

29.3 Mirrors

☑ **Mirrors produce only virtual images.**

- A **virtual image** is an image that appears in a location where light does not really reach.

- Your eye cannot ordinarily tell the difference between an object and its virtual image because the light that enters your eye is entering in exactly the same manner as it would without the mirror if there really were an object where you see the image.

- The virtual image formed by a *convex* mirror (a mirror that curves outward) is smaller and closer to the mirror than the object is. When the object is close to a *concave* mirror (a mirror that curves inward like a "cave"), the virtual image is larger and farther away than the object is.

Chapter 29   Reflection and Refraction

29.4 Diffuse Reflection

☑ **When light is incident on a rough surface, it is reflected in many directions.**

- **Diffuse reflection** is the reflection of light from a rough surface. Although each ray obeys the law of reflection, the many different angles that incident light rays encounter at the surface cause reflection in many directions.

- Whether a surface is a diffuse reflector or a polished reflector depends on the wavelength of the waves it reflects.

- We see most of the things around us by diffuse reflection.

29.5 Reflection of Sound

☑ **Sound energy not reflected is absorbed or transmitted.**

- An echo is reflected sound. The fraction of sound energy reflected from a surface is greater when the surface is rigid and smooth, and smaller when the surface is soft and irregular.

- The study of the reflective properties of surfaces and sound is called *acoustics.*

- When the walls of a room, auditorium, or concert hall are too reflective, the sound becomes garbled. This is due to multiple reflections of sound waves called **reverberations.** In the design of an auditorium or concert hall, a balance between reverberation and absorption is desired.

- Both sound and light obey the same law of reflection, so if a reflector is oriented so that you can *see* a particular musical instrument, you will *hear* it also. Sound from the instrument will follow the line of sight to the reflector and then to you.

29.6 Refraction

☑ **When a wave that is traveling at an angle changes its speed upon crossing a boundary between two media, it bends.**

- Water waves bend, or refract, when one part of each wave is made to travel slower (or faster) than another part.

- **Refraction** is the bending of a wave as it crosses the boundary between two media at an angle.

- In wave drawings, **wave fronts** are lines that are drawn to represent the positions of different crests.

29.7 Refraction of Sound

☑ **Sound waves are refracted when parts of a wave front travel at different speeds.**

- Sound wave refraction occurs in uneven winds or when sound is traveling through air of uneven temperature.

Chapter 29   Reflection and Refraction

- On a cold day or night, when the layer of air near the ground is colder than the air above it, the speed of sound near the ground is reduced. The higher speeds of the wave fronts above cause a bending of the sound toward Earth. When this happens, sound can be heard over considerably longer distances.

29.8 Refraction of Light

✔ **Changes in the speed of light as it passes from one medium to another, or variations in the temperatures and densities of the same medium, cause refraction.**

- When light rays enter a medium in which their speed decreases, as when passing from air into water, the rays bend toward the normal.
- When light rays enter a medium in which their speed increases, as when passing from water into air, the rays bend away from the normal.

29.9 Atmospheric Refraction

✔ **A mirage is caused by the refraction of light in Earth's atmosphere.**

- The appearance of a distorted image that forms as the result of atmospheric refraction is called a **mirage.**
- On hot days, there may be a layer of very hot air in contact with the ground. Since molecules in hot air are farther apart, light travels faster through this air than through the cooler air above it. The speeding up of the part of the wave nearest the ground produces a gradual bending of the light rays, which can produce a mirage.
- When you watch the sun set, you see the sun for several minutes after it has really sunk below the horizon. This is because light is refracted by Earth's atmosphere.

29.10 Dispersion in a Prism

✔ **Since different frequencies of light travel at different speeds in transparent materials, they will refract differently and bend at different angles.**

- The average speed of light is less than c in a transparent medium.
- Light of frequencies closer to the natural frequency of the electron oscillators in a medium travels more slowly in the medium. This is because there are more interactions between the light and the medium.
- Since the natural or resonant frequency of most transparent materials is in the ultraviolet part of the spectrum, visible light of higher frequencies travels more slowly than light of lower frequencies.
- When light is bent twice at nonparallel boundaries, as in a prism, the separation of the different colors of light is quite apparent. This separation of light into colors arranged according to their frequency is called **dispersion.**

Chapter 29   Reflection and Refraction

29.11 The Rainbow

☑ **In order for you to see a rainbow, the sun must be shining in one part of the sky, and the water droplets in a cloud or in falling rain must be in the opposite part of the sky.**

• In an individual spherical raindrop, some of the light is reflected and the rest is refracted into the drop. At the first refraction, the light is dispersed into its spectral colors. At the second refraction, light is concentrated in a narrow range of angles.

• Each raindrop disperses a full spectrum of colors. An observer, however, is in a position to see only a single color from any one drop. If violet light from a single drop enters your eye, red light from the same drop falls below your eye.

• The dispersed light of other colors in a rainbow is along similar arcs, each at their own slightly different angle. Altogether, the arcs for each color form the familiar rainbow shape.

29.12 Total Internal Reflection

☑ **Total internal reflection occurs when the angle of incidence is larger than the critical angle.**

• The critical angle is the angle of incidence that results in light being refracted at an angle of 90° with respect to the normal.

• When a flashlight submerged in water is tipped beyond the critical angle (48° from the normal in water), the beam of light cannot enter the air; it is only reflected. The beam is experiencing **total internal reflection,** which is the complete reflection of light back into its original medium.

• Total internal reflection is as the name implies: total—100%. Silvered or aluminized mirrors reflect only 90 to 95% of incident light, and are marred by dust and dirt. Prisms, on the other hand, are more efficient and thus are often used instead of mirrors in many optical instruments.

• The critical angle for a diamond is 24.6°, smaller than in other common substances. This means that light inside a diamond is more likely to be totally internally reflected than to escape. A diamond's small critical angle, plus the pronounced refraction within the material, produces wide dispersion and a wide array of brilliant colors.

• **Optical fibers,** sometimes called *light pipes,* are transparent fibers that pipe light from one place to another.

Chapter 29   Reflection and Refraction

Exercises

29.1 Reflection (page 579)

1. What usually happens when a wave reaches a boundary between
   two media?

   _____

   _____

2. The return of a wave back to its original medium is called _____.

3. Explain what happens when a spring is attached to a wall and you send
   a pulse along the spring's length.

   _____

   _____

   _____

4. Is the following sentence true or false? Shiny metals, such as
   aluminum and silver, reflect almost all the frequencies of visible light.

   _____

5. When light strikes glass perpendicularly, much of its energy is

   _____.

29.2 The Law of Reflection (page 580)

6. On the diagram below, label the following: *normal, incident ray, angle of
   incidence, reflected ray, and angle of reflection.*

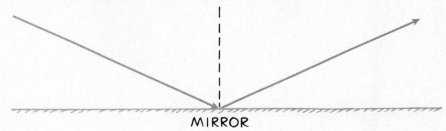

MIRROR

Match each phrase with the correct term or terms.

Phrase	Terms
_____ 7. a line perpendicular to a surface	a. angle of reflection
_____ 8. the angle between the incident ray and the normal	b. angle of incidence
_____ 9. the angle between the reflected ray and the normal	c. law of reflection
_____ 10. the relationship between the angle of incidence and angle of reflection	d. normal

Chapter 29   Reflection and Refraction

29.3 Mirrors (pages 580–581)

11. A _____ is an image that appears to be in a location
where light does not really reach.

12. Can your eye tell the difference between an object and its virtual
image? Explain.

_____

_____

_____

13. The virtual image formed by a _____ mirror (a mirror
that curves outward) is _____ and _____
to the mirror than the object is.

14. When an object is close to a _____ mirror (a mirror
that curves inward), the virtual image is _____ and
_____ than the object is.

15. Identify which mirror is concave and which mirror is convex.

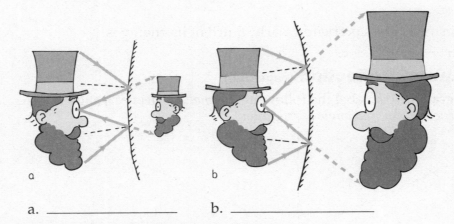

a. _____   b. _____

29.4 Diffuse Reflection (pages 582–583)

16. What is diffuse reflection? _____

17. Explain why light is reflected in many directions when striking a
rough surface.

_____

_____

18. Is the following sentence true or false? If the differences in elevations in a
surface are small (less than about one-eighth the wavelength of the light
that falls on it), the surface is considered polished. _____

19. An open-mesh parabolic dish acts like a _____ reflector
for visible light waves but like a _____ reflector for long-
wavelength radio waves.

20. What determines whether a surface is a diffuse reflector or a polished
reflector?

_____

Chapter 29   Reflection and Refraction

29.5 Reflection of Sound (pages 583–584)

21. Is the following sentence true or false? The fraction of sound energy reflected from a surface is less when the surface is rigid and smooth, and more when the surface is soft and irregular. _____

22. Sound energy not reflected is _____ or _____.

23. _____ is the study of reflective properties of surfaces and sound.

24. Define reverberations.

_____

_____

25. What properties of sound must be considered when designing an auditorium or concert hall?

_____

_____

26. Explain why being able to see a reflection of a musical instrument means, you will also be able to hear it.

_____

_____

29.6 Refraction (pages 584–585)

27. What is refraction?

_____

_____

28. Circle the letter of each statement that is true about refraction.

a. When a wave that is traveling at an angle changes its speed upon crossing a boundary between two media, it continues in a straight line.

b. Water waves bend, or refract, when one part of each wave is made to travel slower (or faster) than another part.

c. Refraction is the same as reflection.

d. Water waves are refracted as they move from deep water into shallow water.

29. On a wave diagram, it is convenient to draw lines, called _____, which represent the positions of different crests.

30. Is the following sentence true or false? At each point along a wave front, the wave is moving parallel to the wave front. _____

29.7 Refraction of Sound (page 586)

31. Sound waves are refracted when parts of a wave front travel at _____.

Chapter 29   Reflection and Refraction

32. How does a sound wave become refracted?

_____

_____

33. How does a layer of warm air on top of a layer of colder air near the ground affect sounds waves?

_____

_____

_____

29.8 Refraction of Light (pages 587–588)

34. Changes in the speed of light as it passes from one medium to another, or variations in the temperatures and densities of the same medium, cause _____.

35. Is the following sentence true or false? The wave fronts of light from the sun look like straight lines because the source of light is so far away.

_____

36. When light rays enter a medium in which their speed decreases, the rays bend toward the _____.

37. Circle the letter of each statement that is true.

   a. If a laser beam enters a container of water at the left and exits at the right, the path would be the same as if the light entered from the right and exited at the left.

   b. Light paths are reversible for reflection but not refraction.

   c. The apparent depth of a glass block is less than the real depth because of refraction.

   d. A full glass mug appears to hold more colored liquid than it actually does because of reflection.

29.9 Atmospheric Refraction (pages 588–590)

38. What is a mirage?

_____

39. Since molecules in hot air are farther apart, light travels _____ through it than through the cooler air above, resulting in a _____ of the light rays.

40. Is the following sentence true or false? Because of refraction, we see the sun for several minutes after the sunset. _____

29.10 Dispersion in a Prism (page 590)

41. Light of frequencies closer to the natural frequency of the electron oscillators in a medium travels more _____ in the medium.

42. Why is the statement in Question 41 true?

_____

_____

Chapter 29   Reflection and Refraction

43. Is the following sentence true or false? Since the natural frequency of most transparent materials is in the ultraviolet part of the spectrum, visible light of higher frequencies travels more slowly than light of lower frequencies. _____

44. What is dispersion?

_____

_____

29.11 The Rainbow (pages 591–593)

45. What needs to happen in order for a person to see a rainbow?

_____

_____

46. Why aren't rainbows completely round?

_____

_____

47. Explain why, if each drop of water disperses a full spectrum of colors, an observer can only see a single color from any one drop.

_____

_____

_____

48. How does a secondary rainbow form?

_____

29.12 Total Internal Reflection (pages 593–595)

Match each phrase with the correct term or number.

Phrase	Terms and Numbers
_____ **49.** the angle of incidence that results in light being refracted at an angle of 90° with respect to the normal	a. 24.6°
	b. critical angle
_____ **50.** the complete reflection of light back into its original medium	c. 43°
	d. total internal reflection
_____ **51.** critical angle for glass	
_____ **52.** critical angle for diamond	

53. What are optical fibers?

_____

_____

54. What are two applications for optical fibers?

_____

_____

_____

Chapter 29 Reflection and Refraction

Reflective Sounds

If you shout down a long hallway, and hear the echo 0.25 second later, how long is the hallway? The speed of sound in air at 20°C is about 343 m/s.

1. Read and Understand

What information are you given?

time for sound to travel down the hallway and back = 0.25 s

time for sound to travel the length of the hallway = 0.25 s/2 = 0.125 s

$v = 343$ m/s

2. Plan and Solve

What unknown are you trying to calculate?

length of hallway = ?

What mathematical expression can you use to calculate the unknown?

$d = v \times t$

$d = (343$ m/s$)(0.125$ s$) = 43$ m

3. Look Back and Check

Is your answer reasonable?

Yes, the length is reasonable and the units indicate distance.

Math Practice

On a separate sheet of paper, solve the following problems.

1. If you shout across a canyon, and you hear the echo 3.00 seconds later, how wide is the canyon? The speed of sound in the air is 343 m/s.

2. A boat captain sounds the ship's horn and you hear it 2.25 seconds later. How far away from the boat are you? The speed of sound in the air is 343 m/s.

3. A boat emits a sonar signal and it strikes an underwater object 4.67 seconds later. How far is the underwater object from the boat? The speed of sound in the seawater is 1533 m/s.

Chapter 30   Lenses

Summary

THE BIG IDEA : Lenses change the path of light.

30.1 Converging and Diverging Lenses

☑ **A lens forms an image by bending parallel rays of light that pass through it.**

- A **lens** is a piece of glass or plastic that refracts light.
- A **converging lens,** also known as a **convex lens,** is thicker in the middle, causing rays of light that are initially parallel (straight wave fronts) to meet at a single point.
- A **diverging lens,** also known as a **concave lens,** is thinner in the middle, causing rays of light to appear to originate from a single point.
- The **principal axis** of a lens is a line joining the centers of curvature of its surfaces.
- For a converging lens, the **focal point** is the point at which a beam of light parallel to the principal axis converges.
- The **focal plane** is a plane perpendicular to the principal axis that passes through either focal point of a lens. When the lens of a camera is set for distant objects, the film (or electronic sensor) is in the focal plane behind the lens in the camera.
- The **focal length** of a lens, whether converging or diverging, is the distance between the center of the lens and its focal point.

30.2 Image Formation by a Lens

☑ **The type of image formed by a lens depends on the shape of the lens and the position of the object.**

- A magnifying glass is simply a converging lens that increases the angle of view and allows more detail to be seen.
- A converging lens will magnify only when the object is between the focal point and the lens. The magnified image will be farther from the lens than the object and right-side up (erect). The image is virtual.
- When the object is far enough away to be beyond the focal point of a converging lens, light originating from the object and passing through the lens converges and can be focused on a screen. An image formed by converging light is called a **real image.**
- A real image formed by converging light is upside down (inverted).
- When a diverging lens is used alone, the image is always virtual, right-side up, and smaller than the object.

Chapter 30   Lenses

30.3 Constructing Images Through Ray Diagrams

✓ The size and location of the object, its distance from the center of the lens, and the focal length of the lens are used to construct a ray diagram.

- **Ray diagrams** show the principle rays that can be used to determine the size and location of an image.

- An arrow is used to represent the object; for simplicity, one end of the object is placed on the principal axis. To locate the position of the image, you only need to know the paths of two rays from a point on the object.

- There are three rays useful for the construction of a ray diagram:

  1. A ray parallel to the principal axis that passes through the focal point on the opposite side.

  2. A ray passing through the center of the lens that is undeflected.

  3. A ray through the focal point in front of the lens that emerges parallel to the principal axis after refraction by the lens.

- In a ray diagram that shows an image formed by a converging lens, all the images that are formed are real and inverted.

- The method of drawing ray diagrams applies also to diverging lenses. The image formed by a diverging lens is always virtual, reduced, and right-side up.

30.4 Image Formation Summarized

✓ A converging lens forms either a real image or a virtual image. A diverging lens always forms a virtual image.

- A converging lens is a simple magnifying glass when the object is within one focal length of the lens. The image is then virtual, magnified, and right-side up.

- When the object is beyond one focal length, a converging lens produces a real, inverted image.

- When an object is viewed with a diverging lens, the image is virtual, reduced, and right-side up.

30.5 Some Common Optical Instruments

✓ Optical instruments that use lenses include the camera, the telescope (and binoculars), and the compound microscope.

- A camera consists of a lens and sensitive film (or light-detecting chip) mounted in a lighttight box. The lens in a camera forms a real, inverted image on the film or chip.

- A simple telescope uses a lens to form a real image of a distant object. A second lens called the **eyepiece** is positioned so that the image produced by the first lens is within one focal length of the eyepiece. The eyepiece forms an enlarged virtual image of the real image.

Chapter 30   Lenses

- A third lens or a pair of reflecting prisms is used in the terrestrial telescope, which produces an image that is right-side up. A pair of terrestrial telescopes, side by side, makes up a pair of *binoculars.*
- A compound microscope uses two converging lenses of short focal length. The first lens in a microscope, called the **objective lens,** produces a real image of a close object. A second lens in a microscope, the eyepiece, forms a virtual image of the first image, further enlarged.

30.6 The Eye

✓ **The main parts of the eye are the cornea, the iris, the pupil, and the retina.**

- Light enters the eye through the transparent covering called the **cornea.**
- The amount of light that enters is regulated by the **iris,** the colored part of the eye that surrounds the pupil.
- The **pupil** is the opening of the eyeball through which light passes.
- Light passes through the pupil and lens and is focused on a layer of tissue at the back of the eye—the **retina**—that is extremely sensitive to light.
- The *fovea* is a small region in the center of our field of view where we have the most distinct vision.
- The *blind spot* is the spot in the retina where the nerves carrying all the information leave the eye in a narrow bundle.
- Adjustments in focusing of the image on the retina are made by changing the thickness and shape of the lens to regulate its focal length.

30.7 Some Defects in Vision

✓ **Three common vision problems are farsightedness, nearsightedness, and astigmatism.**

- A **farsighted person** has trouble focusing on nearby objects because the eyeball is too short and images form behind the retina. The remedy for farsightedness is to increase the converging effect of the eye by wearing eyeglasses or contact lenses with converging lenses.
- A **nearsighted person** can see nearby objects clearly, but does not see distant objects clearly because they are focused too near the lens, in front of the retina. A remedy for nearsightedness is to wear corrective lenses that diverge the rays from distant objects so that they focus on the retina instead of in front of it.
- **Astigmatism** of the eye is a defect that results when the cornea is curved more in one direction than the other, somewhat like the side of a barrel. The remedy for astigmatism is cylindrical corrective lenses that have more curvature in one direction than in another.

Chapter 30   Lenses

30.8 Some Defects of Lenses

☑ **Two types of aberration are spherical aberration and chromatic aberration.**

- The distortions in an image are called **aberrations**.

- *Spherical aberration* results when light passes through the edges of a lens and focuses at a slightly different place from light passing through the center of the lens.

- *Chromatic aberration* is the result of the different speeds of light of various colors and hence the different refractions they undergo.

- In the eye, vision is sharpest when the pupil is smallest because light then passes through only the center of the eye's lens, where spherical and chromatic aberrations are minimal.

Chapter 30 Lenses

Exercises

30.1 Converging and Diverging Lenses (pages 603–604)

1. A(n) _____ is a piece of glass or plastic that refracts light.

2. Describe how a lens is able to form images.

   _____

   _____

3. Is the following sentence true or false? A converging lens is also known as a concave lens. _____

4. A converging lens is _____ in the middle.

5. A(n) _____ lens causes rays of light that are initially parallel to meet at a single point.

6. A diverging lens is also known as a(n) _____ lens.

Use the illustration below to answer Questions 7 and 8.

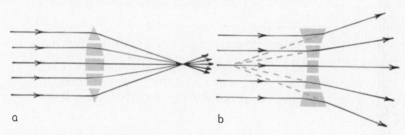

a   b

7. The lens on the left is a(n) _____ lens.

8. Is the following sentence true or false? The lens on the right causes rays to appear as if they come from a single point. _____

Match each term to its definition.

Term	Definition
_____ 9. principal axis	a. line joining the centers of curvature of a lens
_____ 10. focal point	b. distance between the center of the lens and its focal point
_____ 11. focal plane	c. plane perpendicular to the principal axis that passes through either focal point
_____ 12. focal length	d. location where a beam of light parallel to the principal axis converges

13. Is the following sentence true or false? A lens has two focal points and two focal planes. _____

Chapter 30   Lenses

30.2 Image Formation by a Lens (pages 604–606)

14. Is the following sentence true or false? When you are closer to an object, you view it through a smaller angle of view. _____

15. Explain how the angle of view of a lens is related to magnification.

_____

_____

16. Circle the letter of each factor that affects the type of image formed.

a. shape of lens   b. type of object observed

c. position of lens   d. how object is illuminated

17. A converging lens only forms magnified images when the object is located between the _____ and the _____.

18. A small handheld magnifying lens is used to view an insect. Explain what will be seen if a white screen is placed at the location of the enlarged focused image of the insect.

_____

_____

19. Is the following sentence true or false? A converging lens cannot form an image that can be projected onto a wall. _____

20. Circle the letter of each characteristic that describes the image formed when light originating from an object that is far from a converging lens passes through the lens.

a. virtual

b. formed by converging light rays

c. upside down

d. can be projected on a wall

21. Circle the letter of each characteristic that describes the image formed by a diverging lens.

a. virtual

b. smaller than object

c. upside down

d. formed by converging light rays

22. Is the following sentence true or false? A diverging lens forms images only when the object is located between the lens and the focal point.

_____

23. Why are diverging lenses often used in the viewfinder of cameras?

_____

_____

30.3 Constructing Images Through Ray Diagrams
(pages 606–609)

24. What is a ray diagram?

_____

Chapter 30   Lenses

Use the illustration below to answer Questions 25–28. The illustration shows several rays from an object passing through a convex lens.

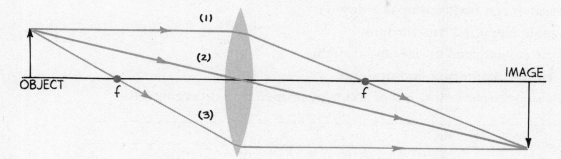

25. Circle the letter of the ray that travels parallel to the principal axis and is then refracted by the lens through the focal point.

   a. ray (1)   b. ray (2)

   c. ray (3)   d. ray (1) and ray (3)

26. Circle the letter of the ray that passes through the focal point and is then refracted parallel to the principal axis.

   a. ray (1)   b. ray (2)

   c. ray (3)   d. ray (1) and ray (3)

27. Circle the letter of the ray that is not refracted in any significant way.

   a. ray (1)   b. ray (2)

   c. ray (3)   d. ray (1) and ray (3)

28. Circle the letter of each statement about the image formed that is true.

   a. The image is upside down.

   b. The image is virtual.

   c. The image is real.

   d. The image is formed by converging rays.

29. Is the following sentence true or false? Ray diagrams cannot be drawn for diverging lenses because the lenses cause light rays to spread apart.

   _____

30. Is the following sentence true or false? Ray diagrams can be used to determine the size and location of real and virtual images. _____

30.4 Image Formation Summarized (page 610)

31. Identify each type of lens capable of forming a real image.

   _____

32. Identify each type of lens capable of forming a virtual image.

   _____

Chapter 30   Lenses

33. Circle the letter that describes the image formed when a converging lens is used as a magnifying glass.

    a. real, magnified, and upside down

    b. real, magnified, and upright

    c. virtual, reduced in size, and upright

    d. virtual, magnified, and upright

34. Describe the characteristics of an image formed by a diverging lens.

    _____

    _____

35. Circle the letter of the required location of an object in front of a diverging lens such that the lens forms a virtual image.

    a. less than f b. at f

    c. beyond f d. anywhere

30.5 Some Common Optical Instruments (pages 610–612)

36. Circle the letter of each optical instrument that uses lenses.

    a. camera   b. binoculars

    c. microscope   d. telescope

37. Is the following sentence true or false? A camera's diaphragm controls the size of the opening the light passes through. _____

38. Describe the function of the eyepiece lens in a telescope.

    _____

    _____

39. Is the following sentence true or false? When looking through a telescope, you see an image of an image. _____

40. Circle the letter of the optical instrument most closely related to binoculars.

    a. camera   b. terrestrial telescope

    c. microscope   d. astronomical telescope

41. Circle the letter that best describes a compound microscope.

    a. uses lenses to form enlarged images

    b. uses two converging lenses to form magnified images of faraway objects

    c. uses two converging lenses to form magnified images of close objects

    d. uses diverging lenses to create enlarged virtual images

42. Describe the function of the objective lens in a compound microscope.

    _____

Chapter 30   Lenses

30.6 The Eye (pages 612–613)

Match each term to its definition.

Term	Definition
_____ 43. cornea	a. light-sensitive layer
_____ 44. iris	b. regulates the amount of light entering the eye
_____ 45. pupil	
_____ 46. retina	c. region of retina with no vision
_____ 47. fovea	d. transparent covering of the eye
_____ 48. blind spot	e. region of retina with clearest vision
	f. the opening in the eyeball through which light passes

49. Describe how the eye changes its focus.

_____

_____

30.7 Some Defects in Vision (pages 614–615)

50. Circle the letter of the reason a farsighted person has trouble focusing on nearby objects.

   a. images form in front of retina   b. no images form

   c. iris opening too small   d. eyeball too short

51. A _____ person does not see distant objects clearly.

52. Is the following sentence true or false? Images formed by someone who is nearsighted form in front of the retina. _____

53. Describe the shape of the cornea that results in astigmatism.

_____

Match each vision defect to its corrective remedy.

Defect	Remedy
_____ 54. nearsightedness	a. converging lenses
_____ 55. farsightedness	b. lenses with uneven curvature
_____ 56. astigmatism	c. diverging lenses

30.8 Some Defects of Lenses (pages 615–616)

57. What is an aberration?

_____

58. _____ aberration occurs when light passing through the edges of a lens does not focus in the same location as light that passes through the center of the lens.

59. _____ aberration is caused by light of different colors traveling at different speeds.

Chapter 30   Lenses

Percent Transmission of Light

No glass lens is perfectly transparent, that is, the lens does not transmit 100% of the light that strikes it through the lens. Consider the two lenses in a telescope, the objective lens and the eyepiece lens. If the objective lens transmits 96% of the light, and the eyepiece lens transmits 97%, what percent of light from a distant source reaches your eye?

1. Read and Understand

What information are you given?
   Transmission of objective lens = 96%
   Transmission of eyepiece lens = 97%

2. Plan and Solve

What unknown are you trying to calculate?
   Percent of light transmitted through two-lens system = ?

What formula contains the given quantity and the unknown?
   Transmitted light = Incident light × Percent transmission

Substitute the known values and solve.

   For light passing through two lenses, multiply the incident light by the percent transmission of each lens. Assume the amount of incident is unity, or 1.

   Transmitted light = Incident light × Percent transmission$_{objective}$ × Percent transmission$_{eyepiece}$

   Transmitted light = $1 \times 0.96 \times 0.97$

   Transmitted light = 0.93 or 93% of the light passes through the two-lens system

3. Look Back and Check

Is your answer reasonable?
   Yes, it makes sense that the amount of light that passes through is less than the percent transmission value for each lens.

Math Practice

On a separate sheet of paper, solve the following problems.

1. The diaphragm of a digital camera limits the lens opening to allow only 50% of the incident light to enter the lens. If the percent transmission of the multi-lens optical system used in the camera is 88%, what percent of the total incident light makes its way to the electronic sensor?

2. Light passing through one side of a binocular passes through an objective lens, two prisms, and an eyepiece lens. The objective lens, prism 1, prism 2, and eyepiece lens have percent transmission of 98%, 95%, 95%, and 94%, respectively. What percent of the light from an object makes it to your eyes?

Chapter 31   Diffraction and Interference

Summary

THE BIG IDEA : The wave model of light explains diffraction and interference.

31.1 Huygens' Principle

☑ Huygens stated that light waves spreading out from a point source may be regarded as the overlapping of tiny secondary wavelets, and that every point on any wave front may be regarded as a new point source of secondary waves.

- The idea that wave fronts are made up of tinier wave fronts is called **Huygens' principle.**

- Each point along a wave front is the source of a new wavelet that spreads out in a sphere from that point.

- Huygens' principle can be observed in water waves that are made to pass through a narrow opening.

31.2 Diffraction

☑ The extent of diffraction depends on the relative size of the wavelength compared with the size of the obstruction that casts the shadow.

- Any bending of a wave by means other than reflection or refraction is called **diffraction.**

- If waves pass through an opening that is large compared with the wavelength of light, the spreading effect is small. As the opening becomes smaller, the diffraction of waves becomes more pronounced.

- When light is of a single color, diffraction can produce sharp *diffraction fringes* at the edge of the shadow. In white light, the fringes merge together to create a fuzzy blur at the edge of a shadow.

- When the wavelength is long compared with an obstruction that casts a shadow, the wave diffracts more. Short wavelengths don't diffract as much.

31.3 Interference

☑ Within an interference pattern, wave amplitudes may be increased, decreased, or neutralized.

- If you drop a couple of stones into water at the same time, the two sets of waves that result cross each other and produce what is called an *interference pattern.*

- When the crest of one wave overlaps the crest of another, their individual effects add together; this is *constructive interference.*

- When the crest of one wave overlaps the trough of another, their individual effects are reduced; this is *destructive interference.*

Chapter 31   Diffraction and Interference

31.4 Young's Interference Experiment

✅ **Young's interference experiment convincingly demonstrated the wave nature of light originally proposed by Huygens.**

- In 1801 the British physicist and physician Thomas Young discovered that when **monochromatic** light—light from a single color—was directed through two closely spaced pinholes, fringes of brightness and darkness were produced on a screen behind.

- A multitude of closely spaced parallel slits makes up what is called a **diffraction grating.**

- Many spectrometers use diffraction gratings rather than prisms to disperse light into colors. Whereas a prism separates the colors of light by refraction, a diffraction grating separates colors by interference.

31.5 Interference From Thin Films

✅ **The colors seen in thin films are produced by the interference in the films of light waves of mixed frequencies.**

- The phenomenon in which the interference of light waves of mixed frequencies produces a spectrum of colors is known as **iridescence.**

- A thin film, such as a soap bubble, has two closely spaced surfaces. Light that reflects from one surface may cancel light that reflects from the other surface.

- Interference provides the principal method for measuring the wavelengths of visible light as well as the wavelengths of light in other regions of the electromagnetic spectrum.

31.6 Laser Light

✅ **Laser light is emitted when excited atoms of a solid, liquid, or gas emit photons.**

- Light emitted by a common lamp is incoherent. In **incoherent** light, the crests and troughs of the light waves don't line up with one another (and there are many different frequencies as well).

- A beam of light that has the same frequency, phase, and direction is said to be **coherent.**

- Coherent light is produced by a **laser** (whose name comes from *light amplification by stimulated emission of radiation*). A laser is not a source of energy. It is simply a converter of energy. Lasers come in many types and have many different uses.

31.7 The Hologram

✅ **A hologram is produced by the interference between two laser light beams on photographic film.**

- A **hologram** is a three-dimensional version of a photograph that contains the whole message or entire picture in every portion of its surface.

- To the naked eye, it appears to be an imageless piece of transparent film, but on its surface is a pattern of microscopic interference fringes.

Chapter 31   Diffraction and Interference

Exercises

31.1 Huygens' Principle (pages 623–624)

1. What does Huygens' principle state?

   _____

   _____

   _____

2. Describe what the dots on spherical wave front AA' represent in the illustration below.

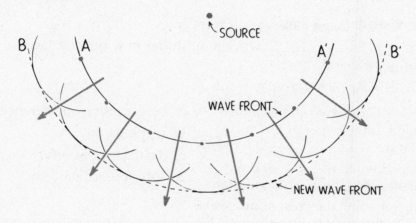

   _____

   _____

   _____

3. Is the following sentence true or false? When water waves are forced through a narrow opening, the wave fronts spread out into the "shadow region" in accord with Huygens' principle. _____

31.2 Diffraction (pages 625–627)

4. Any bending of a wave by means other than reflection or refraction is called _____.

5. What happens when light passes through a narrow slit?

   _____

   _____

6. Explain why many areas have poor FM radio reception, but good AM reception.

   _____

   _____

   _____

7. Is the following sentence true or false? If the size of an object viewed in a microscope is the same as the wavelength of light, the image of the object will be blurred by diffraction. _____

Chapter 31   Diffraction and Interference

8. Circle the letter of each statement that is true.

   a. When light is of a single color, diffraction can produce sharp diffraction fringes at the edge of the shadow.

   b. In white light, the fringes merge together to create a fuzzy blur at the edge of a shadow.

   c. The extent of diffraction does not depend on the relative size of the wavelength compared with the size of the obstruction that casts the shadow.

   d. When the wavelength is long compared with the obstruction, the wave diffracts less.

31.3 Interference (page 628)

9. Within a(n) _____, wave amplitudes may be increased, decreased, or neutralized.

Match each phrase with the correct word or words.

_____ 10. produced when two stones are dropped in the water at the same time

_____ 11. produced when the crest of one wave overlaps the crest of another

_____ 12. produced when the crest of one wave overlaps the trough of another

_____ 13. used to produce water waves under carefully controlled conditions

a. constructive interference

b. ripple tank

c. destructive interference

d. interference pattern

14. The number of regions of destructive interference in an interference pattern depends on the wavelength of the waves and _____

_____.

31.4 Young's Interference Experiment (pages 629–630)

15. What is monochromatic light? _____

16. What did Thomas Young discover in 1801?

_____

_____

17. Young realized that the bright fringes of light resulted from _____ and that the dark areas resulted from _____.

Chapter 31   Diffraction and Interference

18. A multitude of closely spaced parallel slits make up what is called a(n) _____.

19. A prism separates colors of light by _____; a diffraction grating separates colors by _____.

31.5 Interference From Thin Films (pages 631–632)

20. How are the colors seen in thin films produced?

_____

_____

21. When gasoline drips on a wet street, you can see a beautiful spectrum of colors. Circle the letter of the word that describes this phenomenon.

   a. reflection

   b. iridescence

   c. incoherence

   d. refraction

22. Is the following sentence true or false? In a soap bubble, light that reflects from one surface may cancel light that reflects from the other surface. _____

23. Extremely small distances (millionths of a centimeter) are measured with instruments called _____.

31.6 Laser Light (pages 633–634)

24. Is the following sentence true or false? Light emitted by a common lamp is coherent. _____

25. What is incoherent light?

_____

_____

26. _____ within a beam of incoherent light is rampant, and a beam spreads out after a short distance, becoming wider and wider and less intense with increased distance.

27. What type of light is illustrated in the drawing below?

_____

Chapter 31 Diffraction and Interference

28. Coherent light is many different rays of light that all have the same _____. Circle the correct answer(s).

   a. frequency

   b. phase

   c. wavelength

   d. direction

29. Is the following sentence true or false? Only a beam of coherent light will not spread and diffuse. _____

30. What do the letters in *laser* stand for?

   _____

31. When is laser light emitted?

   _____

32. What are two applications for lasers?

   _____

   _____

31.7 The Hologram (pages 635–636)

33. What is a hologram?

   _____

   _____

34. Why are holograms used on credit cards?

   _____

   _____

35. How is a hologram produced?

   _____

   _____

36. Is the following statement true or false? If a hologram is made on film, you can cut it in half and see the entire image on each half. _____

37. Is a hologram made with X-rays smaller or larger than a hologram made with visible light? _____

Chapter 32   Electrostatics

Summary

THE BIG IDEA : Electrostatics involves electric charges, the forces between them, and their behavior in materials.

32.1 Electrical Forces and Charges

☑ The fundamental rule at the base of all electrical phenomena is that like charges repel and opposite charges attract.

- **Electrostatics** is electricity at rest.
- **Electrical forces** arise from particles in atoms.
- In the simple model of the atom, protons in the nucleus attract the electrons and hold them in orbit. Electrons are attracted to protons, but electrons repel other electrons.
- The fundamental electrical property to which the mutual attractions or repulsions between electrons or protons is attributed is called **charge.**
- By convention, electrons are *negatively* charged and protons *positively* charged. Neutrons have no charge and are neither attracted nor repelled by charged particles.

32.2 Conservation of Charge

☑ An object that has unequal numbers of electrons and protons is electrically charged.

- An atom with a net positive charge is a *positive ion*; it has lost one or more electrons. An atom with a net negative charge is a *negative ion*; it has gained one or more electrons.
- The principle that electrons are neither created nor destroyed but are simply transferred from one material to another is known as **conservation of charge.**

32.3 Coulomb's Law

☑ Coulomb's law states that for charged particles or objects that are small compared with the distance between them, the force between the charges varies directly as the product of the charges and inversely as the square of the distance between them.

- The relationship among electrical force, charges, and distance is **Coulomb's law.** Coulomb's law can be expressed as $F = kq_1q_2/d^2$, where d is the distance between the charged particles; q_1 represents the quantity of charge of one particle and q_2 the quantity of charge of the other particle; and k is the proportionality constant.
- The SI unit of charge is the **coulomb,** abbreviated C.
- The proportionality constant k in Coulomb's law is 9.0×10^9 N·m^2/C^2.
- Because most objects have almost exactly equal numbers of electrons and protons, electrical forces usually balance out.

Chapter 32   Electrostatics

32.4 Conductors and Insulators

✔ **Electrons move easily in good conductors and poorly in good insulators.**

- Materials through which electric charge can flow are called **conductors.**

- Metals are good conductors because their outer electrons are "loose."

- Electrons in other materials—rubber and glass, for example—are tightly bound and remain with particular atoms. These materials, known as **insulators,** are poor conductors of electricity.

- **Semiconductors** are materials that can be made to behave sometimes as insulators and sometimes as conductors. Atoms in a semiconductor hold their electrons until given small energy boosts.

32.5 Charging by Friction and Contact

✔ **Two ways electric charge can be transferred are by friction and by contact.**

- Electrons are transferred by friction when one material rubs against another.

- *Charging by contact* occurs when electrons are transferred from one material to another by simply touching. If the object is a good conductor, the charge will spread to all parts of its surface. If it is a poor conductor, the extra charge will stay close to where the object was touched.

32.6 Charging by Induction

✔ **If a charged object is brought *near* a conducting surface, even without physical contact, electrons will move in the conducting surface.**

- Electric charge on a conducting object can be redistributed, or **induced,** by the presence of a charged object nearby.

- **Induction** is the charging of an object without direct contact.

- When we allow charges to move off (or onto) a conductor by touching it, it is common to say that we are **grounding** it.

- Charging by induction occurs during thunderstorms. The negatively charged bottoms of clouds induce a positive charge on the surface of Earth below.

32.7 Charge Polarization

✔ **Charge polarization can occur in insulators that are *near* a charged object.**

- When one side of an atom or molecule is induced to be slightly more positive (or negative) than the other side, the atom or molecule is said to be **electrically polarized.**

- A molecule with a little more negative charge on one side than the other is an *electric dipole.*

Chapter 32 Electrostatics

Exercises

32.1 Electrical Forces and Charges (pages 645–646)

1. Circle the letter beside the correct comparison of the strengths of the gravitational force and the electrical force.

   a. The gravitational force is slightly stronger than the electrical force.

   b. The electrical force is slightly stronger than the gravitational force.

   c. The gravitational force is much stronger than the electrical force.

   d. The electrical force is much stronger than the gravitational force.

2. Why don't you feel the electrical forces that act on you all the time?

   _____

   _____

   _____

3. Describe the simple model of the atom proposed in the early 1900s by Rutherford and Bohr.

   _____

   _____

4. _____ is the fundamental electrical property to which the mutual attractions or repulsions between electrons or protons is attributed.

5. By convention, what is the charge of the following?

   a. electrons _____

   b. protons _____

   c. neutrons _____

6. Is the following sentence true or false? The mass of a proton is 2000 times greater than the mass of an electron. _____

7. Circle the letter beside the correct comparison of the *magnitudes* of the charges of a proton and an electron.

   a. The magnitude of the proton's charge is slightly greater.

   b. The magnitude of the electron's charge is slightly greater.

   c. The magnitudes of a proton's charge and an electron's charge are always equal, but they vary for different atoms.

   d. The magnitudes of a proton's charge and an electron's charge are always equal and never change.

8. Like charges _____ and opposite charges _____.

Chapter 32   Electrostatics

32.2 Conservation of Charge (pages 646–647)

9. Explain why there is no net charge in a neutral atom.

_____

_____

10. A charged atom is called a(n) _____.

11. The _____ of many atoms are bound very loosely to an atom and can be easily dislodged. Circle the correct answer.

  a. outermost electrons

  b. innermost electrons

  c. outermost protons

  d. innermost protons

12. If a rubber rod is rubbed by a piece of fur, the rubber becomes _____ charged and the fur becomes _____ charged.

13. What is the principle of conservation of charge?

_____

_____

_____

32.3 Coulomb's Law (pages 648–650)

14. What does Coulomb's law state?

_____

_____

_____

_____

Match each variable or constant in Newton's law of gravitation with its analogous variable or constant in Coulomb's law.

_____ 15. m_1 a. d

_____ 16. m_2 b. k

_____ 17. d c. q_1

_____ 18. G d. q_2

19. The SI unit of charge is the _____.

20. How many electrons are contained in 1 C of charge?

_____

21. Is the following sentence true or false? The electrical force between two protons is very small compared to the gravitational force. _____

Chapter 32   Electrostatics

32.4 Conductors and Insulators (pages 651–652)

22. A material through which electric charge can flow is a(n)
_____.

23. A material that is a poor conductor of electricity is a(n)
_____.

24. Define semiconductor.

_____

_____

_____

25. Classify the following by writing *C* beside each conductor, *I* beside each
insulator, and *S* beside each semiconductor.

_____ a. aluminum   _____ d. glass

_____ b. copper   _____ e. rubber

_____ c. germanium   _____ f. silicon

26. What effect will adding an impurity level of one atom in ten million to a
crystal of semiconductor have?

_____

_____

27. Is the following sentence true or false? Atoms in a semiconductor hold
their electrons until the atoms of the semiconductor are given small
energy boosts. _____

28. Thin layers of semiconducting materials sandwiched together make
up _____, which are used in a variety of electrical
applications.

32.5 Charging by Friction and Contact (page 652)

29. Classify each of the following by writing *F* if it is an example of charging
an object by friction and *C* if it is an example of charging an object by
contact.

_____ a. sliding across the seat of an automobile

_____ b. scuffing your shoes as you walk across a rug

_____ c. touching a charged rod to a metal sphere

_____ d. combing your hair with a plastic comb

_____ e. touching your hand to a slightly charged metal plate

30. One object charges a second object by contact. Describe what will
happen to the charge on the second object in each of the cases below.

a. The second object is a good conductor.

_____

_____

b. The second object is a poor conductor.

_____

_____

Chapter 32   Electrostatics

32.6 Charging by Induction (pages 653–654)

Use the figure below to answer Questions 31–33.

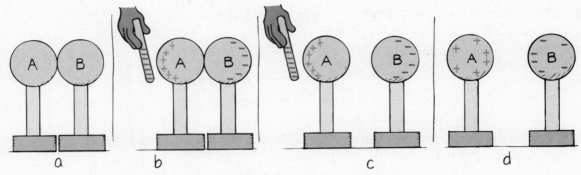

31. Why do the positive and negative charges separate in part (b)?

_____

_____

_____

32. Why do the positive and negative charges spread out on each on the spheres in part (d)?

_____

_____

33. Why is the process illustrated in the figure an example of charging by induction?

_____

_____

_____

34. The _____ is a practically infinite reservoir for electric charge.

35. Circle each letter next to a discovery made by Benjamin Franklin.

   a. electricity   b. Lightning is an electrical phenomenon.

   c. lightning rods   d. Electricity can travel along metal wires.

36. Describe what causes lightning to occur during thunderstorms.

_____

_____

_____

37. Is the following sentence true or false? A lightning rod placed above a building repels electrons in the air to prevent leaking of the charge onto the ground. _____

Chapter 32   Electrostatics

32.7 Charge Polarization (pages 655–657)

38. Describe an electrically polarized atom or molecule.

_____

_____

_____

39. Why can an insulator become polarized when you bring a conducting rod near it?

_____

_____

40. Circle the letter beside the sentence that explains why a charged comb attracts an uncharged piece of paper.

   a. The forces of attraction and repulsion on opposite sides of the paper cancel.

   b. The forces of attraction and repulsion on the paper disappear with the comb nearby.

   c. The force of attraction for the closer charge is greater than the force of repulsion for the farther charge.

   d. The force of repulsion for the closer charge is greater than the force of attraction for the farther charge.

41. Explain why the bits of paper sometimes suddenly fly off when a comb attracts bits of uncharged paper.

_____

_____

_____

42. When you rub an inflated balloon on your hair and it becomes negatively charged, the charge on the balloon induces a _____ charge on the surface of the wall.

43. Why is the water molecule shown in the figure above an electric dipole?

_____

44. What are the three ways objects can become electrically charged?

   a. _____

   b. _____

   c. _____

Chapter 32 Electrostatics

Coulomb's Law

Consider a pair of charged particles separated by a distance *d*. If the distance between the particles is multiplied by 4, how will the electrostatic force between the particles change?

1. Read and Understand

What information are you given?

Two charged particles, q_1 and q_2, are a distance *d* apart.

An electrostatic force, *F*, exists between the particles.

The final distance equals 4*d*.

2. Plan and Solve

What unknown are you trying to calculate?

Electrostatic force after the distance changes, $F_{new} = ?$

What mathematical relationship can you use to find the unknown?

Coulomb's law: $F = k\dfrac{q_1 q_2}{d^2}$

Apply this law to find the new force after the distance changes.

$$F_{new} = k\frac{q_1 q_2}{(4d)^2} = k\frac{q_1 q_2}{16d^2} = \left(\frac{1}{16}\right)F$$

3. Look Back and Check

Is your answer reasonable?

Yes, the distance increased by a factor of 4, so the force should decrease by a factor of 4 squared, or 16.

Math Practice

On a separate sheet of paper, solve the following problems. Consider a pair of particles separated by a distance d.

1. If the charge of each particle tripled and the distance also tripled, how would the electrostatic force between the particles change?

2. If the charge of one particle doubled and the charge of the other particle tripled, how would the electrostatic force between the particles change?

3. If the charge of one particle were reduced to one-half the original charge and the distance between the charges were multiplied by 2, how would the electrostatic force between the particles change?

Chapter 33   Electric Fields and Potential

Summary

THE BIG IDEA : An electric field is a storehouse of energy.

33.1 Electric Fields

☑ The magnitude (strength) of an electric field can be measured by its effect on charges located in the field. The direction of an electric field at any point, by convention, is the direction of the electrical force on a small *positive* test charge placed at that point.

- An **electric field** is a force field that surrounds an electric charge or group of charges.

- An electric field has both magnitude and direction.

- Consider a small positive "test charge" that is placed in an electric field. Where the force is greatest on the test charge, the field is strongest. Where the force on the test charge is weak, the field is small.

- If a test charge q experiences a force F at some point in space, then the electric field E at that point is $E = \dfrac{F}{q}$.

- If the charge that sets up an electric field is positive, the field points away from that charge. If the charge that sets up the field is negative, the field points toward that charge.

33.2 Electric Field Lines

☑ You can use the electric field lines (also called lines of force) to represent an electric field. Where the lines are farther apart, the field is weaker.

- Since an electric field has both magnitude and direction, it is a vector quantity and can be represented by vectors.

- In a vector representation of an electric field, the length of the vectors indicates the magnitude of the field. In a lines-of-force representation, the distance between field lines indicates magnitudes.

33.3 Electric Shielding

☑ If the charge on a conductor is not moving, the electric field inside the conductor is exactly zero.

- The absence of electric field within a conductor holding static charge does not arise from the inability of an electric field to penetrate metals. It comes about because free electrons within the conductor can "settle down" and stop moving only when the electric field is zero.

- Consider a charged hollow metal sphere. Because of mutual repulsion, the electrons spread as far apart from one another as possible, distributing themselves uniformly over the surface of the sphere. The forces on a test charge located inside a charged hollow sphere cancel to zero.

- If a conductor is not spherical, then the charge distribution will not be uniform. The exact charge distribution over the surface is such that the electric field everywhere inside the conductor is zero.

33.4 Electrical Potential Energy

✔ **The electrical potential energy of a charged particle is increased when work is done to push it against the electric field or something else that is charged.**

- A charged object can have potential energy by virtue of its location in an electric field.

- Suppose you have a small positive charge located at some distance from a positively charged sphere. If you push the small charge closer to the sphere, you expend energy to overcome electrical repulsion. The work is equal to the energy gained by the charge.

- The energy a charge has due to its location in an electric field is called **electrical potential energy.**

33.5 Electric Potential

✔ **Electric potential is *not* the same as electrical potential energy. Electric potential is electrical potential energy per charge.**

- The concept of electrical potential energy per charge has a special name, **electric potential:** electric potential = electrical potential energy/charge.

- The SI unit of measurement for electric potential is the **volt.**

- Since potential energy is measured in joules and charge is measured in coulombs, 1 volt = 1 joule/coulomb.

- Since electric potential is measured in volts, it is commonly called **voltage.**

33.6 Electrical Energy Storage

✔ **The energy stored in a capacitor comes from the work done to charge it.**

- Electrical energy can be stored in a common device called a **capacitor.**

- The simplest capacitor is a pair of conducting plates separated by a small distance, but not touching each other. When the plates are connected to a charging device such as a battery, charge is transferred from one plate to the other. The greater the battery voltage and the larger and closer the plates, the greater the charge that is stored.

33.7 The Van de Graaff Generator

✔ **The voltage of a Van de Graaff generator can be increased by increasing the radius of the sphere or by placing the entire system in a container filled with high-pressure gas.**

- In a Van de Graaff generator, a moving rubber belt carries electrons from the voltage source to a conducting sphere.

- Van de Graaff generators in pressurized gas can produce voltages as high as 20 million volts. These devices accelerate charged particles used as projectiles for penetrating the nuclei of atoms.

Chapter 33   Electric Fields and Potential

Exercises

33.1 Electric Fields (pages 665–666)

1. What is an electric field?

   _____

   _____

2. Like a gravitational field, an electric field has both _____ and _____.

3. How can the magnitude of an electric field be measured?

   _____

   _____

4. Is the following statement true or false? The direction of an electric field at any point, by convention, is the direction of the electrical force on a small *negative* test charge, placed at that point. _____

5. Consider the electric field around a small positive charge. How can you describe the direction of the field?

   _____

   _____

   _____

33.2 Electric Field Lines (pages 666–667)

6. Since an electric field has both magnitude and direction, it is a

   _____.

7. Is the following sentence true or false? In a vector representation of an electric field, the magnitude of an electric field is indicated by the length of the vector arrows. _____

8. Electric fields can also be described by using field lines (or lines of force). In a field lines representation of an electric field, the field is weaker where the lines are _____.

Match the illustrations to the correct description.

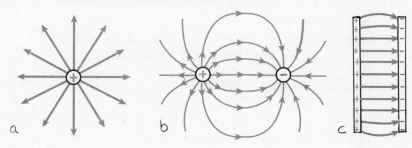

9. _____ The field lines emanate from the positive charge and terminate on the negative charge.

10. _____ Field lines are evenly spaced between two oppositely charged plates.

11. _____ The field lines extend to infinity.

Chapter 33   Electric Fields and Potential

33.3 Electric Shielding (pages 668–669)

12. If the charge on a conductor is not moving, the electric field inside the conductor is exactly _____.

13. Circle the letter of each statement that is true about charged conductors.

   a. The absence of an electric field within a conductor holding static charge arises from the inability of an electric field to penetrate metals.

   b. The absence of an electric field comes about because free electrons within the conductor stop moving when the electric field is zero.

   c. The charges arrange themselves to ensure a zero field within the material.

   d. If the conductor is not spherical, then the charge distribution will not be uniform.

14. Why are some electronic components and some cables encased in a metal covering?

   _____

   _____

   _____

33.4 Electrical Potential Energy (pages 669–670)

15. Is the following sentence true or false? A charged object has potential energy by virtue of its location in an electric field. _____

16. Circle the letter of each statement that is true.

   a. No work is required to push a charged particle against the electric field of a charged body.

   b. The electrical potential energy of a charged particle decreases when work is done to push it against the electric field of something else that is charged.

   c. The energy a charge has due to its location in an electric field is called electrical potential energy.

   d. If a charge with electrical potential energy is released, its electrical potential energy will transform into kinetic energy.

33.5 Electric Potential (pages 670–671)

17. What is electric potential?

   _____

   _____

   _____

18. Is the following sentence true or false? Electric potential is *not* the same as electrical potential energy. _____

19. The SI unit of measurement for electric potential is the _____.

Chapter 33   Electric Fields and Potential

20. Write an equation that expresses the relationship between volts, joules, and coulombs.

_____

21. What is voltage?

_____

_____

33.6 Electrical Energy Storage (pages 672–673)

22. What are two applications of capacitors?

_____

_____

23. The diagram shows a simple capacitor. Explain how the capacitor is charged.

_____

_____

_____

_____

_____

_____

24. A charged capacitor is discharged when a _____ is provided between the plates.

25. The energy stored in a capacitor comes from the _____ done to charge it.

33.7 The Van de Graaff Generator (pages 673–674)

26. Is the following sentence true or false? In a Van de Graaff generator, as electrons leak off the belt and onto the conducting sphere, the electric field inside the sphere steadily increases in magnitude.

_____

27. How can the voltage of a Van de Graaff generator be increased?

_____

_____

_____

_____

Chapter 33   Electric Fields and Potential

Electric Fields

A 2.5-µC charge in an electric field experiences a force of 3.0×10^{-4} N. What is the strength of the electric field at the location of the test charge?

1. Read and Understand

What information are you given?

test charge, $q = 2.5$ µC $= 2.5 \times 10^{-6}$ C

force on test charge, $F = 3.0 \times 10^{-4}$ N

2. Plan and Solve

What unknown are you trying to calculate?

electric field strength, $E = ?$

What equation can you use to calculate the unknown?

$$E = \frac{F}{q}$$

$$E = \frac{3.0 \times 10^{-4}\,\text{N}}{2.5 \times 10^{-6}\,\text{C}} = 1.2 \times 10^2\,\frac{\text{N}}{\text{C}}$$

3. Look Back and Check

Is your answer reasonable?

Yes, the units indicate a force (in newtons) per unit charge.

Math Practice

On a separate sheet of paper, solve the following problems.

1. An electric field exerts a force of 2.6×10^{-4} N on a test charge of 5.5×10^{-6} C. What is the strength of the electric field at the location of the test charge?

2. When placed near a second charge, a 60-µC charge experiences a force of 0.30 N. What is the electric field strength at the location of the 60-µC charge? What is the strength of the electric field at the location of the test charge?

3. A 10-µC charge is located in 400-N/C electric field. What is the force experienced by the charge?

Chapter 34 Electric Current

Summary

THE BIG IDEA Voltage is an "electric pressure" that can produce a flow of charge, or current, within a conductor.

34.1 Flow of Charge

✓ When the ends of an electric conductor are at different electric potentials, charge flows from one end to the other.

- Charge flows when there is a **potential difference**, or difference in potential (voltage), between the ends of a conductor.

- The flow of charge will continue until both ends reach a common potential. When there is no potential difference, there is no longer a flow of charge through the conductor.

- To attain a sustained flow of charge in a conductor, some arrangement must be provided to keep one end at a higher potential than the other.

34.2 Electric Current

✓ A current-carrying wire has a net electric charge of zero.

- **Electric current** is the flow of electric charge.

- In solid conductors, the electrons carry the charge through the circuit because they are free to move throughout the atomic network. These electrons are called *conduction electrons*.

- In fluids, such as the electrolyte in a car battery, positive and negative ions as well as electrons may compose the flow of electric charge.

- Electric current is measured in **amperes**, for which the SI unit is symbol A. An ampere is the flow of 1 coulomb of charge per second.

34.3 Voltage Sources

✓ Voltage sources such as batteries and generators supply energy that allows charges to move steadily.

- Something that provides a potential difference is known as a **voltage source**.

- The potential energy per coulomb of charge available to electrons moving between terminals is the voltage (sometimes called the *electromotive force*, or *emf*).

- Charges *flow* through a circuit because of an applied voltage *across* the circuit. Voltage doesn't go anywhere, for it is the charges that move. Voltage causes current.

Chapter 34   Electric Current

34.4 Electric Resistance

✓ **The resistance of a wire depends on the conductivity of the material used in the wire (that is, how well it conducts) and also on the thickness and length of the wire.**

- The amount of charge that flows in a circuit depends on the voltage provided by the voltage source. The current also depends on the resistance that the conductor offers to the flow of charge—**the electric resistance**.

- The resistance of some materials becomes zero at very low temperatures, a phenomenon known as **superconductivity**.

- Electric resistance is measured in units called **ohms**.

34.5 Ohm's Law

✓ **Ohm's law states that the current in a circuit is directly proportional to the voltage impressed across the circuit, and is inversely proportional to the resistance of the circuit.**

- The relationship among voltage, current, and resistance is called **Ohm's law**. In short, current = voltage/resistance.

- The relationship among the units of measurement for current, voltage, and resistance is: 1 ampere = 1 volt/ohm.

34.6 Ohm's Law and Electric Shock

✓ **The damaging effects of electric shock are the result of current passing through the body.**

- From Ohm's law, we can see that a damaging electric current depends on the voltage applied, and also on the electrical resistance of the human body.

- The resistance of the human body depends on its condition and ranges from about 100 ohms if it's soaked with salt water to about 500,000 ohms if the skin is very dry.

- Drops of water that collect around on/off switches of devices such as a hair dryer can conduct current to the user. Handling electric devices while taking a bath is extremely dangerous.

- If a bird is perched on a highline wire, the bird will not receive a shock unless there is a *difference* in potential between one part of its body and another part.

- Mild shocks occur when the surfaces of appliances are at an electrical potential different from that of the surfaces of other nearby devices.

34.7 Direct Current and Alternating Current

✓ **Electric current may be DC or AC.**

- **Direct current** is a flow of charge that *always flows in one direction*. Electrons always move through the circuit in the same direction, from the repelling negative terminal and toward the attracting positive terminal.

Chapter 34   Electric Current

- **Alternating current** (AC) is electric current that repeatedly reverses direction. Electrons in the circuit move first in one direction and then in the opposite direction, alternating back and forth about relatively fixed positions.

- Nearly all commercial AC circuits in North America involve voltages and currents that alternate back and forth at a frequency of 60 cycles per second. This is 60-hertz current.

- Voltage of AC in North America is normally 120 volts. Power transmission is more efficient at higher voltages, so Europe adopted 220 volts as its standard.

- The primary use of electric current, whether DC or AC, is to transfer energy quietly, flexibly, and conveniently from one place to another.

34.8 Converting AC to DC

✅ **With an AC-DC converter, you can operate a battery-run device on AC instead of batteries.**

- In addition to a transformer to lower the voltage, an AC-DC converter uses a **diode,** a tiny electronic device that acts as a one-way valve to allow electron flow in only one direction. Since alternating current vibrates in two directions, only half of each cycle will pass through a diode. The output is a rough DC, off half the time.

- To maintain continuous current while smoothing the rough DC, a capacitor is used.

34.9 The Speed of Electrons in a Circuit

✅ **In a current-carrying wire, collisions interrupt the motion of the electrons so that their actual *drift speed*, or *net speed* through the wire due to the field, is extremely low.**

- Energy is transported through the connecting wires at nearly the speed of light. The electrons that make up the current, however, do not move at this high speed.

- A pulsating electric field can travel through a circuit at nearly the speed of light. The electrons continue their random motions in all directions while simultaneously being nudged along the wire by the electric field. Conduction electrons are accelerated by an electric field.

- Before the electrons gain appreciable speed, they "bump into" the anchored metallic ions in their paths and transfer some of their kinetic energy to them. This is why current-carrying wires become hot.

- In an AC circuit, the conduction electrons don't make any net progress in any direction. They oscillate rhythmically to and fro about relatively fixed positions. When you talk to your friend on a conventional telephone, it is the *pattern* of oscillating motion that is carried across town at nearly the speed of light.

Chapter 34 Electric Current

34.10 The Source of Electrons in a Circuit

✓ **The source of electrons in a circuit is the conducting circuit material itself.**

- When you plug a lamp into an AC outlet, *energy* flows from the outlet into the lamp, not electrons. Energy is carried by the electric field and causes a vibratory motion of the electrons that already exist in the lamp filament.

- When you are jolted by an AC electric shock, the electrons making up the current in your body originate in your body. Electrons do not come out of the wire and through your body and into the ground; energy does.

34.11 Electric Power

✓ **Electric power is equal to the product of current and voltage.**

- **Electric power** is the rate at which electrical energy is converted into another form such as mechanical energy, heat, or light. In equation form, electric power = current × voltage.

- If the voltage is expressed in volts, and the current in amperes, then the power is expressed in watts: 1 watt = (1 ampere) × (1 volt).

- A *kilowatt-hour* represents the amount of energy consumed in 1 hour at the rate of 1 kilowatt, or 1000 watts.

Chapter 34   Electric Current

Exercises

34.1 Flow of Charge (page 681)

1. Charge flows when there is a _____ between the ends of a conductor.

2. Explain what would happen if a Van de Graaff generator charged to a high potential was connected to a ground wire.

   _____

   _____

3. Explain how the sustained flow of charge is analogous to the flow of water from a higher reservoir to a lower one, as shown in the illustration below.

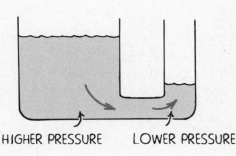

HIGHER PRESSURE   LOWER PRESSURE

a

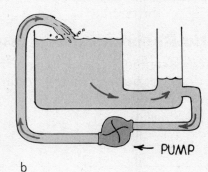

← PUMP

b

_____

_____

_____

_____

_____

_____

34.2 Electric Current (page 682)

Match each phrase with the correct term or terms. Terms may be used more than once.

Phrase	Terms
_____ 4. the flow of electric charge	a. ampere
_____ 5. particles within a solid conductor that carry charge through a circuit	b. zero
_____ 6. SI unit used to measure electric current	c. conduction electrons
_____ 7. equivalent to 1 coulomb of charge per second	d. electric current
_____ 8. the net charge in a current-carrying wire	

Chapter 34 Electric Current

34.3 Voltage Sources (page 683)

9. What is a voltage source? _____

_____

10. How do batteries and generators supply electrical energy?

_____

_____

_____

11. Is the following sentence true or false? The potential energy per coulomb of charge available to electrons moving between the terminals of a battery or generator is the voltage. _____

12. Charges flow _____ a circuit because of an applied voltage _____ the circuit.

34.4 Electric Resistance (page 684)

13. Is the following sentence true or false? The amount of charge that flows in a circuit does not depend on the voltage provided by the voltage source. _____

14. What is electric resistance?

_____

_____

15. Circle the letter of each statement that is true.

a. The resistance of a wire depends on the conductivity of the material used in the wire.

b. The resistance of a wire does not depend on the thickness of the wire.

c. Longer wires have less resistance than short wires.

d. Electric resistance depends on the temperature of the wire.

16. The resistance of some materials becomes zero at very low temperatures, a phenomenon known as _____.

17. Electric resistance is measured in units called _____.

34.5 Ohm's Law (page 685)

18. The relationship among current, voltage, and _____ is called Ohm's law.

19. State Ohm's law.

_____

_____

20. How can you express Ohm's law mathematically?

_____

_____

Chapter 34   Electric Current

21. What is the relationship among the units of measurement for the three quantities related by Ohm's law?

_____

22. What are resistors?

_____

34.6 Ohm's Law and Electric Shock (pages 686–688)

23. The damaging effects of electric shock are the result of _____ passing through the body.

24. Is the following sentence true or false? The resistance of your body is much greater when you're soaked with water than when your skin is dry. _____

25. Explain why it is dangerous to handle electric devices while taking a bath.

_____

_____

_____

_____

26. Is the following sentence true or false? A bird perched on a high-voltage wire is not shocked because there is not a potential difference between one part of its body and another part. _____

27. What is the purpose of the third prong on a three-prong electric plug?

_____

34.7 Direct Current and Alternating Current (pages 688–689)

28. Circle the letter of each statement that is true.

   a. Direct current refers to a charge that always flows in one direction.

   b. In a DC circuit, electrons always move from the positive terminal toward the negative terminal.

   c. A battery produces direct current.

   d. AC is current that repeatedly reverses direction.

29. Circle the letter of the correct answer. A 60-hertz current means that the current

   a. equals 60 amperes.

   b. alternates back and forth at 60 cycles per second.

   c. changes direction once every 60 seconds.

   d. travels at a speed of 60 meters per second.

30. Circle the letter of the correct answer. What is the standard voltage of AC in the United States?

   a. 9 V   b. 12 V

   c. 110–120 V   d. 220–240 V

Chapter 34 Electric Current

31. Will an appliance that operates on 220–240 volts work when plugged into a wall socket in the United States? Explain your answer.

_____

_____

_____

_____

_____

34.8 Converting AC to DC (page 690)

32. The current in laptops and cell phones is _____.

33. With an _____, you can operate a battery-run device on AC instead of batteries.

34. In addition to a transformer to lower the voltage, an AC-DC converter uses a _____, which acts as a one-way valve to allow electron flow in only one direction.

The diagrams below show the effect of an AC–DC converter on alternating current. Match the letter of each diagram to the correct description.

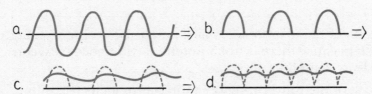

_____ **35.** Charging and discharging of a capacitor provides continuous but bumpy current.

_____ **36.** Only half of each cycle of AC passes through the diode, resulting in a pulsating DC.

_____ **37.** The input to the diode is AC.

_____ **38.** By using a pair of diodes, there are no gaps in the current output.

34.9 The Speed of Electrons in a Circuit (pages 691–692)

39. Circle the letter of each statement that is true.

    a. Energy is transported through connecting wires of a circuit at nearly the speed of light.

    b. The electrons that make up an electric current travel at the speed of light.

    c. The electric field inside a current-carrying wire has no effect on the motion of conduction electrons.

    d. The random thermal motion of the electrons inside a wire is what produces current.

40. Is the following statement true or false? A pulsating electric field can travel through a circuit at nearly the speed of light. _____

Chapter 34   Electric Current

41. Explain why current-carrying wires become hot.

_____

_____

_____

_____

42. In a current-carrying wire, collisions interrupt the motion of the electrons so that their actual _____, or net speed through the wire due to the field, is extremely low.

43. In an AC circuit, do the conduction electrons make any net progress in a single direction? Explain your answer.

_____

_____

34.10 The Source of Electrons in a Circuit (page 693)

44. The source of electrons in a circuit is the

_____.

45. When you plug a lamp into an AC outlet, _____ flows from the outlet into the lamp, not _____.

46. If 120 volts AC are impressed on a lamp, then an average of _____ joules of energy are dissipated by each coulomb of charge that is made to vibrate.

47. When you turn on an electric lamp, what two forms of energy are produced? _____

48. Explain what happens in your body when you are jolted by an AC electric shock.

_____

_____

_____

34.11 Electric Power (pages 693–694)

49. Define electric power.

_____

_____

50. Electric power = current × _____

51. Express the equation in Question 50 in terms of units.

_____

52. One kilowatt-hour is the amount of energy consumed in _____ hour at the rate of _____ watts.

53. If the power and voltage on a lightbulb read "60 W, 120 V," how much current will flow through the bulb?

_____

Chapter 34   Electric Current

Calculating Power

If four 1.5-V batteries deliver 1.25-A current to a small motor, what is the power provided to the motor?

1. Read and Understand

What information are you given?
   voltage = V = 4 × 1.5 V = 6.0 V

   current = I = 1.25 A

2. Plan and Solve

What unknown are you trying to calculate?
   power = P = ?

What mathematical expression can you use to calculate the unknown?
   $P = VI$

   P = (6.0 V)(1.25 A) = 7.5 W

3. Look Back and Check

Is your answer reasonable?
   Yes, the number calculated is a product of current and voltage and the units indicate power.

Math Practice

On a separate sheet of paper, solve the following problems.

1. An 8.0-V power supply delivers a 1.75-A current to a circuit. Calculate the power provided to the circuit.

2. How much power is used by a set of lights operating on a 12-V battery and 2.75 A?

3. A 15-W motor draws a current of 1.25 A. What is the voltage impressed across the circuit?

Chapter 35   Electric Circuits

Summary

THE BIG
IDEA : Any path along which electrons can flow is a circuit.

35.1 A Battery and a Bulb

☑ **In a flashlight, when the switch is turned on to complete an electric circuit, the mobile conduction electrons already in the wires and the filament begin to drift through the circuit.**

- There must be a complete path, or **circuit,** for a bulb in a simple circuit to light.

- In a simple circuit, electrons flow from the negative part of a battery through a wire or foil to the side (or bottom) of a bulb, through a filament inside the bulb, and out the bottom (or side) and through the other piece of wire or foil to the positive part of the battery. The current then passes through the interior of the battery to complete the circuit.

35.2 Electric Circuits

☑ **For a continuous flow of electrons, there must be a complete circuit with no gaps.**

- A gap is usually provided by an electric switch that can be opened or closed to either cut off or allow electron flow.

- When connected **in series,** the devices in a circuit form a single pathway for electron flow between the terminals of the battery, generator, or wall socket. When connected **in parallel,** the devices form branches, each of which is a separate path for the flow of electrons.

35.3 Series Circuits

☑ **If one device fails in a series circuit, current in the whole circuit ceases and none of the devices will work.**

- In a **series circuit,** devices are arranged so that charge flows through each in turn.

- The current passing through each device in a series circuit is the same.

- In a series circuit, the total resistance to current is the sum of the individual resistances along the circuit path.

- The current in a series circuit is numerically equal to the voltage supplied by the source divided by the total resistance. This is Ohm's law. Ohm's law also applies separately to each device.

- The *voltage drop*, or potential difference, across each device connected in series depends directly on its resistance. The total voltage across a series circuit divides among the individual devices.

Chapter 35   Electric Circuits

35.4 Parallel Circuits

✓ In a parallel circuit, each device operates independent of the other devices. A break in any one path does not interrupt the flow of charge in the other paths.

- In a **parallel circuit,** each electric device is connected to the same two points of the circuit. The voltage is therefore the same across each device connected in parallel.

- The total current in a parallel circuit divides among the branches. Ohm's law applies separately to each branch.

- The overall resistance of a parallel circuit is less than the resistance of any one of its branches.

35.5 Schematic Diagrams

✓ In a schematic diagram, resistance is shown by a zigzag line, and ideal resistance-free wires are shown with solid straight lines. A battery is represented with a set of short and long parallel lines.

- Electric circuits are frequently described by simple diagrams, called **schematic diagrams,** using special symbols to represent certain circuit elements.

35.6 Combining Resistors in a Compound Circuit

✓ The equivalent resistance of resistors connected in series is the sum of their values. The equivalent resistance for a pair of equal resistors in parallel is half the value of either resistor.

- The *equivalent resistance* of a circuit with several resistors is the value of a single resistor that would comprise the same load to the battery or power source.

- The equivalent resistance for a pair of 1-ohm resistors in series is 2 ohms.

- The equivalent resistance for a pair of 1-ohm resistors in parallel is 0.5 ohm.

35.7 Parallel Circuits and Overloading

✓ To prevent overloading in circuits, fuses or circuit breakers are connected in series along the supply line.

- Electric current is usually fed into a home by wires called lines, which supply 110–120 V. This voltage is applied to devices that are connected in parallel by plugs to these lines.

- As more devices are connected to the lines, more pathways are provided for current. The combined resistance of the circuit is thereby lowered, and a greater amount of current occurs in the lines. Lines that carry more than a safe amount of current are said to be *overloaded*.

- When insulation that separates the wires in a circuit wears away and allows the wires to touch, the path of the circuit is shortened. This is called a short circuit, and it can draw a dangerously large current.

Chapter 35 Electric Circuits

Exercises

35.1 A Battery and a Bulb (pages 703–704)

1. A _____ is a complete path along which charge can flow.

2. Circle the letter of each statement that is true about a completed electric circuit consisting of a battery, a lightbulb, and two wires.

   a. Electrons flow from the positive terminal of the battery to the negative terminal.

   b. The battery acts like a pump, causing current to flow through the circuit.

   c. The conduction electrons tend to pile up inside the bulb.

   d. The conduction electrons that drift through the circuit originate from the wires and the bulb filament.

35.2 Electric Circuits (page 704)

3. A gap in a circuit is usually provided by an electric _____.

Match each switch position with the correct effect on the circuit.

Switch Position	Effect
_____ 4. open	a. cuts off electron flow
_____ 5. closed	b. allows electron flow

6. When connected in _____, devices in a circuit form a single pathway for electron flow.

7. When connected in _____, devices in a circuit form branches, each of which is a separate path for the flow of electrons.

35.3 Series Circuits (pages 705–706)

8. Suppose you have a completed circuit with three lamps connected in series. Circle the letter of the statement that correctly describes what happens if the filament of the middle lamp burns out.

   a. Current ceases, and the remaining two lamps will also go out.

   b. Both of the remaining lamps will stay lit.

   c. Only one of the remaining lamps will stay lit.

   d. The amount of current flowing through the circuit drops by one third.

9. The total resistance to current in a series circuit is the _____ of the individual resistances along the circuit path.

10. The voltage drop across each device in a series circuit depends directly on its _____.

11. Describe the main disadvantage of a series circuit.

   _____

   _____

   _____

Chapter 35   Electric Circuits

35.4 Parallel Circuits (pages 707–708)

Use the figure below to answer Questions 12–17.

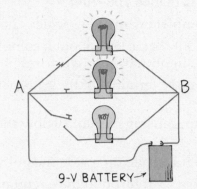

9-V BATTERY

12. Circle the letter of the correct answer. How many *possible* pathways for current are there between points A and B?

    a. 1

    b. 3

    c. 4

    d. 5

13. Is the following sentence true or false? In a parallel circuit like the one shown, each device operates independent of the other devices.

    _____

14. Circle the letter of the correct answer. What is the voltage across each lit bulb in the circuit shown?

    a. 3 volts

    b. 4.5 volts

    c. 6 volts

    d. 9 volts

15. Suppose *I* is the total current in the circuit. Circle the letter of the amount of current through each lit bulb.

    a. $\dfrac{I}{2}$

    b. $\dfrac{I}{3}$

    c. $2I$

    d. $3I$

16. If the switch next to the unlit bulb were closed, the total current through the battery would _____.

17. Is the following sentence true or false? The overall resistance of the circuit is less than the resistance of any one of the branches.

    _____

Chapter 35   Electric Circuits

35.5 Schematic Diagrams (page 709)

18. What is a schematic diagram?

_____

_____

_____

19. Describe how the positive and negative terminals of a battery are indicated on a schematic diagram.

_____

_____

Match each circuit element with the description of its symbol in a schematic diagram.

Circuit Element

_____ **20.** resistance

_____ **21.** connecting wire

_____ **22.** battery

_____ **23.** open switch

Symbol

a. zigzag line

b. broken line with one end tilted up at an angle

c. set of short and long parallel lines

d. solid straight line

35.6 Combining Resistors in a Compound Circuit (pages 710–711)

24. Define equivalent resistance.

_____

_____

_____

25. The equivalent resistance of resistors in series is _____ .

26. The equivalent resistance of two resistors in parallel is _____ .

Chapter 35   Electric Circuits

The diagrams below show how a complex schematic diagram can be simplified by using equivalent resistances. Use these diagrams to answer Questions 27–29.

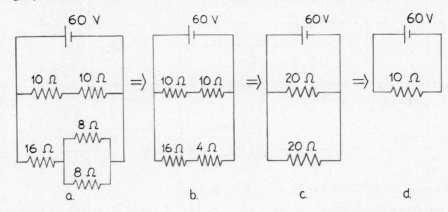

27. Describe how diagram (a) was simplified to make diagram (b).

_____

_____

_____

28. Describe how diagram (b) was simplified to make diagram (c).

_____

_____

_____

29. Describe how diagram (c) was simplified to make diagram (d).

_____

_____

_____

35.7 Parallel Circuits and Overloading (pages 711–712)

30. Is the following sentence true or false? The more devices you connect in parallel to your household supply line, the more you increase the total line current. _____

31. What is the purpose of connecting a fuse or circuit breaker in series along the supply line?

_____

_____

Chapter 35 Electric Circuits

Ohm's Law and Parallel Circuits

The equivalent resistance for resistors in parallel can be found using the following equation.

$$\frac{1}{R_{eq}} = \frac{1}{R_1} + \frac{1}{R_2} + \frac{1}{R_3} + \ldots + \frac{1}{R_n}$$

Calculate the current in a 48-V battery that powers three 15-Ω resistors connected in parallel.

1. Read and Understand

What information are you given?
voltage = V = 48 V

individual resistances: $R_1 = R_2 = R_3 = 15\ \Omega$

2. Plan and Solve

What unknown are you trying to calculate?
current = I = ?

What equation can you use to find the unknown?
Ohm's law: $V = IR$

For a parallel circuit, $V = IR_{eq}$, where R_{eq} is the equivalent resistance.

Rearranging the equation gives you $I = \dfrac{V}{R_{eq}}$.

First, find the equivalent resistance R_{eq}.

$$\frac{1}{R_{eq}} = \frac{1}{15\ \Omega} + \frac{1}{15\ \Omega} + \frac{1}{15\ \Omega} = \frac{1}{5\ \Omega}$$

$R_{eq} = 5\ \Omega$

Then substitute for V and R_{eq} to solve for I.

$$I = \frac{48\ V}{5\ \Omega} = 9.6\ A$$

3. Look Back and Check

Is your answer reasonable?
Yes, a current of 9.6 A is reasonable, and the units are $\dfrac{V}{\Omega}$, or A, which is reasonable.

Math Practice

On a separate sheet of paper, solve the following problems.

1. Calculate the current in a 9-V battery that powers three 6-Ω resistors in parallel.

Chapter 35   Electric Circuits

2. Calculate the voltage impressed across a circuit in which three 1.5-Ω resistors in parallel draw a current of 12 A.

3. Calculate the current in 12-V battery that powers four 10-Ω resistors in parallel.

Chapter 36 Magnetism

Summary

THE BIG IDEA : A moving electric charge is surrounded by a magnetic field.

36.1 Magnetic Poles

☑ **Like poles repel; opposite poles attract.**

- Magnets can both attract and repel without touching. The strength of the interaction between two magnets depends on the distance between them.

- Regions called **magnetic poles** produce magnetic forces.

- If you suspend a bar magnet from its center by a piece of string, it will act as a compass. The end that points northward is called the *north pole*. The end that points south is called the *south pole*. All magnets have a north and a south pole.

- If the north pole of one magnet is brought near the north pole of another magnet, they repel. The same is true of a south pole near a south pole. If opposite poles are brought together, however, attraction occurs.

- A north magnetic pole never exists without the presence of a south pole, and vice versa. If you break a bar magnet, each piece still behaves as a complete magnet.

36.2 Magnetic Fields

☑ **The direction of the magnetic field outside a magnet is from the north to the south pole.**

- The space around a magnet, in which a magnetic force is exerted, is filled with a **magnetic field.** The shape of the field is revealed by *magnetic field lines* that spread out from the north pole, curve around the magnet, and return to the south pole.

- Where the magnetic field lines are closer together, the field strength is greater than where the lines are farther apart.

36.3 The Nature of a Magnetic Field

☑ **A magnetic field is produced by the motion of electric charge.**

- Just as an electric charge is surrounded by an electric field, a moving electric charge is surrounded by a magnetic field.

- Both the orbital motion and the spinning motion of every electron in an atom produce magnetic fields.

- Every spinning electron is a tiny magnet. Multiple electrons spinning in the same direction make a stronger magnet, but electrons spinning in opposite directions work against one another. Their magnetic fields cancel. This is why most substances are not magnets.

Chapter 36   Magnetism

36.4 Magnetic Domains

✓ **Permanent magnets are made by simply placing pieces of iron or certain iron alloys in strong magnetic fields.**

- The magnetic fields of individual atoms are sometimes so strong that interactions among adjacent atoms cause large clusters of them to line up. These clusters of aligned atoms are called **magnetic domains.**

- The difference between ordinary iron and an iron magnet is the alignment of domains.

- Iron can be magnetized by placing it in a strong magnetic field or by stroking it with a magnet.

36.5 Electric Currents and Magnetic Fields

✓ **An electric current produces a magnetic field.**

- If you arrange magnetic compasses around a current-carrying wire, the compasses will align with the magnetic field around the wire.

- A current-carrying coil of wire with many loops is an **electromagnet.** A piece of iron inside the coil increases the magnetic field intensity.

36.6 Magnetic Forces on Moving Charged Particles

✓ **A moving charge is deflected when it crosses magnetic field lines but not when it travels parallel to the field lines.**

- A charged particle at rest will not interact with a static magnetic field. However, if the charged particle *moves* in a magnetic field, the particle experiences a deflecting force. The direction of the deflecting force is always perpendicular to both the magnetic field lines and the velocity of the charged particle.

- Examples of magnetic forces acting on moving charged particles include the deflection of electrons in TV tubes and the deflection of cosmic radiation by Earth's magnetic field.

36.7 Magnetic Forces on Current-Carrying Wires

✓ **Since a charged particle moving through a magnetic field experiences a deflecting force, a current of charged particles moving through a magnetic field also experiences a deflecting force.**

- A current-carrying wire experiences a force in a magnetic field. If the direction of current in the wire is reversed, the deflecting force acts in the opposite direction. The force is maximum when the current is perpendicular to the magnetic field lines.

Chapter 36   Magnetism

36.8 Meters to Motors

☑ **The principal difference between a galvanometer and an electric motor is that in an electric motor the current is made to change direction every time the coil makes a half revolution.**

- A sensitive current-indicating instrument is called a *galvanometer*. A galvanometer calibrated to measure current (amperes) is called an *ammeter*. A galvanometer calibrated to measure electric potential (volts) is called a *voltmeter*.

- If the design of the galvanometer is slightly modified, you have an electric motor. Unlike a galvanometer, the current in an electric motor is reversed during each half revolution by means of stationary contacts on the shaft.

36.9 Earth's Magnetic Field

☑ **A compass points northward because Earth itself is a huge magnet.**

- A compass aligns with the magnetic field of Earth. The discrepancy between the orientation of a compass and true north is known as the *magnetic declination*.

- Convection currents in the molten parts of Earth's interior may produce Earth's magnetic field.

- The magnetic field of Earth is not stable; it has flip-flopped throughout geologic time. These changes are recorded in Earth's rocks.

Chapter 36   Magnetism

Exercises

36.1 Magnetic Poles (pages 721–722)

1. List two ways that magnets are like electric charges.

   a. _____

   _____

   b. _____

   _____

2. Regions that produce magnetic forces are called magnetic

   _____ .

3. Is the following sentence true or false? Every magnet, regardless of its shape, has both a north pole and a south pole. _____

4. Write *attract* or *repel* to describe the effect of bringing the poles listed below together.

   _____ a. the north pole of a bar magnet near the north pole of another bar magnet

   _____ b. the north pole of a bar magnet near the south pole of another bar magnet

   _____ c. the south pole of a bar magnet near the south pole of another magnet

5. Describe what happens if you break a bar magnet in half and then break each of the halves in half.

   _____

   _____

   _____

   _____

36.2 Magnetic Fields (pages 722–723)

6. Define *magnetic field*.

   _____

   _____

   _____

7. The direction of the magnetic field outside a magnet is from the _____ pole to the _____ pole.

8. Circle the letter of each statement about magnetic fields that is correct.

   a. Where the magnetic field lines are close together, the field strength is great.

   b. Where the magnetic field lines are far apart, the field strength is weak.

   c. Where the magnetic field lines are parallel, the field strength is zero.

   d. The field strength around a magnetic pole does not vary with distance.

Chapter 36 Magnetism

9. Describe what happens if you place a magnetic compass near a bar magnet.

_____

_____

_____

36.3 The Nature of a Magnetic Field (pages 723–724)

10. Describe the two types of electron motion that produce the magnetic field in a bar magnet.

a. _____

_____

b. _____

_____

11. Of the two types of electron motion you described above, which one is more important in terms of the material's overall magnetic field?

_____

_____

12. Explain why certain substances such as iron are magnetic but most substances are not.

_____

_____

_____

_____

36.4 Magnetic Domains (pages 724–725)

13. What are magnetic domains?

_____

_____

14. Is the following sentence true or false? The difference between a piece of ordinary iron and an iron magnet is the alignment of the magnetic domains. _____

15. Describe what happens to the magnetic domains in an iron nail that is brought near a strong magnet.

_____

_____

_____

_____

Chapter 36   Magnetism

16. If an ordinary iron nail is removed from a strong magnet, the nail will lose its magnetism. Explain why this happens.

_____

_____

_____

17. How can you make a permanent magnet weaker?

_____

_____

_____

36.5 Electric Currents and Magnetic Fields (pages 726–727)

Use the diagrams below to answer Questions 18 and 19. Each diagram shows magnetic compasses placed around a conducting wire.

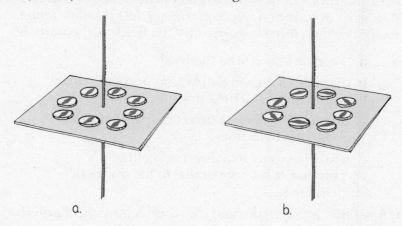

a.   b.

18. Which of the diagrams shows a current-carrying wire? How do you know?

_____

_____

_____

_____

19. Circle the letter of each sentence that correctly describes diagram (b).

   a. The compass needles are aligned with Earth's magnetic field.

   b. There is no current passing through the wire.

   c. At the location of each compass, the magnetic field produced by the wire is stronger than Earth's magnetic field.

   d. Charges moving through the wire produce a magnetic field pattern in the form of concentric circles about the wire.

20. Is the following sentence true or false? If a current-carrying wire is bent into a loop, the magnetic field strength inside the loop cancels to zero.

   _____

Chapter 36   Magnetism

21. Describe a simple electromagnet.

_____

_____

_____

22. Describe some uses for superconducting electromagnets.

_____

_____

_____

_____

36.6 Magnetic Forces on Moving Charged Particles (page 728)

23. Listed below are descriptions of how a charged particle moves within a magnetic field. For each description, write *maximum, less than maximum,* or *zero* to describe how much force is exerted by the field on the particle.

_____ a. Particle is at rest in the field.

_____ b. Particle moves in a direction perpendicular to the magnetic field lines.

_____ c. Particle moves in a direction parallel to the magnetic field lines.

_____ d. Particle moves in a direction neither perpendicular nor parallel to the magnetic field lines.

24. The direction of force that a magnetic field exerts on a moving charged particle is always perpendicular to _____ and _____.

25. Explain how the effect of magnetic forces on charged particles helps protect Earth from cosmic radiation.

_____

_____

_____

_____

36.7 Magnetic Forces on Current-Carrying Wires (page 729)

26. Is the following sentence true or false? A conducting wire experiences no deflecting force by a magnetic field as long as the wire carries current.

_____

Chapter 36   Magnetism

27. Circle the letter of each correct statement about a current-carrying wire in a magnetic field.

    a. The force on the wire is maximum when the current is perpendicular to the magnetic field lines.

    b. The force on the wire is parallel to the current.

    c. If the direction of current in the wire is reversed, the deflecting force on the wire cancels to zero.

    d. If the direction of current in the wire is reversed, the deflecting force on the wire acts in the opposite direction.

28. Is the following sentence true or false? Just as a current-carrying wire will deflect a magnetic compass, a magnet will deflect a current-carrying wire. _____

36.8 Meters to Motors (pages 730–731)

29. What is a galvanometer?

_____

_____

30. If a galvanometer is calibrated to measure current, it is called a(n) _____. If a galvanometer is calibrated to measure electric potential, it is called a(n) _____.

31. The diagram below shows a simplified DC motor. Explain the purpose of the stationary contacts.

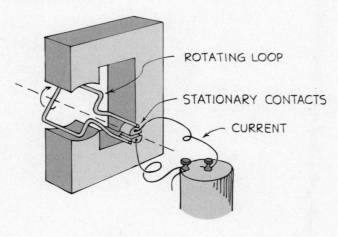

ROTATING LOOP

STATIONARY CONTACTS

CURRENT

_____

_____

_____

_____

Chapter 36 Magnetism

36.9 Earth's Magnetic Field (pages 732–733)

32. The discrepancy between the orientation of a compass and true north is called the _____.

33. Describe some possible explanations for why Earth itself is a magnet.

_____

_____

_____

_____

34. How do rock strata provide evidence that Earth's magnetic field is not stable?

_____

_____

_____

_____

Chapter 37   Electromagnetic Induction

Summary

THE BIG IDEA : Magnetism can produce electricity, and electricity can produce magnetism.

37.1 Electromagnetic Induction

☑ **Electric current can be produced in a wire by simply moving a magnet into or out of a wire coil.**

- Voltage is induced by the relative motion of a wire with respect to a magnetic field. The amount of voltage induced depends on how quickly the magnetic field lines are traversed by the wire. Very slow motion produces hardly any voltage at all. Quick motion induces a greater voltage.

- The greater the number of loops of wire that move in a magnetic field, the greater are the induced voltage and the current in the wire.

- Work is done in pushing a magnet into a loop of wire. That's because the induced current in the loop creates a magnetic field that repels the approaching magnet.

- The force that you exert on the magnet multiplied by the distance that you move the magnet is your input work. This work is equal to the energy expended (or possibly stored) in the circuit to which the coil is connected.

- The phenomenon of inducing voltage by changing the magnetic field around a conductor is **electromagnetic induction.**

37.2 Faraday's Law

☑ **Faraday's law states that the induced voltage in a coil is proportional to the product of the number of loops, the cross-sectional area of each loop, and the rate at which the magnetic field changes within those loops.**

- The amount of current produced by electromagnetic induction depends not only on the induced voltage but also on the resistance of the coil and the circuit to which it is connected.

37.3 Generators and Alternating Current

☑ **Whereas a motor converts electrical energy into mechanical energy, a generator converts mechanical energy into electrical energy.**

- A machine that produces electric current by rotating a coil within a stationary magnetic field is called a **generator.** It is essentially the opposite of a motor.

- When the loop of wire of a simple generator is rotated in the magnetic field, there is a change in the number of magnetic field lines within the loop. The voltage induced by the generator alternates, and the current produced is alternating current (AC).

Chapter 37   Electromagnetic Induction

37.4 Motor and Generator Comparison

✔ **Moving charges experience a force that is perpendicular to both their motion and the magnetic field they traverse.**

- The motor effect occurs when a current-carrying wire moves through a magnetic field, and the wire is deflected.

- In the generator effect, a wire with no current is moved downward through a magnetic field. The electrons in the wire experience a force along the wire, resulting in a current.

- The electrical part of a hybrid automobile's engine is both a motor and a generator.

37.5 Transformers

✔ **A transformer works by inducing a changing magnetic field in one coil, which induces an alternating current in a nearby second coil.**

- Consider a pair of coils, side by side. The primary (input) coil is connected to a battery, and the secondary (output) is connected to a galvanometer. As soon as the switch is closed in the primary and current passes through its coil, a current occurs in the secondary also—even though there is no material connection between the two coils.

- If an alternating current is used to power the primary, the rate of the magnetic field changes is equal to the frequency of the alternating current, creating a transformer. A **transformer** is a device for increasing or decreasing voltage through electromagnetic induction.

- A step-up transformer has a greater number of turns on the secondary than on the primary.

- A step-down transformer has fewer turns on the secondary than on the primary.

- The relationship between primary and secondary voltages with respect to the relative number of turns is: primary voltage divided by number of primary turns equals secondary voltage divided by number of secondary turns.

- The rate at which energy is transferred from the primary to the secondary in a transformer is the power.

37.6 Power Transmission

✔ **Almost all electric energy sold today is in the form of alternating current because of the ease with which it can be transformed from one voltage to another.**

- Power is transmitted great distances at high voltages and correspondingly low currents, a process that otherwise would result in large energy losses owing to heating of the wires.

- Power may be carried from power plants to cities at about 120,000 volts or more, stepped down to 2400 volts in the city. Most household use requires around 120 volts.

Chapter 37   Electromagnetic Induction

37.7 Induction of Electric and Magnetic Fields

✓ **A magnetic field is created in any region of space in which an electric field is changing with time.**

- Faraday's law states that an electric field is created in any region of space in which a magnetic field is changing with time. The magnitude of the created electric field is proportional to the rate at which the magnetic field changes. The direction of the created electric field is at right angles to the changing magnetic field.

- If electric charge happens to be present where the electric field is created, this charge will experience a force.

- British physicist James Clerk Maxwell advanced a counterpart to Faraday's law, in which the roles of electric and magnetic fields are interchanged. The magnitude of the created magnetic field is proportional to the rate at which the electric field changes. The direction of the created magnetic field is at right angles to the changing electric field.

37.8 Electromagnetic Waves

✓ **An electromagnetic wave is composed of oscillating electric and magnetic fields that regenerate each other.**

- Electromagnetic waves move outward from a vibrating charge. No medium is required. At any point on the wave, the electric field is perpendicular to the magnetic field, and both are perpendicular to the direction of motion of the wave.

- Electromagnetic waves move at the speed of light—no matter what the frequency or wavelength or intensity of the radiation.

- In an electromagnetic wave, the changing electric field induces a magnetic field. The changing magnetic field acts back to induce an electric field.

- Light is simply electromagnetic waves with frequencies in the range of 4.3×10^{14} to 7×10^{14} vibrations per second. Radiation of any frequency would propagate at the same speed as light.

- Radio waves are radiation which can be generated by causing electric charges to move up and down an antenna.

Chapter 37   Electromagnetic Induction

Exercises

37.1 Electromagnetic Induction (pages 741–742)

1. Circle the letter beside the names of the two scientists who, in 1831, independently discovered that electric current can be produced in a wire by simply moving a magnet into or out of a wire coil.

   a. Einstein and Faraday   b. Faraday and Henry

   c. Henry and Newton   d. Maxwell and Newton

2. Is the following sentence true or false? Voltage is induced whether the magnetic field of a magnet moves past a stationary conductor, or the conductor moves through a stationary magnetic field. _____

Use the figure to answer Questions 3 and 4.

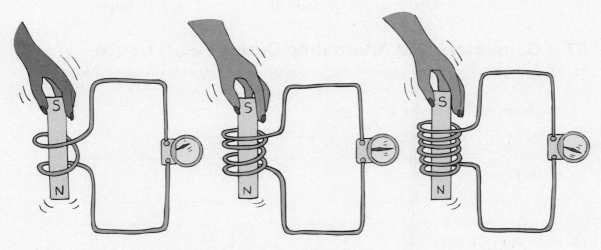

3. When the magnet is pushed into the middle coil, _____ as much voltage is induced as in the coil on the left.

4. When the magnet is pushed into the coil on the right, _____ as much voltage is induced as in the coil on the left.

5. Describe how the speed at which the person pushes the magnet affects the voltage that is induced in the coils.

   _____

   _____

   _____

6. Explain why producing voltage by pushing a magnet through a wire loop doesn't violate the law of conservation of energy.

   _____

   _____

   _____

7. The phenomenon of inducing voltage by changing the magnetic field around a conductor is _____.

Chapter 37 Electromagnetic Induction

37.2 Faraday's Law (page 743)

8. Faraday's law states that the induced voltage in a coil is proportional to the product of what three things?

   a. _____

   b. _____

   c. _____

9. The amount of current produced by electromagnetic induction depends not only on the induced voltage but also on what two things?

   a. _____

   b. _____

10. Is the following sentence true or false? You induce the same voltage when you plunge a magnet in and out of a closed rubber loop as you do when you plunge the magnet in and out of a closed loop of copper.

   _____

37.3 Generators and Alternating Current (pages 743–745)

11. Describe how each of the following changes as a magnet is plunged into and out of a coil of wire.

   a. Magnetic field strength:

   _____

   _____

   b. Voltage:

   _____

   _____

12. What is a generator?

   _____

   _____

13. Complete the table to describe the difference in a motor and a generator.

Device	Converts	Into
Motor	_____ energy	_____ energy
Generator	_____ energy	_____ energy

14. When the loop of wire of a simple generator is rotated in the magnetic field, there is a change in the number of _____.

15. Circle the letter beside the number of times each second that standard alternating current in North America changes its magnitude and direction.

   a. 20   b. 60

   c. 120   d. 240

16. Complex generators used in power plants are connected to an assembly of paddle wheels called a(n) _____.

17. Is the following sentence true or false? Electricity is a source of energy.

   _____

Chapter 37 Electromagnetic Induction

37.4 Motor and Generator Comparison (page 746)

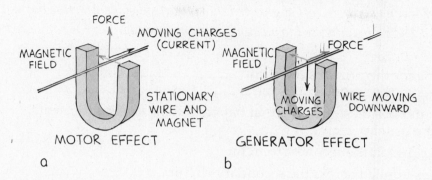

18. Describe the following effects shown in the figure above.

    a. Motor effect:

    _____

    _____

    _____

    b. Generator effect:

    _____

    _____

    _____

19. In both the motor effect and the generator effect, the moving charges experience a force that is _____ to both their motion and the magnetic field they traverse.

20. Circle the letter beside another name for the generator effect.

    a. conservation of charge

    b. Coulomb's law

    c. conservation of energy

    d. law of induction

21. An example of a device functioning as both a motor and a generator is found in hybrid automobile. Explain this effect in each case below.

    a. Acting as a motor:

    _____

    _____

    _____

    b. Acting as a generator:

    _____

    _____

    _____

Chapter 37   Electromagnetic Induction

37.5 Transformers (pages 747–749)

For questions 22–25, consider two coils of wire that are placed side by side, close but not touching. The primary coil is connected to a battery and the secondary coil is connected to a galvanometer.

22. Another name for the primary coil is the _____ coil, and another name for the second coil is the _____ coil.

23. Circle each letter beside something that happens *at the moment* the switch is closed in the primary circuit.

    a. A current flows in the secondary circuit.

    b. A voltage is applied across the secondary circuit.

    c. A magnetic field exists around the primary coil.

    d. A magnetic field exists around the secondary coil.

24. Circle each letter beside something that *continues to happen* as long as the switch is closed in the primary circuit.

    a. A current flows in the secondary circuit.

    b. A voltage is applied across the secondary circuit.

    c. A magnetic field exists around the primary coil.

    d. A magnetic field exists around the secondary coil.

25. What effect would an iron core placed inside the primary and secondary coils have on magnetic fields and the galvanometer reading?

    _____

    _____

26. A transformer is a device for increasing or decreasing _____ through _____.

27. A transformer works by inducing _____ in one coil, which induces _____ in a nearby second coil.

28. A step-up transformer has a _____ number of turns on the secondary than on the primary.

29. A step-down transformer has a _____ number of turns on the secondary than on the primary.

30. Complete the table to describe the relationship between voltage and turns in different transformers.

Primary Voltage	Secondary Voltage	Number of Primary Turns	Number of Secondary Turns
3 volts		6	18
	30 volts	2	10
9 volts	27 volts	8	

31. Power in a transformer is the rate at which _____ is transferred from one coil to the other in a transformer.

Chapter 37   Electromagnetic Induction

37.6 Power Transmission (page 750)

32. Almost all electric energy sold today is in the form of _____.

33. Power is transmitted great distances at high voltage and low _____.

34. Why would transmitting electric energy at low voltages result in large energy losses?

_____

35. Circle the letter beside a typical voltage at which power is carried from power plants to cities.

    a. 3600 volts

    b. 120,000 volts

    c. 760,000 volts

    d. 2,400,000 volts

36. Circle the letter beside the typical voltage to which a common neighborhood transformer steps down for houses and small businesses.

    a. 20 volts

    b. 60 volts

    c. 120 volts

    d. 240 volts

37.7 Induction of Electric and Magnetic Fields (page 751)

37. According to Faraday's law, an electric field is created in any region in space where a magnetic field is _____, and the magnitude of the electric field is proportional to _____.

38. What does an electric charge present where an electric field is created experience? _____.

39. Express the law described by James Clerk Maxwell, which is a companion to Faraday's law.

_____

_____

_____

40. According to Maxwell, the magnitude of a created magnetic field is proportional to _____.

41. What is the direction of the magnetic field that is created by a changing electric field?

_____

_____

Chapter 37   Electromagnetic Induction

37.8 Electromagnetic Waves (pages 753–755)

42. Is the following sentence true or false? It is possible to produce electromagnetic waves by shaking a charged rod back and forth in empty space. _____

43. Circle the letter beside each statement that correctly describes electromagnetic waves.

   a. No medium is required to produce the waves.

   b. The waves move outward in all directions from the vibrating charge that created them.

   c. The electric field is parallel to the magnetic field in the waves.

   d. Both electric and magnetic fields are perpendicular to the direction of motion of the wave.

44. How fast does an electromagnetic wave move? _____

45. Is the following sentence true or false? The speed of light depends on the frequency, wavelength, and intensity of the radiation. _____

46. Circle the letter beside the name of the scientist who discovered the speed of electromagnetic waves.

   a. Albert Einstein   b. Michael Faraday

   c. James Clerk Maxwell   d. Isaac Newton

47. Describe what would happen to an electromagnetic wave if the following were true.

   a. The wave traveled at less than the speed of light.

   _____

   _____

   b. The wave traveled at a speed greater than the speed of light.

   _____

   _____

48. Describe how a sending antenna is used to produce radio waves.

   _____

   _____

   _____

   _____

49. What happens when a radio wave hits a receiving antenna?

   _____

   _____

Chapter 37   Electromagnetic Induction

Transformers

A transformer has 50 turns on its primary coil and 500 turns on its secondary coil. If the input current is 1.4 A, what is the output current?

1. Read and Understand

What information are you given?

Number of turns on the primary coil = N_p = 50

Number of turns on the secondary coil = N_s = 500

Input current = I_p = 1.4 A

2. Plan and Solve

What unknown are you trying to calculate?

Output current = I_s = ?

You can relate the voltage and number of turns on each coil.

$$\frac{V_p}{N_p} = \frac{V_s}{N_s}$$

You can also relate the voltage and current of each coil.

$$V_p \times I_p = V_s \times I_s$$

Combining these, you can relate the current and the number of turns on each coil.

$$\frac{N_p}{N_s} = \frac{I_s}{I_p}$$

Solve for the unknown.

$$I_s = I_p \frac{N_p}{N_s}$$

Substitute known values in for each variable.

$$I_s = 1.4 \text{ A} \left(\frac{50}{500}\right) = 0.14 \text{ A}$$

3. Look Back and Check

Is your answer reasonable?

The ratio of current in the two coils of a transformer is inversely proportional to the ratio of number of turns. Because the number of turns increases by a factor of 10, the current should decrease by a factor of 10, which it does, so the answer is reasonable.

Math Practice

On a separate sheet of paper, solve the following problems.

1. A transformer has 300 turns on its primary coil and 60 turns on its secondary coil. If the input current is 0.8 A, what is the output current?

Chapter 37   Electromagnetic Induction

2. A transformer has 400 turns on its primary coil and 20 turns on its secondary coil. If the primary voltage is 120 V, what is the secondary voltage?

3. A transformer has 70 turns on its primary coil and 14 turns on its secondary coil. If the input current is 2.8 A, what is the output current?

Chapter 38   The Atom and the Quantum

Summary

THE BIG IDEA : Material particles and light have both wave properties and particle properties.

38.1 Models

☑ **Through the centuries there have been two primary models of light: the particle model and the wave model.**

- To visualize the processes that occur in the subatomic realm, we construct models.

- A useful model of the atom must be consistent with a model for light, for most of what we know about atoms we learn from the light and other radiations they emit. Most light has its source in the motion of electrons within the atom.

38.2 Light Quanta

☑ **The energy of a photon is directly proportional to the photon's frequency.**

- Einstein visualized particles of light as concentrated bundles of electromagnetic energy.

- Einstein built on the idea that atoms do not emit and absorb light continuously, but do so in little chunks. Each chunk is considered a **quantum**, or a fundamental unit. Einstein proposed that light itself is composed of quanta.

- One quantum of light energy is called a **photon.**

- The energy in a light beam is quantized and comes in packets, or quanta; only a whole number of quanta can exist.

- The total energy of a photon is the same as its kinetic energy.

- When the energy E of a photon is divided by its frequency f, the quantity that results is known as **Planck's constant**, h.

- The energy of every photon is $E = hf$.

38.3 The Photoelectric Effect

☑ **The photoelectric effect suggests that light interacts with matter as a stream of particle-like photons.**

- The **photoelectric effect** is the ejection of electrons from certain metals when light falls on them. These metals are described as being photosensitive. Energy from light shining on the metal gives electrons bound in the metal enough energy to escape.

- High-frequency light, even from a dim source, is capable of ejecting electrons from a photosensitive metal surface. Low-frequency light, even from a very bright source, cannot dislodge electrons from a photosensitive metal surface.

Chapter 38   The Atom and the Quantum

- The *number* of photons that hit the metal has nothing to do with whether a given electron will be ejected. If the energy of the individual photons is large enough, the electron will be ejected from the metal.

- From the equation $E = hf$, the critical factor in the photoelectric effect is the frequency, or color, of the light. Only high-frequency photons have the energy needed to pull loose an electron.

- The number of photons in a light beam controls the brightness of the *whole* beam, but the frequency of the light controls the energy of each *individual* photon.

38.4 Waves as Particles

✓ **Light behaves like waves when it travels in empty space, and like particles when it interacts with solid matter.**

38.5 Particles as Waves

✓ **French physicist Louis de Broglie suggested that all matter could be viewed as having wave properties.**

- All particles—electrons, protons, atoms, marbles, and even humans— have a wavelength that is related to the momentum of the particles by:

$$\text{wavelength} = \frac{h}{\text{momentum}}$$

- A particle of large mass and ordinary speed has too small a wavelength to be detected by conventional means. A tiny particle—such as an electron—moving at typical speed has a detectable wavelength.

- Because the wavelength of electron beams is so much shorter than the wavelength of visible light, electron microscopes can show greater detail than is possible with optical microscopes.

38.6 Electron Waves

✓ **According to de Broglie's theory of matter waves, electron orbits exist only where an electron wave closes in on itself in phase.**

- An electron can be boosted by various means to a higher energy level. As the electrons return to lower levels, photons are emitted.

- The characteristic pattern of lines in the spectrum of an element corresponds to electron transitions between the energy levels of the atoms of that element.

- The wavelength of the electron wave must fit evenly into the circumferences of the orbits. Orbit circumferences are whole-number multiples of the electron wavelengths, which differ for the various elements.

- Since the circumferences of electron orbits are discrete, it follows that the radii of these orbits, and hence the energy levels, are also discrete.

Chapter 38   The Atom and the Quantum

38.7 Relative Sizes of Atoms

✅ **The radii of the electron orbits in the Bohr model of the atom are determined by the amount of electric charge in the nucleus.**

- As the nuclear charge increases and additional electrons are added in outer orbits, the inner orbits shrink in size because of the stronger electrical attraction to the nucleus.

- Heavier elements are not much larger in diameter than the lighter elements.

- Each element has an arrangement of electron orbits unique to that element.

- The *ionization energy* of the hydrogen atom is the energy needed to knock the electron out of the atom completely.

38.8 Quantum Physics

✅ **The subatomic interactions described by quantum mechanics are governed by laws of probability, not laws of certainty.**

- The study of the motion of particles in the microworld of atoms and nuclei is called **quantum mechanics.**

- The branch of physics that is the general study of the microworld of photons, atoms, and nuclei is simply called **quantum physics.**

- In the subatomic domain, the uncertainties in many measurements are comparable to the magnitudes of the quantities themselves.

38.9 Predictability and Chaos

✅ **Predictability in orderly systems, both Newtonian and quantum, depends on knowledge of initial conditions.**

- Some systems are inherently unpredictable; these systems are called "chaotic systems."

- A feature of chaotic systems is that slight differences in initial conditions result in wildly different outcomes.

- Weather is chaotic. Small changes in one day's weather can produce big (and largely unpredictable) changes a week later.

- The *butterfly effect* refers to situations where very small effects can amplify into very big effects.

Chapter 38   The Atom and the Quantum

Exercises

38.1 Models (page 767)

1. Models are assessed more in terms of their _____ than their _____.

2. Explain why scientists construct models.

   _____

   _____

3. Is the following sentence true or false? A model of the atom does not need to be consistent with a model for light because they are not related.

   _____

4. Is the following sentence true or false? The emission of light is seldom related to the motion of electrons in atoms. _____

5. Circle the letter of each of the primary models of light.
   a. particle model   b. light model
   c. matter model   d. wave model

38.2 Light Quanta (page 768)

6. What is a quantum?

   _____

   _____

7. One quantum of light energy is also called a(n) _____.

8. Is the following sentence true or false? Many quantities are quantized, including mass, energy, and angular momentum. _____

9. The energy of a photon is directly proportional to its

   _____.

10. What is Planck's constant?

    _____

    _____

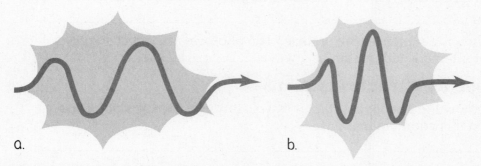

a.   b.

11. Which photon in the illustration above has greater energy and why?

    _____

Chapter 38   The Atom and the Quantum

38.3 The Photoelectric Effect (pages 769–770)

12. What is the photoelectric effect?

_____

_____

13. Circle the letter(s) of the conditions that would cause the most number of electrons to be ejected from a photosensitive metal via the photoelectric effect.

    a. dim, low-frequency light   b. bright, low-frequency light

    c. dim, high-frequency light   d. bright, high-frequency light

14. Is the following sentence true or false? The absorption of a photon by a metal atom is an all-or-nothing process. _____

15. When red light is shined onto the surface of a certain photosensitive metal, no electrons are ejected. Predict the effect of increasing the intensity, or brightness, of the light.

_____

_____

Use the illustration below to answer question 16. The illustration shows two tests for the photoelectric effect. The test shown on the left does not cause the photoelectric effect to occur. The test shown on the right does cause the photoelectric effect to occur. The same type of photosensitive metal is used in both tests.

16. Describe the difference between the light source on the left and the light source on the right.

_____

_____

17. Is the following sentence true or false? The photoelectric effect suggests that light interacts with matter as a wave. _____

38.4 Waves as Particles (page 770)

18. Describe how light behaves when it travels through the vacuum of space and when it encounters matter.

_____

_____

Chapter 38   The Atom and the Quantum

38.5 Particles as Waves (page 771)

19. According to de Broglie, all particles can be viewed as having _____ properties.

20. Is the following sentence true or false? The wavelengths of particles with large mass and ordinary speed can always be observed and measured. _____

21. All particles have a wavelength that is related to the momentum of the particles by wavelength $= \dfrac{h}{\text{momentum}}$, where h is _____.

22. The wavelength of a particle is called the _____ wavelength.

23. A beam of electrons can be diffracted. From this observation, you can deduce that a beam of electrons behaves like _____.

24. The electron microscope makes use of the _____ nature of electrons.

25. Explain why an electron microscope can distinguish much more detail than an optical microscope.

_____

_____

38.6 Electron Waves (pages 772–773)

26. The _____ model of the atom, which was developed by Niels Bohr, is helpful for explaining the atomic spectra of elements.

27. Describe the Bohr model in terms of energy levels of electrons.

_____

_____

28. When electrons move down from a high-energy orbit to a lower-energy orbit, _____ are emitted.

29. Describe how the lines in an atom's line emission spectrum are related to electron orbit transitions.

_____

_____

30. Is the following sentence true or false? Electron orbits only exist where an electron wave closes in on itself in phases. _____

31. Orbit circumferences are _____ multiples of the electron wavelengths.

32. Is the following sentence true or false? Each element has characteristic discrete energy levels. _____

33. Explain why an electron in a low-energy orbit does not spiral into the nucleus.

_____

_____

_____

Chapter 38   The Atom and the Quantum

38.7 Relative Sizes of Atoms (pages 774–775)

34. What is the determining factor of the radii of electron orbits in the Bohr model?

_____

35. Circle the letter that describes what happens to the size of inner electron orbits when the charge in the nucleus increases.

a. The inner electron orbits are unaffected. They do not change.

b. The inner electron orbits become larger.

c. The inner electron orbits collapse and fall into the nucleus.

d. The inner electron orbits become smaller.

36. Circle the letter that best describes the size of atoms of heavier elements compared to the size of atoms of lighter elements.

a. the same   b. much larger

c. much smaller   d. somewhat larger

37. Is the following sentence true or false? All elements have the same arrangement of electron orbits. _____

38.8 Quantum Physics (page 776)

38. _____ is the study of the motion of particles in the microworld of atoms and nuclei.

39. What is quantum physics?

_____

40. Is the following sentence true or false? When dealing with particles in the subatomic world, measurements become more uncertain.

_____

41. Are the subatomic interactions described by quantum mechanics governed by laws of probability or laws of certainty?

_____

38.9 Predictability and Chaos (pages 776–777)

42. Circle the letter(s) of examples of orderly systems.

a. the flight of a rocket

b. the motion of the planets

c. the decay of radioactive particles

d. the flow of water in a stream

43. What is a chaotic system?

_____

_____

44. Is the following sentence true or false? Weather is a chaotic system.

_____

45. What is the butterfly effect?

_____

Chapter 39 The Atomic Nucleus and Radioactivity

Summary

THE BIG IDEA : Certain elements radiate particles and turn into other elements.

39.1 The Atomic Nucleus

☑ **The principal role of the neutrons in an atomic nucleus is to act as a sort of nuclear cement to hold the nucleus together.**

- The nucleus is composed of particles called **nucleons**, which when electrically charged are protons, and when electrically neutral are neutrons.

- Neutrons and protons have close to the same mass. Nucleons have nearly 2000 times the mass of electrons, so the mass of an atom is practically equal to the mass of its nucleus alone.

- In an electrically neutral atom, there are as many protons in the nucleus as there are electrons outside the nucleus.

- Nucleons are bound together by an attractive nuclear force appropriately called the **strong force**. The nuclear force of attraction is strong only over a very short distance.

- A nucleus needs a certain balance of neutrons and protons for stability.

- The more protons there are in a nucleus, the more neutrons are needed to hold them together.

39.2 Radioactive Decay

☑ **The atoms of radioactive elements emit three distinct types of radiation called *alpha particles*, *beta particles*, and *gamma rays*.**

- A lone neutron will decay into a proton plus an electron.

- Particles that decay by spontaneously emitting charged particles and energy are said to be **radioactive**.

- Particles decay only when their combined products have less mass after decay than before.

- All elements heavier than bismuth (atomic number 83) decay in one way or another.

- **Radiation** is the name given to the charged particles and energy emitted by an unstable nucleus or particle.

- Alpha particles have a positive electric charge, beta particles are negative, and gamma rays are electrically neutral.

- An alpha particle is made of two protons and two neutrons and is identical to the nucleus of a helium atom. A beta particle is simply an electron ejected from the nucleus when a neutron is transformed into a proton. A gamma ray is massless energy; gamma rays are simply photons.

Chapter 39   The Atomic Nucleus and Radioactivity

39.3 Radiation Penetrating Power

☑ **The penetrating power of radiation depends on its speed and its charge.**

- There is a great difference in the penetrating power of three types of radiation.

- An alpha particle is easy to stop because it is relatively slow and its double-positive charge interacts with molecules in encounters along its path. It will come to a stop after only a few centimeters and become a harmless helium atom.

- A beta particle normally moves at a much faster speed than an alpha particle, carries only a single negative charge, and is able to travel much farther (than an alpha particle) through the air.

- Gamma rays are the most penetrating of the three types of radiation because they have no charge. Dense materials such as lead are good absorbers of gamma rays.

39.4 Radioactive Isotopes

☑ **Isotopes of an element are chemically identical but differ in the number of neutrons.**

- An **isotope** is a form of an element having a particular number of neutrons in the nuclei of its atoms.

- All isotopes of hydrogen are chemically identical.

- The symbols $_1^1H$, $_1^2H$, and $_1^3H$ are used to distinguish the isotopes of hydrogen.

- The lower number ($_1^1H$) is the **atomic number** or the number of protons.

- The higher number ($_1^1H$) is the **atomic mass number** or the total number of nucleons in the nucleus.

- The common isotope of hydrogen, $_1^1H$, is a stable element.

- All elements have isotopes; some are radioactive and some are not.

- The common isotope of uranium is $_{92}^{238}U$, or U-238 for short.

39.5 Radioactive Half-Life

☑ **Rates of radioactive decay appear to be absolutely constant, unaffected by any external conditions.**

- Since some radioactive nuclei are more stable than others, they decay at different rates.

- The **half-life** of a radioactive material is the time needed for half of the radioactive atoms to decay.

- Each isotope of a radioactive element has its own characteristic half-life.

- High or low pressure, high or low temperatures, strong magnetic or electric fields, and even violent chemical reactions have no detectable effect on the rate of decay of an element.

- The half-life can be computed from the rate of disintegration, which can be measured in the laboratory.

Chapter 39   The Atomic Nucleus and Radioactivity

39.6 Natural Transmutation of Elements

✔ **When a radioactive isotope undergoes alpha or beta decay, it changes to an isotope of a different element.**

- The changing of one element into another is called **transmutation**.

- In alpha decay, an alpha particle is ejected. The nucleus loses two protons and two neutrons; the protons and neutrons left behind are the nucleus of a new element.

$$^{238}_{92}U \rightarrow ^{234}_{90}Th + ^{4}_{2}He$$

- In beta decay, an electron is ejected from the nucleus and a neutron changes into a proton.

$$^{234}_{90}Th \rightarrow ^{234}_{91}Pa + ^{0}_{-1}e$$

- Radioactive elements decay forward and backward in the periodic table.

- A radioactive nucleus may emit gamma radiation along with an alpha particle or a beta particle.

- Gamma emission has no effect on the mass number or the atomic number.

- A radioactive decay series describes the steps in the decay process.

39.7 Artificial Transmutation of Elements

✔ **The elements beyond uranium in the periodic table—the *transuranic* elements—have been produced through artificial transmutation.**

- In 1919, Ernest Rutherford was the first physicist to succeed in artificially transmuting a chemical element. He bombarded nitrogen nuclei with alpha particles and then found oxygen and hydrogen atoms that were not there before.

$$^{14}_{7}N + ^{4}_{2}H \rightarrow ^{17}_{8}O + ^{1}_{1}H$$

39.8 Carbon Dating

✔ **Scientists can figure out how long ago a plant or animal died by measuring the ratio of carbon-14 to carbon-12 in the remains.**

- Most of the carbon that exists on Earth is the stable $^{12}_{6}C$, carbon-12.

- Less than one-millionth of 1% of carbon in the atmosphere is carbon-14. The ratio of carbon-14 to carbon-12 in living things is the same as the ratio of carbon-14 to carbon-12 in the atmosphere.

- The longer an organism has been dead, the less carbon-14 that remains.

- Archaeologists use the carbon-14 dating technique to establish the dates of wooden artifacts and skeletons.

Chapter 39   The Atomic Nucleus and Radioactivity

39.9 Uranium Dating

☑ **The dating of very old, nonliving things is accomplished with radioactive minerals, such as uranium.**

- Most of the Pb-206 and Pb-207 isotopes that exist were at one time uranium.

- From the half-lives of uranium isotopes and the percentage of lead isotopes in uranium-bearing rocks, you can calculate when the rock was formed.

39.10 Radioactive Tracers

☑ **Scientists can analyze biological or mechanical processes using small amounts of radioactive isotopes as tracers.**

- Tracers are used in medicine to study the process of digestion and the way in which chemicals move about in the body.

- Radioactive isotopes can prevent food from spoiling quickly. The food is only a receiver of radiation and is in no way transformed into an emitter of radiation.

- There are hundreds of examples of the use of radioactive isotopes.

39.11 Radiation and You

☑ **Sources of natural radiation include cosmic rays, Earth minerals, and radon in the air.**

- Radioactivity has been around longer than humans have.

- Much of the radiation we are exposed to is cosmic radiation streaming down through the atmosphere. At higher altitudes, cosmic radiation is more intense.

- We are bombarded most by neutrinos. About once a year on average, a neutrino triggers a nuclear reaction in your body.

- Gamma radiation is the most dangerous; exposure to gamma radiation should be minimized.

- People who receive high doses of radiation (on the order of 1000 times natural background or more) run a greater risk of cancer and have a shorter life expectancy than people who are not so exposed.

Chapter 39   The Atomic Nucleus and Radioactivity

Exercises

39.1 The Atomic Nucleus (pages 783–784)

1. Circle the letter of each nucleon.

   a. proton   b. neutron

   c. electron   d. positron

2. Is the following sentence true or false? The mass of a proton and an electron are nearly the same. _____

3. Most of an atom's mass is located in its _____.

4. Describe the relationship between the number of protons and the number of electrons in a neutral atom.

   _____

5. Circle the letter of the particle that determines the kind of element and the chemical properties of an atom.

   a. proton   b. neutron

   c. electron   d. positron

6. Describe the primary role of the neutrons in the nucleus of an atom.

   _____

7. Circle the letter that best describes the strong force.

   a. an attractive magnetic force

   b. a repulsive electric force

   c. an attractive nuclear force

   d. an attractive gravitational force

8. Is the following sentence true or false? The strong force acts across large distances. _____

9. The two major forces that act on a nucleus are the strong force and _____.

10. A nucleus needs a certain ratio of _____ to _____ to make it stable.

39.2 Radioactive Decay (pages 785–786)

11. What will a lone neutron decay into?

    _____

    _____

12. Particles that decay spontaneously and emit particles and energy are said to be _____.

13. Explain what is meant by saying that radioactivity is governed by mass-energy equivalence.

    _____

    _____

14. All atoms with atomic numbers greater than _____ decay in one way or another.

Chapter 39   The Atomic Nucleus and Radioactivity

15. Circle the letter of the name given to the charged particles and energy emitted by an unstable nucleus.

    a. radiation   b. Planck emission

    c. transmutation   d. transuranium

16. Circle the letter of the type of radiation that has a positive charge.

    a. alpha particle   b. gamma ray

    c. neutrino   d. beta particle

17. Is the following sentence true or false? Gamma rays have no charge. _____

18. The types of radiation that are deflected by a magnetic field are _____ and _____.

19. Is the following sentence true or false? An alpha particle is identical to a helium nucleus. _____

20. A(n) _____ is ejected from a nucleus when a neutron is converted into a proton.

21. Is the following sentence true or false? Gamma rays have zero mass. _____

22. Compare and contrast gamma rays and visible light rays. How are they similar? How are they different?

    _____

    _____

39.3 Radiation Penetrating Power (pages 786–787)

23. Is the following sentence true or false? Alpha, beta, and gamma radiation have roughly equal abilities to penetrate matter. _____

24. Radiation with a large _____ and a small _____ will have the greatest penetrating ability.

25. Based on the figure to the right, circle the letter that correctly ranks the types of radiation from least penetrating to most penetrating.

    a. alpha particles, gamma rays, beta particles

    b. gamma rays, beta particles, alpha particles

    c. alpha particles, beta particles, gamma rays

    d. gamma rays, alpha particles, beta particles

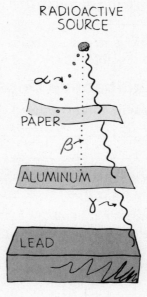

Chapter 39   The Atomic Nucleus and Radioactivity

26. Is the following sentence true or false? Gamma rays are not stopped unless they directly strike a metal surface. _____

39.4 Radioactive Isotopes (pages 788–789)

27. Circle the letter that best describes isotopes of an element.

   a. same composition and chemical properties

   b. differing composition and identical chemical properties

   c. differing composition and differing chemical properties

   d. same composition and physical properties

28. The atomic number of an atom is the number of _____ in the nucleus.

29. The atomic mass number of an atom is the total number of _____ in the nucleus.

30. In isotope notation form, the 2 in ^2_1H is the _____ and the 1 is the _____.

31. Is the following sentence true or false? All isotopes are radioactive. _____

39.5 Radioactive Half-Life (pages 790–791)

32. Is the following sentence true or false? All radioactive nuclei decay at the same constant rate. _____

33. Define half-life. _____

Use the following graph to answer Questions 34 and 35.

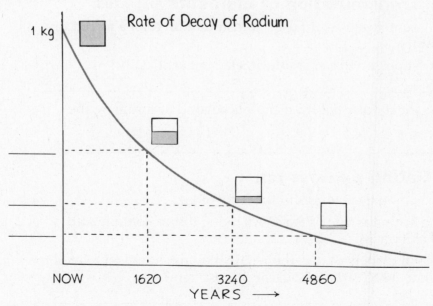

34. The boxes in the graph above represent how much of a sample of radium has decayed over time. What is the half-life of radium? _____

35. Insert the missing masses on the lines next to the vertical axis of the graph.

36. The _____ of a particular radioisotope is constant and not affected by external conditions.

Chapter 39   The Atomic Nucleus and Radioactivity

39.6 Natural Transmutation of Elements (pages 792–794)

37. What is transmutation?

_____

38. Circle the letter that describes how an atom changes when it undergoes alpha decay.

   a. its atomic number increases by 2

   b. its atomic number decreases by 2

   c. its mass number increases by 2

   d. its mass number increases by 4

39. Circle the letter that describes how an atom changes when it undergoes beta decay.

   a. its mass number increases by 1

   b. its atomic number increases by 1

   c. its mass number decreases by 1

   d. its mass number increases by 4

40. Is the following sentence true or false? Beta emission has almost no effect on the mass of the nucleus. _____

41. Is the following sentence true or false? Radioactive nuclei always decay down the periodic table, in the direction of decreased mass.

_____

39.7 Artificial Transmutation of Elements (page 795)

42. Is the following sentence true or false? Transmutation can be forced to occur in laboratory. _____

43. Who was the first person to transmute an element artificially?

_____

44. What is significant about all of the elements beyond uranium on the periodic table?

_____

39.8 Carbon Dating (pages 796–797)

45. Most of the carbon on Earth exists in the form of _____.

46. Is the following sentence true or false? All living things contain both carbon-12 and carbon-14. _____

47. How is the ratio of carbon-14 to carbon-12 in a living organism related to the ratio of carbon-14 to carbon-12 in the atmosphere?

_____

Chapter 39   The Atomic Nucleus and Radioactivity

48. How do scientists figure out how long ago a plant or animal died using carbon dating?

_____

_____

49. Is the following sentence true or false? Archeologists use carbon dating techniques on skeletons. _____

39.9 Uranium Dating (page 798)

50. What is uranium dating?

_____

_____

51. How is the percentage of lead isotopes in an ancient uranium-bearing rock related to its age?

_____

_____

52. Circle the letter of the age of the oldest rocks on Earth that have been dated using uranium dating.

    a. 1.2 million years   b. 2.2 million years

    c. 4.2 billion years   d. 12.2 billion years

39.10 Radioactive Tracers (pages 798–799)

53. Describe what a tracer is.

_____

_____

54. Describe two uses of radioactive tracers.

_____

_____

39.11 Radiation and You (pages 800–801)

55. What are three sources of natural background radiation?

_____

56. Is the following sentence true or false? Cosmic radiation is more intense at lower elevations than at higher elevations. _____

57. Our bodies are bombarded most by massless chargeless particles called
_____.

58. Circle the letter of the most damaging form of radiation.

    a. alpha particles   b. gamma rays

    c. beta particles   d. positrons

59. Is the following sentence true or false? People who receive high doses of radiation have shorter life expectancies than those who do not.

_____

Chapter 39   The Atomic Nucleus and Radioactivity

Half-Life

A lab has 525-g sample of radium. The half-life of radium is 1620 years. How much of the sample will remain after 3 half-lives have passed? How many years are needed for 3 half-lives of radium to pass?

Read and Understand

What information are you given?

Mass of radium = 525 g

Half-life of radium = 1620 years

Plan and Solve

What unknown are you trying to calculate?

Mass of radium remaining after 3 half-lives = ?

Time for 2 half-lives to pass = ?

What formula contains the given quantity and the unknown?

Amount remaining = (initial amount)$\left(\frac{1}{2}\right)^n$, where n = number of half-lives

Substitute the known values and solve.

Amount remaining = $(525 \text{ g})\left(\frac{1}{2}\right)^3$

Amount remaining = 65.5 g

Time for 3 half-lives to pass = 3(1620 years) = 3240 years

Look Back and Check

Is your answer reasonable?

Yes, the mass is a small fraction of the original as expected.

Math Practice

On a separate sheet of paper, solve the following problems.

1. The half-life of carbon-14 is 5730 years. If a sample of carbon-14 has a mass of 100.0 g today, what will its mass be after 4 half-lives have passed?

2. What percentage of a radioactive sample remains after 5 half-lives have passed?

3. The half-life of carbon-14 is 5730 years. If a sample of carbon-14 has a mass of 100.0 g today, what mass did it have 2 half-lives into the past?

4. One-eighth of a radioactive sample exists 9 days after it was first brought into the lab. What is the half-life of the radioactive substance?

Chapter 40   Nuclear Fission and Fusion

Summary

THE BIG IDEA : Nuclear fission and nuclear fusion reactions release huge amounts of energy.

40.1 Nuclear Fission

☑ **Nuclear fission occurs when the repelling electrical forces within a nucleus overpower the attracting nuclear strong forces.**

- The splitting of atomic nuclei is called **nuclear fission.**

- The energy that is released by the fission of one U-235 atom is enormous—about seven million times the energy released by the explosion of one TNT molecule.

- One neutron starts the fission of a uranium atom, and three more neutrons are produced when the uranium fissions.

- A **chain reaction** is a self-sustaining reaction in which one reaction event stimulates one or more additional reaction events to keep the process going.

- Fission occurs mainly for the rare isotope U-235; only 1 part in 140 of the uranium in pure uranium metal is U-235.

- The **critical mass** is the amount of mass for which each fission event produces, on average, one additional fission event. A *subcritical* mass is one in which the chain reaction dies out. A *supercritical* mass is one in which the chain reaction builds up explosively.

40.2 Uranium Enrichment

☑ **In order to sustain a chain reaction in uranium, the sample must contain a higher percentage of U-235 than occurs naturally.**

- Since U-235 and U-238 are virtually identical chemically, they cannot be separated by a chemical reaction. They must be separated by physical means.

- Gaseous diffusion offers one way to separate U-235 and U-238; a newer method involves gas centrifuges.

- It may require thousands of stages before the uranium is sufficiently enriched to be used as fuel.

40.3 The Nuclear Fission Reactor

☑ **A nuclear fission reactor generates energy through a controlled nuclear fission reaction.**

- A fission reactor is simply a nuclear furnace, doing nothing more elegant than boiling water to produce steam for a turbine. A reactor contains three main components: the nuclear fuel combined with a moderator, the control rods, and water.

- The nuclear fuel is uranium, with its fissionable isotope U-235 enriched to about 3%.

Chapter 40   Nuclear Fission and Fusion

- Control rods that can be moved in and out of the reactor control the "multiplication" of neutrons. Heated water around the nuclear fuel is kept under high pressure and brought to a high temperature without boiling.
- A major drawback to fission power is the generation of the radioactive waste products of fission.

40.4 Plutonium

✓ Pu-239, like U-235, will undergo fission when it captures a neutron.

- It is relatively easy to separate plutonium from uranium.
- Plutonium combines with oxygen to form three compounds, PuO, PuO_2, and Pu_2O_3, all of which are chemically relatively benign.
- Plutonium, in any form, is radioactively toxic.
- The greatest danger plutonium presents to humans is its potential for use in nuclear fission bombs. Its usefulness is in breeder reactors.

40.5 The Breeder Reactor

✓ A breeder reactor converts a nonfissionable uranium isotope into a fissionable plutonium isotope.

- A **breeder reactor** is a nuclear fission reactor that produces more nuclear fuel than it consumes.
- After a few years of operation, breeder-reactor power utilities breed twice as much fuel as they start with.
- Fission power has several benefits: it supplies plentiful electricity; it conserves coal, oil, and natural gas; it does not produce sulfur oxides and other poisons; and it produces no greenhouse gases.
- Fission power has several drawbacks: storing radioactive wastes; danger of nuclear weapons proliferation; low-level release of radioactive materials; and the risk of accidental release of large amounts of radioactivity.

40.6 Mass-Energy Equivalence

✓ During fission, the total mass of the fission fragments (including the ejected neutrons) is less than the mass of the fissioning nucleus.

- Imagine removing the nucleons from a U-238 nucleus. The separated nucleons have a total mass greater than the mass of the original nucleus.
- The mass difference is related to the "binding energy" of the nucleus. The binding energy per nucleon is greatest in the nucleus of iron.
- The masses of ions of isotopes of various elements can be accurately measured with a *mass spectrometer*.
- For elements lighter than iron and heavier than iron, the binding energy per nucleon is less than it is in iron.

Chapter 40   Nuclear Fission and Fusion

- The mass per nucleon in the fission fragments (of a uranium nucleus) is less than the mass per nucleon when the same set of nucleons is combined in the uranium nucleus.

- This decrease in mass (from fission), when multiplied by the speed of light squared, is equal to the energy yielded by each uranium nucleus that undergoes fission.

- Any nuclear transformation that moves nuclei toward iron (on the mass per nucleon graph) releases energy.

40.7 Nuclear Fusion

☑ **After fusion, the total mass of the light nuclei formed in the fusion process is less that the total mass of the nuclei that fused.**

- The process in which the nuclei of light atoms fuse is **nuclear fusion.**

- Nuclear fusion is the opposite of nuclear fission, although both produce energy.

- For fusion to occur, atomic nuclei must collide at very high speed; the high speed corresponds to extremely high temperatures.

- Fusion brought on by high temperatures is called **thermonuclear fusion.**

- In the central part of the sun, fusion reactions convert 657 million tons of hydrogen into 653 million tons of helium each second. The missing 4 million tons of mass is discharged as radiant energy.

40.8 Controlling Nuclear Fusion

☑ **Producing thermonuclear fusion reactions under controlled conditions requires temperatures of hundreds of millions of degrees.**

- No matter how the temperature is produced, a problem is that all materials melt and vaporize at the temperatures required for fusion; one solution is to confine the reaction in a magnetic field.

- At about 350 million degrees, fusion reactions will produce enough energy to be self-sustaining.

- Fusion has been achieved, but instabilities in the plasma have thus far prevented a sustained reaction.

- We are still waiting for the "Break-Even Day" when one of the variety of fusion schemes will sustain a yield of at least as much energy as is required to initiate it.

- Fusion power is nearly ideal: reactors cannot become "supercritical"; there is no air pollution; and the by-products are not radioactive.

- The fuel for nuclear fusion is hydrogen—in particular, its heavier isotopes, deuterium (H-2) and tritium (H-3).

Chapter 40   Nuclear Fission and Fusion

Exercises

40.1 Nuclear Fission (pages 809–811)

1. What is nuclear fission? _____

2. Is the following sentence true or false? A delicate balance between the strong force and electrical forces of repulsion exists inside a nucleus. _____

3. Circle the letter that describes why nuclear fission occurs.

    a. the electrical forces and nuclear strong forces repel each other

    b. the electrical forces decrease suddenly

    c. repelling electrical forces overpower the attracting nuclear strong forces

    d. repelling nuclear strong forces overpower the attracting electrical forces

4. Is the following sentence true or false? The energy released by the fission of one U-235 atom is approximately equal to the energy released by the explosion of one TNT molecule. _____

Use the illustration below to answer questions 5 through 7. The illustration shows the fission of a U-235 nucleus.

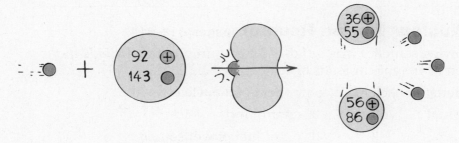

5. Circle the letter of each product of the fission reaction.

    a. $^{91}_{36}\text{Kr}$ b. $^{142}_{56}\text{Ba}$

    c. neutrons   d. electrons

6. Circle the letter of the nucleus that undergoes fission.

    a. $^{91}_{36}\text{Kr}$ b. $^{142}_{56}\text{Ba}$

    c. $^{235}_{92}\text{U}$ d. neutrons

7. Circle the letter of the reaction particle capable of starting another fission reaction.

    a. electron   b. $^{142}_{56}\text{Ba}$

    c. $^{91}_{36}\text{Kr}$ d. neutron

8. Describe what a chain reaction is.

_____

_____

Chapter 40   Nuclear Fission and Fusion

9. Is the following sentence true or false? Most of the uranium in a uranium metal sample is U-235. _____

Match each term with its definition.

Term	Definition
_____ **10.** critical mass	a. amount of mass in which the chain reaction dies out
_____ **11.** subcritical mass	b. amount of mass required for a self-sustaining chain reaction
_____ **12.** supercritical mass	c. amount of mass in which the chain reaction builds explosively

40.2 Uranium Enrichment (page 812)

13. If a sample of uranium is to sustain a chain reaction it must have a higher percentage of _____ than occurs naturally.

14. Is the following sentence true or false? U-235 nuclei cannot be separated from U-238 nuclei by chemical means. _____

15. Describe two methods used to separate U-235 from U-238.

_____

_____

_____

40.3 The Nuclear Fission Reactor (pages 812–814)

16. Is the following sentence true or false? 1 kg of uranium fuel yields more energy than 30 freight-car loads of coal. _____

17. Circle the letter of each main component of a nuclear reactor.

a. nuclear fuel   b. control rods

c. water   d. fossil fuel power source

18. Circle the letter of the fissionable percentage of the nuclear fuel used in a nuclear reactor.

a. 1%   b. 3%

c. 97%   d. 100%

19. The energy conversion that occurs at a nuclear fission power plant is from _____ energy to _____ energy.

20. _____ are used to adjust the production of, or multiplication of, neutrons inside the reactor.

21. Describe the current policy of the United States for handling radioactive wastes from nuclear reactors.

_____

_____

Chapter 40   Nuclear Fission and Fusion

40.4 Plutonium (pages 814–815)

22. The isotope plutonium-239 undergoes nuclear fission when it captures a
    _____.

23. Is the following sentence true or false? Plutonium cannot easily be
    separated from uranium. _____

24. Circle the letter of the statement that is true for *all* forms of plutonium.

    a. They are liquids.

    b. They are chemically benign.

    c. They are radioactively toxic.

    d. They dissolve easily in water.

25. Circle the letter describing the greatest risk plutonium presents for
    humans.

    a. use in nuclear weapons

    b. chemical toxicity

    c. low-level radiation exposure

    d. cancer

40.5 The Breeder Reactor (page 816)

26. Circle the letter that describes a key feature of breeder reactors.

    a. they produce no waste products

    b. they produce no radioactive waste products

    c. they do not require nuclear fuel

    d. they produce more nuclear fuel than they use

27. Is the following sentence true or false? A breeder reactor converts a
    fissionable plutonium isotope into a nonfissionable uranium isotope.

    _____

28. Is the following sentence true or false? If a breeder reactor operates for
    several years it will likely produce twice as much nuclear fuel as it had
    when it began operating. _____

29. What are three benefits of fission power?

    _____

    _____

30. Circle the letter of each disadvantage or potential risk of fission power.

    a. radioactive wastes produced

    b. inexpensive electrical power

    c. buildup of nuclear weapons

    d. low-level radioactive substances leak into environment

Chapter 40   Nuclear Fission and Fusion

40.6 Mass-Energy Equivalence (pages 817–820)

31. Describe how the mass of the nucleons in a nucleus is related to their mass outside the nucleus. Assume the nucleons are placed outside the nucleus so they are separated from one another.

_____

_____

32. Is the following sentence true or false? The work done to remove a nucleon from a nucleus adds to the nucleon's mass. _____

33. The mass difference of nucleons inside and outside the nucleus is related to the _____ energy of the nucleus.

34. Circle the letter that describes what a mass spectrometer is used for.

   a. it measures the masses of the ions of isotopes

   b. it measures the binding energy of isotopes

   c. it measures the density of isotopes

   d. it determines the color of light emitted during fission

35. Is the following sentence true or false? Less work is required per nucleon to pull apart an iron nucleus than any other nucleus. _____

Use the graph of mass per nucleon of the elements to answer questions 36 and 37.

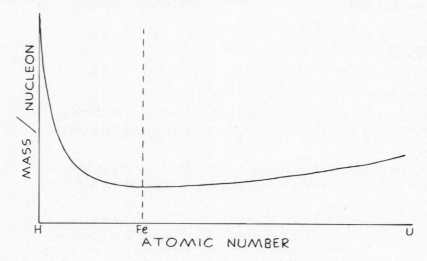

36. Circle the letter of the element with the greatest mass per nucleon.

   a. H   b. Fe

   c. Pu   d. U

37. Circle the letter of the element with the least mass per nucleon.

   a. H   b. Fe

   c. Pu   d. U

38. Is the following sentence true or false? After a large nucleus undergoes fission, the resulting fission fragments have less mass than the original nucleus. _____

Chapter 40 Nuclear Fission and Fusion

39. Iron is located at the bottom of the mass per nucleon graph, meaning it has the greatest _____ per nucleon.

40. Is the following sentence true or false? Any nuclear transformation that moves nuclei away from iron on the mass per nucleon graph releases energy. _____

40.7 Nuclear Fusion (pages 821–822)

41. What is nuclear fusion?

_____

42. Is the following sentence true or false? Nuclear fission and nuclear fusion are virtually the same process. _____

43. Circle the letter that describes the condition needed for light nuclei to overcome electrical forces of repulsion during fusion.

a. extremely low pressure

b. extremely high pressure

c. extremely high temperature

d. extremely low temperature

44. A fusion reaction that occurs at an extremely high temperature is known as _____ fusion.

45. Is the following sentence true or false? Thermonuclear fusion occurs in the sun. _____

40.8 Controlling Nuclear Fusion (pages 822–824)

46. Producing thermonuclear fusion reactions requires temperatures of

_____.

47. What are plasmas? _____

48. _____ are sometimes used to contain fusion reactions during research.

49. Explain what *ignition temperature* is as it relates to a fusion reaction.

_____

_____

50. Is the following sentence true or false? Fusion has never been achieved inside a laboratory. _____

51. Circle the letter of each likely benefit of fusion as a potential energy source.

a. cannot become supercritical as a nuclear fission reactor can

b. produces non-radioactive by-products

c. does not cause air pollution

d. power plants are inexpensive to build and operate

52. Is the following sentence true or false? Helium is the most commonly used fuel for a fusion reactor. _____

Chapter 40   Nuclear Fission and Fusion

Mass-Energy Equivalence

A typical United States 5-cent coin, or nickel, that is in circulation has a mass of approximately 5.0 g. How much energy would be released if all of this mass were converted into energy?

Read and Understand

What information are you given?

Mass of nickel, $m = 5.0$ g

The speed of light is $c = 3.00 \times 10^8$ m/s.

Plan and Solve

What unknown are you trying to calculate?

Energy released when mass is converted to energy, $E = ?$

What formula contains the given quantity and the unknown?

$E = mc^2$

To use the $E = mc^2$ equation, the mass must be in units of kilograms, kg.

$5.0\,\text{g} \times \dfrac{1\,\text{kg}}{1000\,\text{g}} = 0.005\,\text{kg}$

Substitute the known values and solve.

$E = (0.005\,\text{kg})(3.00 \times 10^8\,\text{m/s})^2 = 4.5 \times 10^{14}\,\text{kg·m}^2/\text{s}^2 = 4.5 \times 10^{14}\,\text{J}$

Look Back and Check

Is your answer reasonable?

Yes, the units are correct and a huge value is to be expected because the energy equation involves the square of the speed of light.

Math Practice

On a separate sheet of paper, solve the following problems.

1. A bowler uses a 5.0 kg bowling ball. If the bowling ball could be converted to energy, how much energy would be produced?

2. If the United States uses approximately 1.5×10^{19} J of energy per year, how many bowling balls (as described in Question 1) would be needed to supply this amount of energy?

3. The smallest species of ant has a mass of approximately 0.01 mg. How much energy is released if the ant were converted to energy?